GETTING THE MOST OUT OF LIFE

An Anthology
from
The Reader's Digest

THE READER'S DIGEST ASSOCIATION, INC.
Pleasantville, New York

PRINTED IN U. S. A.

CONTENTS

THE TURNING POINT OF MY CAREER .... *A. J. Cronin* 1

BUILDING A PERSONALITY .... *Harry Emerson Fosdick, D.D.* 7
Condensed from Physical Culture

FAMILY SESSION, INC. .... *Frances Newton* 11
Condensed from Your Life

TAKE A DEEP BREATH .... *Helen Durham* 15
Condensed from Collier's

YOU WON'T BE SNUBBED .... *Henry Morton Robinson* 19

"I OWE MY CAREER TO LOSING A LEG"... *Major Alexander P. de Seversky* 23
Condensed from Ladies' Home Journal

THE SEVEN POINTS OF DEPARTURE .... *William F. H. Godson, Jr.* 28
Condensed from The Atlantic Monthly

IDEAS GET THE JOB .... *John R. Tunis* 31
Condensed from Review of Reviews

DON'T BE A "DUCK" .... *J. P. McEvoy* 35
Condensed from The Rotarian

WAKE UP AND LIVE! .... *Dorothea Brande* 39
Condensed from the book of the same title

FATHER FORGETS .... *W. Livingston Larned* 55
Condensed from People's Home Journal

THE BUSINESS OF LIVING A LONG TIME .... *Raymond Pearl* 57
Condensed from The Forum

HE BROUGHT THEM BACK TO HEALTH .... *M. K. Wisehart* 61
Condensed from The American Magazine

I AM THE MOTHER-IN-LAW IN THE HOME .... *Anonymous* 64
Condensed from The Saturday Evening Post

IT'S MORE FUN TO BE FIT .... *Gene Tunney* 69

THE WORTH OF BEAUTY .... *James C. Derieux* 74
Condensed from Good Housekeeping

WHAT MAKES A HUSBAND EASY TO LIVE WITH? .... *A Symposium* 78
Condensed from Woman's Home Companion

MARY WHITE .... *William Allen White* 81
Condensed from the Emporia Gazette

Do the Thing You Fear .... Henry C. Link, Ph.D. 85

We Teach Our Children to Pray .... O. K. Armstrong 89
Condensed from Better Homes & Gardens

How Well Do You Read? .... Ruth McCoy Harris 92
Condensed from Liberty

Who Shall Be the Judge? .... Frederic Loomis, M.D. 96
Condensed from the book "Consultation Room"

Every Man His Own Naturalist .... Donald Culross Peattie 101
Condensed from Natural History

Making Habits Work for You .... William James 105
Condensed from the book "Psychology: Briefer Course"

Savings of a Lifetime .... Margaret Culkin Banning 109
Condensed from The Saturday Evening Post

What Are You Really Fitted For? .... Edwin Muller 113
Condensed from Nation's Business

Why We All Have "Ups and Downs" .... Myron Stearns 117
Condensed from Redbook

How to Take a Walk .... Alan Devoe 122
Condensed from Coronet

A Religion That Does Things .... Sir Wilfred Grenfell 125
Condensed from the book "Forty Years for Labrador"

How to Win Friends and Influence People .... Dale Carnegie 129
Condensed from the book of the same title

Lou Gehrig's Epic of Courage .... Paul Gallico 145
Condensed from Cosmopolitan

Education Begins at Home .... Charles F. Kettering 150
Condensed from School and Society

Are You a Man or a Smokestack? .... J. P. McEvoy 154
Condensed from Your Life

The Sexual Relationship in Marriage .... Frederick Harris 158
Condensed from The World Tomorrow

Have You an Educated Heart? .... Gelett Burgess 162
Condensed from the book "The Bromide and Other Theories"

Three Days to See .... Helen Keller 165
Condensed from The Atlantic Monthly

How Your Mind May Make You Ill ... *Elsie McCormick* 170
Condensed from Your Life

"We Have with Us Tonight —" ... *Dale Carnegie* 174
Condensed from The Rotarian

Women over Forty ... *Sarah Trent* 179
Condensed from the book of the same title

One Day Can Change Your Life ... *Henry James Forman* 183
Condensed from Cosmopolitan

Keep Open the Windows of Your Mind ... *Merle Crowell* 186
Condensed from The American Magazine

You Can Sleep ... *J. P. McEvoy* 188
Condensed from The Baltimore Sunday Sun

The Gusher ... *Charles Battell Loomis* 191
Condensed from The Golden Book Magazine

My Child Was Crippled ... *Anonymous* 194
Condensed from The Forum

Music: A Friend for Life ... *Catherine Drinker Bowen* 200
Condensed from the book "Friends and Fiddlers"

Turn Your Sickness into an Asset ... *Louis E. Bisch, M.D.* 205

"We Live in the Slums" ... *Norma Lee Browning* 209
Condensed from The Forum

To Bore or Not to Bore ... *Ralph W. Bergengren* 213
Condensed from The Atlantic Monthly

Youth, Get Your Toe in the Door ... *J. P. McEvoy* 215
Condensed from Forbes

Can You Loaf? ... *Bruce Barton* 219
Condensed from Forbes

"In Sickness and in Health" ... *France Pastorelli* 222
Condensed from the book "Strength out of Suffering"

Children Can Be Taught Life ... *A Symposium* 226

How to Live on 24 Hours a Day ... *Arnold Bennett* 229
Condensed from the book of the same title

My Adventures with a Paint Brush ... *Winston S. Churchill* 246
Condensed from the book "Amid These Storms"

R·D·A

How I learned a humble lesson in the grace of perseverance

The Turning Point of My Career

By A. J. Cronin

Author of "Hatter's Castle," "The Citadel," "The Keys of the Kingdom," etc.

I WAS 33 at the time, a doctor in the West End of London. I had been lucky in advancing through several arduous Welsh mining assistantships to my own practice — acquired on the installment plan from a dear old family physician who, at our first interview, gazed at my cracked boots and frayed cuffs, and trusted me. I think I wasn't a bad doctor. My patients seemed to like me — not only the nice old ladies with nothing wrong with them who lived near the Park and paid handsomely for my cheerful bedside manner, but the cabbies, porters and dead beats in the mews and back streets of Bayswater who paid nothing and often had a great deal wrong with them.

Yet there was something . . . though I treated everything that came my way, read all the medical journals, attended scientific meetings, and even found time to take complex postgraduate diplomas . . . I wasn't quite sure of myself. I didn't stick at anything for long. I had successive ideas of specializing in dermatology, in aural surgery, in pediatrics, but discarded them all. While I worked all day and half of most nights, I really lacked perseverance, stability.

One day I developed indigestion. After resisting my wife's entreaties for several weeks I went, casually, to consult a friendly colleague. I expected a bottle of bismuth and an invitation to bridge. I received instead the shock of my life: a sentence to six months' complete rest in the country on a milk diet. I had a gastric ulcer.

The place of exile, chosen after excruciating contention, was a small farmhouse near the village of Tarbert in the Scottish Highlands. Imagine a lonely whitewashed steading set on a rain-drenched loch amid ferocious mountains rising into gray mist, with long-horned cattle, like elders of the kirk, sternly munching thistles in the foreground. That was Fyne Farm. Conceive of a harassed stranger in city clothes arriving with a pain in his middle and a box of peptonizing powders in his suitcase. That was I.

Nothing is more agonizing to the active man than enforced idleness. A week of Fyne Farm drove me crazy. Debarred from all physical pursuits, I was reduced to feeding the chickens and learning to greet the disapproving cattle by their Christian names. Casting round desperately for something to do, I had a sudden idea. For years, at the back of my mind, I had nursed the vague illusion that I might write. Often, indeed, in unguarded moments, I had remarked to my wife: "You know, I believe I could write a novel if I had time," at which she would smile kindly across her knitting, murmur, "Do you, dear?" and tactfully lead me back to talk of Johnnie Smith's whooping cough.

Now, as I stood on the shore of that desolate Highland loch I raised my voice in a surge of self-justification: "By Heavens! This is my opportunity. Gastric ulcer or no gastric ulcer, I will write a novel." Before I could change my mind I walked straight to the village and bought myself two dozen penny exercise books.

Upstairs in my cold, clean bedroom was a scrubbed deal table and a very hard chair. Next morning I found myself in this chair, facing a new exercise book open upon the table, slowly becoming aware that, short of dog Latin prescriptions, I had never composed a significant phrase in all my life. It was a discouraging thought as I picked up my pen and gazed out of the window. Never mind, I would begin. . . . Three hours later Mrs. Angus, the farmer's wife, called me to dinner. The page was still blank.

As I went down to my milk and junket — they call this "curds" in Tarbert — I felt a dreadful fool. I felt like the wretched poet in Daudet's *Jack* whose immortal masterpiece never progressed beyond its stillborn opening phrase: "In a remote valley of the Pyrenees . . ." I recollected, rather grimly, the sharp advice with which my old schoolmaster had goaded me to action. "Get it down!" he had said. "If it stops in your head it will always be nothing. Get it down." And so, after lunch, I went upstairs and began to get it down.

Perhaps the tribulations of the next three months are best omitted. I had in my head, clear enough, the theme I wished to treat — the tragic record of a man's egoism and bitter pride. I even had the title of the book. But beyond these naïve fundamentals I was lamentably unprepared. I had no pretensions to technique, no knowledge of style or form. I had never seen a thesaurus. The difficulty of simple statement staggered me. I spent hours looking for an adjective. I corrected and recorrected until the page looked like a spider's web, then I tore it up and started all over again.

Yet once I had begun, the thing haunted me. My characters took shape, spoke to me, laughed, wept, excited me. When an idea struck me in the middle of the night I would get up, light a candle, and sprawl on the floor until I had translated it to paper. I was possessed by the very novelty of what I did. At first my rate of progress was some 800 labored words a day. By the end of the second month I was readily accomplishing 2000.

Suddenly, when I was halfway through, the inevitable happened. A sudden desolation struck me like an avalanche. I asked myself:

"Why am I wearing myself out with this toil for which I am so preposterously ill-equipped? What is the use of it? I ought to be resting . . . conserving, not squandering, my energies on this fantastic task." I threw down my pen. Feverishly, I read over the first chapters which had just arrived in typescript from my secretary in London. I was appalled. Never, never had I seen such nonsense in all my life. No one would read it. I saw, finally, that I was a presumptuous lunatic, that all that I had written, all that I could ever write, was wasted effort, sheer futility. I decided to abandon the whole thing. Abruptly, furiously, I bundled up the manuscript, went out and threw it in the ash can.

Drawing a sullen satisfaction from my surrender, or, as I preferred to phrase it, my return to sanity, I went for a walk in the drizzling rain. Halfway down the loch shore I came upon old Angus, the farmer, patiently and laboriously ditching a patch of the bogged and peaty heath which made up the bulk of his hard-won little croft. As I drew near, he gazed up at me in some surprise: he knew of my intention and, with that inborn Scottish reverence for "letters," had tacitly approved it. When I told him what I had just done, and why, his weathered face slowly changed, his keen blue eyes, beneath misted sandy brows, scanned me with disappointment and a queer contempt. He was a silent man and it was long before he spoke. Even then his words were cryptic.

"No doubt you're the one that's right, doctor, and I'm the one that's wrong. . . ." He seemed to look right to the bottom of me. "My father ditched this bog all his days and never made a pasture. I've dug it all *my* days and I've never made a pasture. But pasture or no pasture," he placed his foot dourly on the spade, "I canna help but dig. For my father knew and I know that if you only dig enough a pasture can be made here."

I understood. I watched his dogged working figure, with rising anger and resentment. I was resentful because he had what I had not: a terrible stubbornness to see the job through at all costs, an unquenchable flame of resolution brought to the simplest, the most arid duties of life. And suddenly my trivial dilemma became magnified, transmuted, until it stood as a touchstone of all human conduct. It became the timeless problem of mortality — the comfortable retreat, or the arduous advance without prospect of reward.

I tramped back to the farm, drenched, shamed, furious, and picked the soggy bundle from the ash can. I dried it in the kitchen oven. Then I flung it on the table and set to work again with a kind of frantic desperation. I lost myself in the ferociousness of my purpose. I would not be beaten, I would not give in. I wrote harder than ever. At last, toward the end of the third month, I wrote *finis*. The relief, the sense of emancipation, was unbelievable. I had kept my word. I had created a book. Whether it was good, bad or indifferent I did not care.

I chose a publisher by the simple expedient of closing my eyes and pricking a catalogue with a pin. I dispatched the completed manuscript and promptly forgot about it.

In the days which followed I gradually regained my health, and I began to chafe at idleness. I wanted to be back in harness.

At last the date of my deliverance drew near. I went round the village saying good-bye to the simple folk who had become my friends. As I entered the post office, the postmaster presented me with a telegram — an urgent invitation to meet the publisher. I took it straight away and showed it, without a word, to John Angus.

The novel I had thrown away was chosen by the Book Society, dramatized and serialized, translated into 19 languages, bought by Hollywood. It has sold, to date, some three million copies. It has altered my life radically, beyond my wildest dreams . . . and all because of a timely lesson in the grace of perseverance.

But that lesson goes deeper still. Today, I am glad to recollect it. In this present chaos, with no shining vision to sustain us, the door is wide open to darkness and despair. The way to close that door is to stick to the job that we are doing, no matter how insignificant that job may be, to go on doing it, and to finish it.

Ignatius of Loyola was once playing a game of ball with his fellow students when someone demanded, suddenly and with due solemnity, what each of them would do if he knew he had to die in 20 minutes. All agreed they would rush frantically to church and pray . . . all but Ignatius, who answered: "I should finish my game."

The virtue of all achievement, as known to Ignatius and my old Scots farmer, is victory over oneself. Those who know this victory can never know defeat.

Our Unseeing Eyes

ONE July afternoon at our ranch in the Canadian Rockies I rode toward Helen Keller's cabin. Along the wagon trail that ran through a lovely wood we had stretched a wire, to guide Helen when she walked there alone, and as I turned down the trail I saw her coming.

I sat motionless while this woman who was doomed to live forever in a black and silent prison made her way briskly down the path, her face radiant. She stepped out of the woods into a sunlit open space directly in front of me and stopped by a clump of wolf willows. Gathering a handful, she breathed their strange fragrance; her sightless eyes looked up squarely into the sun, and her lips, so magically trained, pronounced the single word "Beautiful!" Then, still smiling, she walked past me.

I brushed the tears from my own inadequate eyes. For to me none of this exquisite highland had seemed beautiful: I had felt only bitter discouragement over the rejection of a piece of writing. I had eyes to see all the wonders of woods, sky and mountains, ears to hear the rushing stream and the song of the wind in the treetops. It took the sightless eyes and sealed ears of this extraordinary woman to show me beauty, and bravery. — Frazier Hunt in *Redbook Magazine*

BUILDING A PERSONALITY

Condensed from Physical Culture

Harry Emerson Fosdick, D.D.
Pastor of the Riverside Church, New York

A CONSULTING psychologist told me recently that most cases of emotional maladjustment are due to the fact that people will not accept themselves. They resent their limitations. They want to be someone else. They keep daydreaming about what they would do if they had another's chance. And so, disregarding their own possibilities, they never make anything worth while out of themselves.

Well, anybody can find sufficient cause to dislike his own lot. William Wilberforce, diminutive edition of a man, did not like himself. Boswell went to hear him speak once and said afterward, "I saw what seemed a mere shrimp mounted upon the table; but, as I listened, he grew and grew, until the shrimp became a whale." That shrimp of a man never had good health. For 20 years, on doctor's orders, he took opium to keep body and soul together and had courage never to increase the dose. But more than any other Englishman, he stopped the British slave trade; and as one stands in Westminster Abbey beside the grave of "The Attorney General of the unprotected and the friendless," one sees that that sensitive, suffering life translated itself into a persistent, unconquerable sympathy for downtrodden people that a lusty hulk of a man in perfect health probably never would have felt.

The most stimulating successes in history have come from persons who, facing some kind of limitations and handicaps, took them as part of life's game and played splendidly in spite of them. Once when Ole Bull, the great violinist, was giving a concert in Paris, his

A string snapped and he transposed the composition and finished it on three strings. That is life — to have your A string snap and finish on three strings.

As soon as a man begins to accept this positive technique for handling his handicaps, they present themselves to him as opportunities always challenging, sometimes fascinating. Rebellion against your handicaps gets you nowhere. Self-pity gets you nowhere. One must have the adventurous daring to accept oneself as a bundle of possibilities and undertake the most interesting game in the world — making the most of one's best.

In a battle with the Saracens in Spain, so the story runs, the Scots threw the heart of Robert the Bruce ahead of them and then with all their might fought toward it. That is the method of procedure. Take charge of your life, hurl some ideal and hope ahead and then fight toward it; organize your living around a purpose. Many folk fail to become personalities because they think that life is something we *find* instead of something we *create*. The fact is that existence is what we find. The big business of being a person is to take existence and so organize it around our plans and purposes that it becomes a life.

A friend of mine landed in Boston a half century and more ago. His old Scotch father had told him that he was of less than average ability. He began his life in America as a foundryman and he roomed over a saloon. Such was his existence to start with. What he made of it, however, was a great life, for he turned out to be George A. Gordon, one of the best scholars Harvard ever graduated; for over 40 years in the Old South Church in Boston, his pastorate was one of the most notable for intellectual quality and spiritual influence in the annals of American churches. His existence was what he found; his life was what he created. Often the best friend a man has is not comfort, but the challenge of antagonistic environment to awaken his slumbering soul.

At least three factors enter into the achievement of this sort of personality. First, imagination. Great living starts with a picture, held in some person's imagination, of what he would like some day to do or be. Florence Nightingale dreamed of being a nurse, Edison pictured himself an inventor; all such characters escaped the mere shove of circumstance by imagining a future so vividly that they headed for it.

Look at John Keats: orphaned in early boyhood, pressed by poverty, lacerated by the cruelty of his literary critics, disappointed in love, stricken by tuberculosis, and finally shoved off the scene by death at 26. But with all his ill fortune, Keats' life was not driven by circumstance. From that day when, a youth, he picked up a copy of Spenser's *Faërie Queene* and knew beyond doubt that he too was born to be a poet, Keats' life was drawn by a masterful purpose which gave him a lasting place among the world's renowned. "I think," he said once, "that I shall be among the English poets after my death." He got that picture in his imagination, and to him it was like the heart of Robert the Bruce to the fighting Scots.

Hold a picture of yourself long and steadily enough in your mind's eye and you will be drawn toward it. Picture yourself vividly as defeated and that alone will make victory impossible. Picture yourself vividly as winning and that alone will contribute immeasurably to success. Do not picture yourself as anything and you will drift like a derelict.

Second, common sense. There is no use in a round peg's imagining itself fitted in a square hole. As a matter of fact, many people flounder around pitifully before they discover the true direction of their lives. Whistler, the artist, started out to be a general and was dropped from West Point because he could not pass in chemistry. Sir Walter Scott wanted to be a poet and turned to novel writing only when Byron outshone him in his chosen field. Phillips Brooks failed as a teacher before he turned to preaching. Study yourself and use your head in picturing your goal. But whether with wisdom or without, pick a goal; don't drift.

Third, courage. Real personalities always have the kind of faith that produces courage. When his generation was against him, Richard Wagner had faith in his music, and it overcame the world. After centuries had borne unimpeachable testimony to the devastating virulence of yellow fever, a little group of American medical men in Cuba had faith that it could be conquered, and it was. Charles Darwin worked for 20 years in a little English garden succeeding and failing, trying and keeping on because he had faith that he had found a clue, and he conquered. Faith is not credulity. It is creative power. It is vision plus valor.

Imagination, common sense and courage — even a moderate exercise of these will produce remarkable results. If a man is primarily after wealth, the world can whip him; if he is primarily after pleasure, the world can beat him; but if a man is primarily growing a personality, then he can capitalize anything that life does to him.

YOUR MARRIAGE stands a better than average chance of being successful, according to Dr. L. S. Cottrell of Cornell and Prof. E. W. Burgess of the University of Chicago, *IF:*

Your courtship lasted between four and five years.
You are not an only child.
You were married in a church.
You lived in the country during childhood and adolescence.
You are fond of your mother and father.
The wife worked before marriage.
You don't change your residence often.
The wife is a year or more older than the husband.

— *Your Life*

A family vote each month on expenditures is good training for the children and invaluable in balancing the budget

Family Session, Inc.

Condensed from Your Life

Frances Newton

Author of "Light, Like the Sun"

YEARS AGO, one of our close friends died suddenly, in mid-career. My husband, Dan, was executor of his estate and one evening he said to me: "I've been looking into Steve's affairs: his house is mortgaged, there are unpaid installments on his car, he borrowed on his insurance to send his son to college. It's the sort of thing any man does, of course, and Steve would have come out all right if he'd lived. But now I've got to tell Helen that she must support herself. She'll have to give up her house and her boy must leave school."

The picture shocked me beyond measure. I suddenly realized that beyond the amount of Dan's salary I knew little of his affairs. I didn't know how much money he owed, whether the car was paid for, or even the terms of his will.

Some weeks later, after we had discussed the situation at length, Dan called the children and me into the dining room. On the table lay a pile of papers. Then he took up the problem of our future.

"We're going to form a family business," he explained, "with all matters of policy and expenditure decided by vote. Once a month we'll hold a business meeting. You children are to have as much to say about the spending of my salary as your mother and I. We'll call our business 'Family Session, Inc.'

"If I should die tonight, you would have less than an eighth of our present income — far less than you need for the necessities of life. With careful planning I can leave you with about a quarter of the income we now have. But it will mean cutting down all round, so that we can carry more insurance."

An analysis of our finances showed that we were paying too much rent, and that it would be impossible to keep the car *and* a maid. I felt the car was a necessity. My husband thought the maid a greater necessity, since I could then do more for the children during their formative years.

"Think it over and let's have suggestions at the next Family Session."

The youngsters were thrilled. Next morning they were full of plans for a cheaper house, and during the next month we found it — a suburban cottage with an acre of ground and apple trees, and fireplaces in three rooms.

By our second session, Bill and Father had found that the house could be bought, including taxes, interest and insurance, for $23 a month less than we were paying for our larger rented house. The responsibilities of ownership were threshed out: repairs and maintenance costs — with the children digging into the figures as eagerly as Dan and myself. The whole subject was new to them — and enlightening. They found out what taxes meant and what the taxpayer gets for his money. We finally voted for the new house, and I was given a month to solve the maid problem.

I found a high-school girl who, for room and board, would wash dishes, prepare vegetables, and serve the evening meal. A woman came in once a week to do the heavy cleaning. At the third session I presented a daily work sheet of household chores. I was cook. The children made their own beds, one cleaned the fireplaces, another swept the walks. It was not always easy going. Household duties were often vexatious, and curtailed expenditures often represented real denial. The children were given allowances from which all of their personal expenses, including clothes and amusements, had to come. Unpredictable items which called for a budget revision were argued. Often the sessions were acrimonious, but we learned to cultivate a temperate, detached point of view.

The difference in the children at the end of the first year was unbelievable. They had learned to weigh the value of every penny and discovered the effectiveness of pooling their resources for things they could share in common. Our first Annual Meeting showed us with ten payments made on the house, an added insurance policy, a car, a garden, and a tennis court which we had built ourselves.

Bill, our older boy, was now preparing for college. Our discussions of the subject gave the children a comprehensive idea of the costs, and value, of education. Marian felt that she should go to college only if she won a scholarship. As her success in school was a vital part of our family economy, she dug into her work and qualified easily. Meanwhile, Bill got a job which paid for his board and part of his room rent. Later, when both boys were in college, he arranged for a seven-year student loan, to relieve the strain on our budget. The boys learned that debt may be justifiable, but that the inevitable day of reckoning must be planned for.

Sometimes our sessions involved human relations. In a weak moment Marian bought a dress beyond her budget. I was willing to pay for it, but the boys were furious. If Marian was to get an extra dress, why shouldn't they have extra suits? My sympathies were all with my girl, who was feeling her first conquests, but I stuck to our rule. Marian paid for her dress.

When the laundress's daughter had an abortion and desperate illness, her mother came to us for a loan. We called a special session. The man in the case wouldn't help. His attitude brought into open discussion the question of sex. In that one unsavory affair, the children learned the financial cost of a trial flight into free love. As Bill crudely put it, "They could have had a car for all this trouble!" It was not an idealistic comment, but sound protection for a young man at college.

Eventually, the children all graduated from college, helping to pay their way through. Bill married early. He told me he would never have had the courage to face marriage on his tiny salary if it had not been for his training in the Family Session. "I owe my happiness to it," he said.

The children have often commented on the fact that few of their contemporaries knew anything about family finances. When Marian's roommate at college lost her father, the estate, burdened with debts, left the family practically penniless. "If we had known the real condition of Dad's affairs," the girl said bitterly, "we could have cut down expenses long ago. The money we spent for mourning alone would have rented a small apartment for a year."

Why should family money matters be such mysteries?

Well, in the first place, no one likes to discuss the unpleasant possibility of death. This reluctance amounts almost to a taboo. Then again, the average man isn't too efficient about his personal affairs. Usually he merely gambles on living until his children are self-supporting.

A third reason is the work involved. Before our first Family Session, Dan worked for days preparing a statement of our affairs, scheming how to give us a sense of economic reality without spoiling the children's youth and joy, without making them think that money is the only gauge.

Our Family Sessions have meant unremitting work, with long hours of teaching the children and ourselves the management of money. But they have also meant peace of mind, confidence in the future. We haven't lived very differently from our friends. We've had debts and illnesses and ups and downs like everyone else, but we have been fortified by the knowledge that all five members of the family were coöperating to meet these emergencies. Best of all, we have given our children, by experience, an economic training with which to face the hazards of the world.

Take a Deep Breath

Condensed from Collier's

Helen Durham

Breathe to be healthy. Breathe to be handsome. Breathe to stand well, talk well, *be* well. On this point everyone agrees, cultist, faddist and physician.

"To breathe properly is to live properly," says the old Yogi philosopher. "Breath is the stuff of which voice is made," says the voice expert. The posture expert's first command is to fill your lungs. The honest beauty specialist admits that increased circulation brought about by good breathing will do more for your complexion than a lifetime of massage. The psychoanalyst will tell you that an inferiority complex may spring from something as simple as scant breath. As for the doctor, his business is to keep you breathing, from the time he thumps you on the back to get you going until he produces the oxygen to keep you from stopping. Most of us take in enough to sustain life but not enough to live it vigorously. We are like a car chugging along on only half its cylinders. If some of us actually filled our lungs with a great blast of air, we would have an oxygen jag, a lightheaded feeling — that is a physical fact. If you don't believe it try it sometime.

Properly inflated lungs right the body as ballast rights the ship.

We are so accustomed to using only

the tops of our lungs that we get the idea they end at the bust line. But they don't. On either side of the ribs they extend down to the waistline. Unless you constantly make use of this important lower-lung section in your breathing, you are a poor risk for the insurance company and a flop in the beauty contest. The radio announcer knows the value of deep breathing. Go into any broadcasting studio and see the announcer before his mike, waiting to be flashed on the air, one eye on the clock. The back of his coat is rising and falling. He is tuning up his instrument.

The psychoanalyst says it is quite possible to control your mood by your breathing. If you are nervous, excited, angry — breathe deeply. The calming effect is a miracle.

Deep breathing is the actor's first aid against stage fright. Even a seasoned star like Helen Hayes declares she could never face a first-night audience without screwing up her courage by a few deep breaths.

"It was Mary Garden," says Miss Hayes, "who first made me aware of the importance of breath. I was introduced as 'little Miss Hayes, the actress.' Miss Garden's response was to give me a vigorous thump just above the belt. 'Actress?' she said. 'You can't act, my child. You haven't the diaphragm of a baby.'

"For years I could play only ingénue roles because I had only a fluffy little flapper's breath. I could never have played mature parts without the power and poise I acquired from learning how to breathe."

Many people stand badly because they breathe badly. When chests are concave and torsos slump, the first point of attack is the breath. Properly inflated lungs right the body just as proper ballast rights the ship.

Now if you're curious as to whether or not you breathe correctly, unbuckle your belt and slip it up a few inches, halfway between waistline and bust line. Exhale and pull your belt in as tight as you can until you're empty as a pricked balloon. Now take a whopper of a breath and see how many notches you can expand. It is here that chest expansion should be measured, instead of under the armpits as your old gym teacher believed.

Don't try to expand by swelling out in front. The old opera singer with her ample breath pouch over her tummy is an illustration of what abdominal breathing alone will do for you. Expansion should come not only in front but across the back and sides. To see how much rear expansion you get, put your hands at the small of your back, thumbs forward, middle fingers touching behind. Give yourself a tight squeeze, exhaling as much as you can. Then inhale and see how far you can force your hands apart. Your ribs are a flexible cage that protects your lungs. As your lungs expand, the bony cage should expand all around. One way to learn how to breathe deeply is to get the sensation of packing your breath well in against the back of your ribs.

"Ordinary breathing should be unconscious," says Dr. Eugene Lyman Fisk, "but every day deep-breathing exercises should be employed. People who are shut in all day may partly compensate for the evils of indoor living by stepping out of doors and taking a dozen deep breaths whenever the opportunity presents itself."

Without the help of your diaphragm you can never breathe as you should. The diaphragm is the floor of the chest. It is a dome-shaped muscle, with the dome inverted. As we inhale, the dome drops downward, increasing the chest cavity for the air to rush in. As we exhale, the dome flattens upward, forcing the air out. Without the help of this important muscle you cannot make a sound. You cannot pant, sigh, cough, grunt or clear your throat. A man's diaphragm is placed lower than a woman's, which gives his chest more room; and his active habits of life have made this muscle stronger. Women, with a few exceptions, are shallow breathers, apt to neglect their diaphragms.

Happily, nature taught us how to use the diaphragm. Infants breathe correctly; so do sleeping persons. When we grow up or wake up we allow inhibitions to restrict free diaphragmatic action. A good way to re-educate your diaphragm, once it has gone wrong, is to lie flat on your back, discard the cares of the world and let the great muscle work naturally. If you do this until it becomes a habit you will breathe this way on your feet.

The only purpose of breathing is to get oxygen into our systems, for without oxygen we should quickly die. Every vital process in the body is dependent on oxygen for its performance. The more oxygen you have, the brighter will be your color, the more pep you will have; the smarter you'll be. If you're low in body, sunk in mind, awkward, ugly, rasping — "breathe" is the chorus of advice.

Direct Wire

WAITING in a steamship office to be interviewed for a job as wireless operator, a group of applicants filled the room with such a buzz of conversation that they were oblivious to the dots and dashes which began coming over a loudspeaker. About that time another man entered and sat down quietly by himself. Suddenly he snapped to attention, walked into the private office, came out smiling.

"Say," one of the group called out, "how'd you get in ahead of us? We were here first."

"One of you would have got the job," he replied, "if you'd listened to the message from the loudspeaker."

"What message?" they asked in surprise.

"Why, the code," the stranger answered. "It said: 'The man I need must always be on the alert. The first man who gets this message and comes directly into my private office will be placed on one of my ships as operator.' "

— Contributed by Walter C. Mello

You Won't Be Snubbed

By

Henry Morton Robinson

AROUND ME, a bright-mufflered throng of winter-sports enthusiasts loafed in the white Adirondack sunshine. Lean ski jumpers puffed at blunt brown pipes; bobsledders tossed challenges and snowballs at each other; wind-burned débutantes basked in deck chairs. The thin northern air crackled with frost and gaiety; everyone was having fun.

That is, everyone but me. The deck chair beside me was vacant, yet no one sat down in it. For years, no one ever *did* sit down by me voluntarily. For some reason I had always been unable to draw other human beings into warm personal contacts.

But the whole picture changed on that snow-brilliant day when David Jessup sat down in the deck chair beside me. I had particularly observed this man; it was a joy to watch him approach a stranger and melt the icy cellophane that most human beings come wrapped in. I envied him his easy approach to others, yet I would have gone to my grave (so stern were the proprieties of my New England upbringing) before speaking to him or any stranger first.

But evidently my high-fenced reserve was no barrier to Jessup, for he turned his friendly gray eyes on me, and smiled with genuine good nature. There were no inanities about the weather, no self-conscious preliminaries. Like a man imparting news of interest to an old friend, he said without tension or embarrassment: "I saw you watching that bronzed chap mending his snowshoes. He's the Rhodes Scholar from New York. He stroked the Cornell crew last year and was president of the debating club besides. Don't you think he's a splendid type to represent American youth at Oxford?"

Jessup's opening remarks led us at once into a discussion of Cecil Rhodes' dream of cementing Anglo-American friendship. From that take-off, our talk continued through many fields of common interest and special information. When we stopped an hour later we were friends. It was something of a miracle, and I asked Jessup point-blank how he did it.

"Your happy knack of speaking to strangers — how do you manage it? Personally, I'm limited to a small circle of friends, all of the same type. All my life I've wanted to mingle with strangers who could widen my interests and quicken my sense of being alive, yet I've always hung back, afraid of a rebuff. How does one overcome this fear of being snubbed?"

Jessup waved his hand inclusively at the throng around us. "My fear of being snubbed," he said, "completely disappears when I remember that the dearest friends I have were once strangers. If you approach your fellow man with honest sympathy and a desire to be humanly friendly, he is not likely to misread your motive. I have met men of the most formidable self-importance, and found them all responsive, eager to visit with me. Rarely have I encountered even the slightest hint of a snub. No, my friend, you mustn't let fear be the basis of your seclusion. The new, the unusual, is no more dangerous than the familiar, and it has the advantage of being decidedly more exciting."

Subsequent experiences with David Jessup proved how right he was. Wherever he went, he would enter into conversation with all manner of people, and was forever turning up strange new types and odd, stimulating information. On one of our trips together we passed a granite quarry in which a number of men were walking about on tiptoe, carrying red flags and acting like advance messengers of doom. Instead of hurrying past, Jessup spoke to one of the flag-carriers, and in a few moments the man was telling us a hair-curling story. It seems that many years ago engineers had drilled 50 holes in this quarry, packed the holes with dynamite, and wired them for a blast. But some of the wiring was defective, and only half of the dynamite exploded! For 20 years workmen could not be persuaded to go near the quarry; it was now being reopened by men who received double pay because of the attendant danger.

Another time, on the shore of a beautiful lake in a state park, Jessup noticed a man making sketches. Skillfully engaging the man in conversation, Jessup discovered that he was a marine horticulturist with a new idea called "pond-scaping." "On the lakes surrounding the ancient Aztec capital," said the sketcher, "were many floating islands covered with feathery trees and rare flowers. I believe that I have rediscovered how such islands can be constructed and kept in motion, and am now making some sketches to interest the park commission in my idea."

On the way home I remarked, "That was one of the most interesting things that ever happened to me. Both the man and his drawings were fascinating."

Jessup agreed, then added slyly: "And you would never have met him if you had waited for an introduction, would you?"

"Don't rub it in, please. I've always known that I was missing a great deal, but I never knew how to get people started."

"To talk to a stranger," advised Jessup, "begin with a remark that penetrates to the core of his interest. Usually it will be something that applies to his work. Inane general remarks or fussy little questions only irk the busy man. One must be genuinely interested in what the stranger is doing, make an intelligent comment, then wait for him to respond. And he *will* respond, for the simple reason that most human beings are overjoyed when another person shows interest in their work. Take that floating-garden chap: if we had seemed bored he wouldn't even have begun to talk, for no man likes to expose his treasures to the indifferent. But when he saw that we were really deriving pleasure from his conversation, he tried to reward our interest. Why should he do this? Simply because no one has ever yet discovered a keener happiness than giving pleasure to others."

I was always expecting Jessup to be snubbed, but the snub never came. Once a trio of noisy roughs boarded our bus and began to annoy the passengers with a display of downright coarseness. Dignified, serious, Jessup got up and went back to them. "Here," thought

I, "my friend is riding for a fall." But I was wrong. What Jessup said to those fellows I never knew, but within five minutes he had engaged them in an earnest discussion of labor conditions throughout the country and their own chances of employment.

I've seen Jessup address women bred in the strictest code of convention, and wondered how he avoided being cut by them. He explained it in this way: "If in speaking to a woman you reveal that you are primarily interested in her personally or as a member of the opposite sex, she will instantly resent it, as she has every right to do. In effect, you are insulting her by the assumption that her attention may be so cheaply won. But speak to her as one human being to another, as one interested in the same scenery, the same music, or the same social problems, and she will extend her ready fellowship. Both men and women love to use their minds, and women especially regard it as a distinct compliment to be met on the intellectual plane common to both sexes."

Since knowing David Jessup, the stranger at my elbow has become the most interesting and approachable thing in life. And I know if I approach him unaffectedly there is no danger of being snubbed.

For ultimately we are not so different from one another. Training and tradition may have cast us in dissimilar molds, but the basic stuff of our humanity is pathetically the same. It is this realization that now makes every stranger accessible to me. He may be a barber or a banknote-engraver, but it is almost certain that he can tell me something that will heighten my mental stature or increase my spiritual gauge. I may like him or I may not; if he bores me, I can be off. But the thing that constantly surprises me is the scarcity of people who are really boresome or offensive. By far the larger part of our human race is composed of interesting and friendly members, all eager to know each other. And I have yet to see the person who did not become more attractive and more *alive* for laying aside his too-prized reserve and mingling on equal terms with other members of our common, struggling, hungering human family.

Major Alexander P. de Seversky
Author of "Victory Through Air Power"

The well-known aviation expert finds life rich, exciting and dramatic—not in spite of his disability but because of it

"I Owe My Career to Losing a Leg"

Condensed from Ladies' Home Journal

I OWE my career in large measure to the loss of my right leg in the first World War. What seemed a black end was in reality a bright new beginning. I mean it, quite literally. My bodily disability awakened powers and aptitudes within me which were dormant. It focused mental energies which otherwise would probably have been dissipated, enforced studious interests that would have escaped me.

In 1915, when I was in the Russian air force, I volunteered on a bombing expedition against German warships in the Baltic. My plane was hit, and as it landed on the water the bombs still in my bomb rack exploded.

I recall distinctly being hurled into the air and then sliding deep under water. Then I was on the surface, and I mustered strength to pull myself onto a protruding piece of wing.

In a daze of excruciating pain I explored my body. Where my right leg should have been, I found warm and mushy nothingness. The impossible thought pounded through every aching nerve: At the age of 21, I was crippled! My life was ended, even if I were saved.

A Russian destroyer picked me up, and I spent weary months in hospitals. But as I attained skill in the use of crutches, learning even to vault chairs and tables with their aid, my despair receded. What remained was a challenge to everything that was strongest in my character. No matter how often physicians and colleagues assured me to the contrary, I knew that I would fly again. I knew, also, that things which were commonplace for other people would now be haloed with excitement for me by reason of my handicap.

While still on crutches I returned to war work, as Chief Naval Aircraft Inspector for the Petrograd District. Physically earthbound, I found my creative imagination soaring. I became fascinated by the designing, engineering and production sides of aviation. I began to add armament to planes in my charge, provided flexible installations for machine guns, and even fooled around with armor plate for flying boats — at that time a startling innovation.

As a direct result of my incapacity, in short, my mind was conquering a whole new world of interests. Until the crash, aviation had been for me a kind of superior sport. Now I became excitingly aware of the wonders of aerodynamics.

When my artificial leg was finally fitted, I thought I should never be able to manage it. I seemed to be dragging a thousand tons through life; it was hopelessly painful. This was before the truly impressive progress in this field made in the last generation. Slowly I became habituated to the new limb. More important, I began to feel it as a distinction rather than a handicap.

My desire to fly did not abate. In inspecting airplanes, I found ample opportunities to sit in cockpits for hours. Under the pretext of testing the controls, I was actually testing the strength and flexibility of my artificial leg.

One day I was sent down to a naval air station on the Black Sea to supervise the assembly of a batch of heavy flying-boat bombers. On arrival I found that a demonstration before high-ranking army and navy officers was scheduled. The morning of the big show, one of the airplanes gave an exhibition of stunting that astounded the gold-braided dignitaries. It spun, rolled and looped, dived and zoomed. Finally the craft landed. Its pilot stepped out — the one-legged stranger from Petrograd.

In anger because I had taken the airplane up without permission, the commanding officer of the station confined me to my quarters. However, the story reached the ears of Czar Nicholas II, who restored me to full flying duty. Before the end of the war I was in charge of the Naval Fighter Command of the Baltic Sea, with the rank of commander — and with 13 German planes to my credit.

The fact that I had made a record *despite* my handicap meant additional glory that I certainly didn't merit. Personally, I knew that much of my success in combat was achieved *because of* that handicap. It had forced me to take precautions, to develop technical improvements and to undertake training which, had I possessed both my limbs, I would certainly have overlooked.

Because flying was somewhat more difficult for me, I was constantly studying aerodynamic phenomena and experimenting with improvements of aviation gadgets. In order to reduce the load on my wooden leg, I invented the balanced rudders which led to balanced ailerons. I designed retractable and droppable skis for flying boats; they were adopted by the Russian navy, and subsequently improved designs were used by Sir Hubert Wilkins in his Arctic flight. I also conceived a bomb sight which years later served as the basis for the first fully automatic bomb sight.

After Russia stopped fighting, in 1917, I came to the United States and offered my services to the U. S. Air Service, hoping to return to the front. But, because of my artificial leg, I was given an engineering assignment, helping the War Department put SE-5 fighter planes into production. Thus I came into ever closer contact with key figures in Uncle Sam's new air forces. Ultimately I organized the Seversky Aircraft Corporation (now the Republic Aviation Corporation) and built fighter planes for the U. S. Army. I have the supreme satisfaction today, as an American, of knowing that a fighter plane born in my mind fought brilliantly for our country.

I discovered early that the hardest thing to overcome is not a physical disability but the mental condition which it induces. The world, I found, has a way of taking a man pretty much at his own rating. If he permits his loss to make him embarrassed and apologetic, he will draw embarrassment from others. But if he gains his own respect, the respect of those around him comes easily.

After a while I was able to talk about my disability with as little self-consciousness as men do about encroaching baldness or any other unpleasant physical fact. The adjustment wasn't easy. Often my friends exhibited a well-meaning pity which I deeply resented. The basic piece of advice to the sound of limb, in dealing with those who are not, is to ignore the matter — not to avoid it or pretend not to notice, but to treat it as a circumstance of minor importance. In the sum total of a man's abilities and essential character, a leg more or less *is* quite incidental.

Year by year I regained physical skills which I thought had been lost forever. Greater agility and power with my hands and arms became my reward for the loss of a leg. I adjusted myself to the knowledge that I could not move as quickly as others and that this put me at a disadvantage in some sports — tennis, for instance. But in golf, where control, balance and coördination are more important than speed, I could match other people.

The job of relearning how to skate and do fancy figures was not easy; but the pride in achievement once the job was done more than made up for the effort. Swimming, curiously, is the easiest of physical exercises for a legless person. For a swimmer minus one leg, weight is reduced more than total displacement in the water and buoyancy is increased.

The awareness that others were noticing my physical condition, on the beach or on the diving board, ceased to bother me. On the contrary — and that, too, is one of the marvels of human nature — I developed a kind of inner pride about it. It was as if I had with me always the symbol of my victory over difficulties.

I first met Evelyn Olliphant, of New Orleans, on a "blind date" to which I was taken by a friend in the Air Corps. I fell in love with her. I took her flying, driving, swimming. Any shyness either of us might have felt about my condition was thoroughly dissipated as the sense of comradeship grew between us. She is now Mrs. Seversky. Strange though it may sound, I am convinced that the absent limb, if it affected Mrs. Seversky's attitude at all, served only to enhance her tenderness for me.

Today, I feel it a solemn obligation to help those who are newly handicapped. The best that I can do, usually, is to make them understand that life remains rich and exciting and fruitful despite a physical disability: that life has a wonderful, inscrutable way of "paying off" in other things for any physical limitations. I cannot resist the temptation to tell the fathers and mothers and sweethearts of our boys in the services that my own mother, who was in despair when I was wounded, lived long enough to recognize that my "handicap" was in many respects a blessing in disguise.

The Power of Suggestion

DR. BRUCE BRUCE-PORTER, famous English surgeon, once found a slowly dying girl reading a newspaper serial in which the heroine suffered from the same disease she had. Hurrying to the author, he was told that the character died in the last installment. Dr. Bruce-Porter persuaded the writer to change the ending — and the serial's heroine and his patient both lived. — *News Review*

☆

THE SEVEN POINTS OF DEPARTURE

Excerpt from
The Atlantic Monthly

William F. H. Godson, Jr.

EVERY TIME you pay a call, there is a departure to be made. Many other occasions also require departures. In addition to calls, there are many times when people are together and must eventually separate. Who shall make the first move? This is sometimes a hard question, and we shall not attempt to answer it here. Let us beg it by assuming that you are to make the move. Our immediate problem, then, is to determine how to do it.

All of us can call to mind guests who would not (possibly could not) take their leave. We may have lost patience with them. Would it not be fairer, however, to admit that the situation is a difficult one calling for special treatment? Approaching the matter in this frame of mind, I have given it much thought, and I now submit what I believe to be a complete solution. It is a solution, I may add, that has stood the test of actual practice. I shall present it analytically as "the seven points of departure."

One — stand up. Two — hold out your hand. Three — say good-bye. Four — go to the door. Five — open the door. Six — walk out. Seven — walk away. That is all there is to it. It sounds too simple to be true, and that, I admit, is the one weakness of my solution. The neophyte, therefore, must be warned to keep his wits about him, for experience has shown that every stage of this ritual is attended by unsuspected dangers. These will have to be mentioned briefly.

One — stand up. It is not always easy to stand up. As in the case of a plunge into cold water, there is a mental hazard to be overcome. It is easier, of course, to squirm in your seat, to say "Er . . . eh," to look toward the door, to wish that the rug under your feet were the Wishing Rug — to do anything, in short, but rise. To effect the necessary first move, an act of will is called for. Remember that you wish to leave, and that it is difficult to do so without rising. Not impossible, of course. You *could* fall in a faint and be carried out. This maneuver, however, is a delicate one, not to be recommended except in great emergencies. Ordinarily a departure cannot be successfully engineered without rising. So face the inevitable and stand up. The beginner may hearten himself with the knowledge that rising in company becomes increasingly easy with practice.

Two — hold out your hand. Here again there is a mental hazard. Will it help to put your hands in your pocket? Need you wait for the end of the current anecdote? Should you accompany the offer of your hand with some banality such as "I must be running along"? No, all this is quite superfluous. Just hold out your hand. Most well-bred persons will understand the signal. But what if your hand is ignored? After all, one should be prepared for everything. Suppose your hostess is blind, distrait, occupied, rude. Does the rule fit such a situation? Of course it does. You will observe that nothing was said about shaking hands. It is true that this usually occurs; so much the better. If not, your hand will soon get heavy — drop it. This completes the gesture, and you are ready to advance to the next point.

Three — say good-bye. Why say good-bye? People have often asked me this question, and I shall be frank about it. It is not strictly necessary from the utilitarian point of view. But it will save you from being considered queer. Since I devised my system, many of my acquaintances have tried to detain me. None has succeeded. This has occasioned much wonder among them, and yet I dare say that not one has suspected me of having a system. For this desirable state of affairs I give entire credit to the use of the word "Good-bye." I therefore recommend it.

Four — go to the door. If you think it is easy to go to the door, you have never seen a genuine victim of inertia in action. Such a one can spend hours between rising and leaving; he may even sit down again. So do not underestimate the difficulties at this point. Do not forget that in order to get to the door you will have to move your feet. Very well — move them.

Five — open the door. At this point you will get a real thrill of achievement. Like the first streak of daylight which brings hope to the victims trapped in a coal mine, the sight of the door will cheer you with its promise of ultimate escape. Often, of course, someone will take his stand between you and the exit. Go around him. Or, again, someone may reach the door ahead of you, only to possess the knob without turning it. This is not unusual, and you must be prepared to take whatever measures may be required to deal with this situation. Do not hesitate to strike down the offender in cold blood if need be. If the obstructionist is a woman, and you have scruples against hitting a woman, a playful push may do the trick. Choose a method to fit the circumstances, and — open the door.

Six — walk out. The principle that applies here is precisely the same as that which I laid down under rule four. Think of the many groups you have seen leaning against open doors in different stages of exhaustion and boredom. For shame, do not lend yourself to such a scene. If you lose your courage at this point, your hostess will be sure to say sweetly, "Do come in and sit down again." This is a sure sign, which means only one thing — "Walk out!"

Seven — walk away. And to carry off smoothly this final part of the program, you must not leave anything behind — nor must your wife. But if you do leave something, let it go forever. What is a mere cigarette case, or diamond necklace? *Leave it!* I cannot say too emphatically — and I do so without fear of contradiction — that the most important part of my whole system is to walk away.

Condensed from
Review of Reviews

IDEAS *Get the Job*

John R. Tunis

HERE's a true story. There were 70 applicants for the job of salesman for an oil-burner corporation. One chap realized that the usual letter setting forth his age and experience would be just another dust-catcher in the files. So instead of attempting to sell himself, he sold ideas.

First, he carefully studied the company's product. After learning all he could he visited three friends who had installed the burner. Did they like it? Why? Why not? Then he questioned six more friends who had rival burners. After that he went to five people who still used coal. The results of his investigation he put into a report which stated that he had made the study to satisfy himself that the corporation's burner was the best, and that he could enthusiastically recommend and sell it. This report was passed around to every officer in the concern who unanimously voted to hire him.

Out of 70 applicants he was the only one who had used imagination in seeking the job!

The personnel manager of one of New York's largest department stores once said to me, "Not one person in a hundred who comes before my desk has any ideas. Yet it's the girl with ideas who gets the job, the girl who has intelligence and interest enough to spend some time in the store looking around before she comes to me, who can suggest ways we may improve our service, who at least will be able to say: 'I watched the clerks and customers in the jewelry department yesterday and believe I could sell in that line.' Most of them don't even do that."

Here is how one girl from the Middle West approached a New York department store. She had majored in art so she studied the art section of all the rivals of the company. Then she wrote a letter of application in which she set forth some of the best ideas she had observed elsewhere. She got the job.

Your idea must be pertinent to the particular job you want; it should be specific and practical. Even if your idea is valueless, you will nevertheless stand out above the crowd as that oil-burner salesman did. "Anyone with ideas," said the personnel director of one New York bank, "is a refreshing and potentially successful person."

"Ideas!" snorted the president of a publishing house when I brought up the question. "Ideas! Why most job hunters don't even know what the publishing business is. They all want to become editors; they aren't even aware of the existence of our other departments."

When scouting for ideas, first of all study the business that interests you. Read up on it, learn its problems. Then study particularly the concern with which you would like to be associated, and its competitors. Don't go near the firm until you know something about the business, and can demonstrate that you are the person who can be useful to it in some way. Getting a job is an examination in ideas, and you cannot afford to fail.

Especially valuable in your search for ideas are the various trade journals, usually more than one in each branch of industry. References will show books from which you can obtain information that possibly even the man who is hiring you doesn't know. In any event, he will be astonished when he finds an applicant for a job who has some comprehension of what he is to do.

All around us there are businesses in which jobs are being done according to traditional methods. Try to imagine *different* ways of doing them. "What would you do if you had to land a job tomorrow?" I asked the personnel manager of a great public service corporation. "Well," he said, "I'd investigate the cotton brokerage business. Down street is a prominent firm of cotton brokers who produce a specially fine grade of madras cloth that I've found extremely good for wiping my eyeglasses. Trouble is I have to buy the cloth in quantities and cut it up myself. I'd work out an idea for selling this madras in small squares just for that purpose. I'd show how the idea could be sold and publicized, and I believe I'd land a job!"

I think he would. Anyone who can show a man how to improve his business is going to be listened to with respect and attention, whether or not anything comes from the idea in the end. And remember one thing. An employer is not interested in you. His function is not to give out jobs, but to make money. Tell him how to do that and you'll land the job.

Here's another important point. When you land a job don't assume you should stop dealing in ideas. On the contrary, it's just as necessary to concentrate upon ideas after you have a job as it is for the graduate to keep educating himself after he leaves college. The employe with ideas stands out over the rest of the force just as he did among the applicants for the position.

Often the simplest ideas are the best. A clerk in a chain store where the coffee sales were falling away went to the manager with an idea that was ridiculed. But the clerk persisted, and the next Monday morning he and his helpers all wore small bows of red ribbon on the second finger of their right hand. "Why is that red ribbon tied to your finger?" customers asked. "Oh, I nearly forgot. That's to remind me to tell you that we have a very special sale of coffee this week." Instead of the usual 500 pounds the store had sold 1500 by Saturday night.

The man with ideas is rarely out of a job. There was the young shipping clerk who lost his job in a railroad office. He remembered a certain large steel company that had been kicking to the road about discrepancies in the weights of the castings they manufactured, and the high rates charged for freight. Playing a hunch, he investigated in the factory, discovering, as he expected, that the molds in which the metal was cast had become worn and enlarged so that more metal was used than formerly. Hence the catalogue weights did not agree with the actual weights by which they were charged. He went to the sales manager of the company with the facts carefully worked out, and showed how thousands of dollars a year in freight charges and in wasted metal could be saved. Then he asked for a job. No job was available, but one was created.

Be sure of one thing. You cannot start too early in life to begin turning your imagination on the problem of how things can be done better. In school or in college, train yourself to observe people and their methods of doing business.

You should be able by watching a worker in any occupation — a bus driver or a filling station attendant — to think of ways to make his particular job more efficient. The personnel manager of a world-wide corporation told me that not over one percent of the thousands who passed before his desk as applicants ever dealt in ideas.

"How many of those who do have ideas land jobs?" I asked.

"Almost all," was the answer. "It's so unusual to find a youngster with ideas that we grab anyone who has them, even though his actual suggestions may have little value at the moment."

Personality is and always will be a factor in getting a job. But today employers are asking for something more than personality. Every employer will tell you that he has long lists of applicants who will never be considered because their applications show no sense of the importance of ideas.

Do you want to get a job? First go out and get an idea.

You cannot prevent the birds of sorrow from flying over your head, but you can prevent them from building nests in your hair. — Chinese Proverb

A suggestion that will add pleasure and profit to your next trip abroad

Condensed from The Rotarian

Don't Be a "DUCK"

J. P. McEvoy Famous playwright, author and world-traveler

THERE ARE travelers and tourists. Tourists see the sights and miss the country. Travelers see the country and the sights, too. Travelers are received with hospitality because they come with a special interest, tourists with condescension because they come only with curiosity.

One of the wisest travelers I know is a soup taster. He goes all over the world dipping his beak into the peculiar *potage* of each country, tasting, comparing, collecting recipes. Since he travels with an objective his wanderings take him off the beaten tracks.

Do you like gardens? Passionate gardeners in every city in the world will take you to see their gardens. En route you will see the temples, palaces and shrines. You can't miss them. But if you go out only to see the sights you'll miss the gardens — and the delightful people who live in them.

Are you a collector? I have a friend who goes everywhere looking for playing cards — the smallest, the largest, cards made from wood, bone or alligator hide. In every port you'll find a fellow collector, whether it's stamps or coins, old books or old bottles. If he doesn't speak English, he has friends who do; and through him you'll see and hear more than the most indefatigable tourist.

A friend of mine collects missionaries. "They are mighty glad to see me," he says. "I bring news from the outside world and they give me a real insight into the country. Then they pass me on to the next group with letters that insure me warm hospitality. Living in out-of-the-way places, knowing the language, running schools and hospitals, they have intimate everyday knowledge of amazing variety, a fund of stories and experiences that would thrill a tourist — but tourists never see them."

On the other hand, a priest I know never visits a fellow clergyman. He calls on — of all people — jail wardens. I met him in the largest jail in the world, in Shanghai, and he told me his interest in penology had made it possible for him to travel everywhere with pleasure and profit.

Are you a Rotarian? There are clubs everywhere. The members will gladly show you the town, their wives will acquaint your wife with the best shops, the proper prices, the best hairdresser, the place to buy an ice cream soda. In Egypt are the Pyramids. And behind the Pyramids lives Dr. George A. Reisner, the great Egyptologist whose post office address is just that — Pyramids, Egypt. But where did I find Dr. Reisner? At the Rotary Club in Cairo, which he attends every week.

People often say to me, "It's all right for you to talk; you're a writer and all you have to do is to look up some newspaperman when you go into a strange city." Often the speaker is a doctor, a lawyer, a banker, or teacher, and I remind him that he will find doctors, lawyers, bankers and teachers everywhere. "You don't

Travel Hints

» BEFORE I started on my trip around the world, someone gave me one of the most valuable hints I have ever had. It consists merely in shutting your eyes when you are in the midst of a great moment, or close to some marvel of time or space, and convincing yourself that you are at home again with the experience over and past; and what would you wish most to have examined or done if you could turn time and space back again?

— William Beebe in *The Arcturus Adventure*

» EMERSON in his diary tells about a friend who went every year to Europe. He made up his budget in advance, including all foreseeable items of expense. And at the end he added a generous amount "to be robbed of" and set forth to enjoy his travels with no financial irritations. — Bruce Barton in *The Rotarian* have to be a tourist wandering around aimlessly, or being herded here and there," I tell them. "A doctor I know visits hospitals and clinics, exchanging experiences and getting new knowledge. He winds up by being taken to a lot of places his fellow tourists never hear about."

Are you a lawyer? I know one who visits courts in every place he goes. Are you a musician or a music lover? You will find music makers everywhere. Are you interested in art? Don't limit your interest to art galleries. Dig out a few artists and you will unearth the most interesting parts of the country, the best food at the cheapest prices, and a treasury of information. Artists find the picturesque places — because they are artists — and they stay because it is cheap.

Don't be a tourist. Throw away your guidebook and follow an interest. Whether your passion is architecture or orchids, child welfare or rock gardens, fishing or folkdancing, butterflies or bridge, you will find devotees everywhere.

The best-informed person I met in Bali ran a children's clinic as a hobby. To her house every morning at 11 a stream of children with stubbed toes, cuts, bruises and bellyaches come for free treatment. Treating the children, she has made friends with the parents, who invite her to all their family feasts and religious ceremonies, and even send their prettiest village dancer over to entertain when she has company.

Once, while in the greeting-card business, I made a trip to Europe looking for handmade paper and special ribbon. I found villages in France where they made nothing but ribbon, and every household a different kind. I found one family that had been making the same exquisite paper for generations — since before Columbus discovered America. I have toured France many times — one year collecting Gothic cathedrals, another concentrating on the wines of the country — but I saw more of France, the out-of-the-way, the picturesque, when I was on a crass commercial chase for ribbon and paper.

Do you sell? Do you buy? Do you manufacture or ship? Your

rivals and allies are everywhere. Whether you make bricks or lay them or throw them, the sun never sets on your co-workers, collaborators or conspirators.

Don't travel to "get away from it all." Have you an interest? A hobby? A profession? A skill? Take it with you. The Cubans have a word for tourists — "ducks" — in derisive tribute to the way tourists follow each other around, quacking to themselves, and waddling home again blissfully happy — though, while they have looked at everything, they have seen nothing. Travel with design and you broaden your knowledge; tour with idle curiosity and you flatten your arches. Don't be a "duck."

The Voice of Experience

In 1936, when Simon Bolivar Buckner, later lieutenant general commanding our forces in Alaska, was attending a refresher course for colonels, a young instructor remarked that Regimental Headquarters should prepare the programs for company training, because inexperienced captains might make errors if they did their own.

Up rose Buckner and ended all argument by saying: "Uncle Zeke was known in my Kentucky home town for his wisdom. One day a young friend asked him, 'Uncle Zeke, how come you're so wise?'

"'Because I've got good judgment,' the old man replied. 'Good judgment comes from experience, and experience — well, that comes from poor judgment!'"

— Contributed by Brigadier General John W. Lang

Wake Up and Live!

A condensation from the book

DOROTHEA BRANDE

Author of "Becoming a Writer," "Most Beautiful Lady," etc.

In *Wake Up and Live!* Dorothea Brande offers a formula for success which, she says, "is so simple and so obvious that I could hardly believe it responsible for the magical results which followed when I put it into practice."

WAKE UP AND LIVE!

TWO YEARS AGO I was a failure. Oh, nobody knew it except me. I held an interesting position, lived not too dull a life — yet there was no doubt in my own mind, at least, that I had failed. For I had been in a deadlock: I had known what I wanted to do, had equipped myself for my profession — and got nowhere.

Then I found the idea which set me free. I came across a sentence in a book, *Human Personality* by F. W. H. Myers, which was so illuminating that I put the book aside to consider all the possibilities suggested in that one idea. When I picked up the book again I was a different person.

Every aspect of my life was altered. At first I did not realize it. I only knew, with increasing certainty, that at last I had found a talisman for counteracting failure and inertia and discouragement, and that it worked. In the 20 years before I found my formula I had written 17 short stories, 20 book reviews, half a dozen newspaper items, one attempt at a novel. An average of less than two completed pieces of work per year!

For the two years *after* my moment of illumination, this is the record: three books (the first two in less than the first year, and both successful), 24 articles, four short stories, 72 lectures, the scaffolding of three more books, and innumerable letters of consultation and professional advice sent to all parts of the country.

Nor are those the only results of my formula. The tentativeness and timidity which had crippled me dropped away. Interviews, lectures, engagements which I had driven myself to, became pleasurable experiences. I was on good terms with myself at last, no longer exhorting and ruthlessly driving myself, and so no longer unnecessarily bored and tired.

Some months ago I was asked to lecture to a group of booksellers, and the subject I chose was the substance of this book: that we are victims of a Will to Fail; that unless we see this in time and take action against it we die without accomplishing our intentions; that there is a way of counteracting that Will which gives results like magic.

It seemed that my audience, almost to a man, was in the state I had described, that they all were looking for help. I was flooded with messages, questions, letters, telephone calls, requests for interviews from people who realized they were living halting, hesitant lives. What follows is intended to be a practical guide for all like them who would escape futility and begin to live happily and well.

WITH the time and energy we spend in making failure a certainty we might have certain success.

Suppose a man had an appointment a hundred miles north of his home, and that if he kept it he would be sure of having happiness and prosperity. He has just time enough to get there, just enough gas in his car. He drives out, but decides that it would be more fun to go 25 miles south before starting out in earnest. Nonsense, isn't it?

Yet when it comes to going straight to the appointments we make with ourselves and our own fulfillment, we all act very much like the hero of this silly fable: we drive the wrong way. We fail where we might have succeeded by spending the same power and time. And this failure indicates that energy has been poured into the wrong channel. *It takes energy to fail.*

This is something which we seldom see at once. But let any psychologist tell you how much energy a man must expend to resist motion. A powerful struggle must be waged against the forces of life in order to remain inert, although this struggle takes place so far beneath the surface of our lives that we do not always become aware of it. Physical inaction is no true sign that life-force is not being burned away.

When failure comes about through devoting precious hours to

time-killing pursuits, we can all see that energy is being diverted. But there are other ways of killing time which may seem like conscientious hard work. It is only by looking more closely, by discovering that this work both tires us and leaves us unsatisfied, that we see our energy is being devoted to the pursuit of failure.

But why should this be so? Why, if with the same energy we must use in any case, we might be succeeding, do we so seldom live the lives we hoped and planned to live? And why do we think we are being properly philosophical when we give ourselves excuses for failure? We do not truly believe — although our proverbs sound as though we did — that one must choose either success *or* the good life. We know that those who succeed see the same sunsets, breathe the same air, love and are loved no less than failures; and in addition they have something more: the knowledge that they have chosen to move in the direction of life and growth.

Then why do we fail? Especially, why do we work hard at failure? Because, besides being creatures subject to the Will to Live and the Will to Power, we are driven by another Will, the Will to Fail.

This is to many of us a novel idea. Our psychologies make much of the Will to Power. But the Will to Fail is more obscure. To realize that there is this down-dragging, frustrating current is the first step in turning from failure to success. Braced against it, the energy that is now going into failure can be used to healthy ends.

In youth we seldom recognize the symptoms of the Will to Fail in ourselves. We explain our reluctance to getting started as the natural timidity of the tyro. Or we excuse ourselves for never having got to work in earnest because the employment we were able to find when it was imperative that we should begin earning is not work for which we are ideally suited. When marriage and the raising of a family have been undertaken, the necessity is all the more urgent. We might be willing to wait through a few thin years if no one but ourselves would suffer, but to ask others to do so takes more courage than most of us can muster.

Often, at first, we have a firm intention of not losing sight of our real goal, but the nine-to-five work is tiring and exacting; it takes superhuman strength of character to go on working alone when the rest of the world is at play, and when we have never had any evidence that we should be successful if we continued, anyway. And so without realizing it, we slip through the world without making our contribution, without discovering all that there was in us to do, without using a fraction of our abilities.

"Do not act as if you had a thousand years to live," Marcus Aurelius warned himself in his maxims. Wherever we turn we find the remorseless reminder: "It is later than you think." Yet all those in the grip of the Will to Fail spend their precious hours as though the store were inexhaustible. There are, for instance, those who sleep from two to six hours a day more than they need for perfect health. And there are the waking sleepers who indulge in listless, time-killing pursuits: the solitaire players, the pathological bookworms, the endless crossword puzzlers, the jigsaw-puzzle contingent. The line between recreation and obsession is not hard to see once we know it is there. Again there are the relentless movie fans and theater-goers, the eternal embroiderers, the aimless conversationalists, the nightly dancers, all those who count the day lost which has no tea or dinner or cocktail party in it.

There are still more obscure ways of falling victim to the Will to Fail. Consider the innumerable persons, for instance, who deliberately undertake work which calls for only a small part of their abilities and who then drive themselves relentlessly, exhausting themselves over useless details. Consider the takers of eternal post-graduate courses; or the "devoted" daughters and sons and mothers who pour out their lives into the lives of other adults, but whose offering, since they have never truly developed what was most valuable in themselves, adds no richness and only unimportant comfort to the objects of their "self-sacrifice."

It is plain that one motive is at work in all these cases: *the intention, often unconscious, to fill life so full of secondary activities or substitute activities that there will be no time in which to perform the best work of which one is capable.*

The intention, in short, is to fail.

TO UNDERSTAND why so many of us unconsciously conspire with ourselves to fail, it is necessary to examine what may be called the rewards of failure.

Psychology has accustomed us to accepting the idea that we are all, at some level, engaged most of the time in revery. We dream either consciously or unconsciously, awake or asleep, of a situation in which we feel we should be happier than we are in real life.

The inveterate dreamer will do anything halfheartedly to get his bread and butter. Then, when his daily task is over, he will be back at his happy dream again. He succeeds at only one thing — clearing away a little space, gaining each day a few hours of free time, for just one purpose — to go on wasting his life.

Consider, for instance, that if you try for anything just enough to give yourself some justification for saying that you *have* tried, you can fold your hands for the rest of your days. You can thereupon become a dilettante, able to hint at standards of excellence untouched by those who are still out trying to run the dusty race, standards so marvelous, so unattainable, that failure to reach them is more honorable, you imply, than another man's easy success. With not one thing completed, the acclaim you *might* have received, the enormous financial coup you *might* have brought off, the masterpiece you *might* have accomplished, can assume in your revery almost more importance than the real success would have had.

Notice that in these cases your failure will at the very least have rewarded you with escape from the struggle, the pain, the humiliations that attend outward activity.

Yet the rewards of success are so immeasurably more worth having. The smallest task well done, the smallest object, out there in the world where it would not have been if you had not acted, brings in a moment more satisfaction than the failure knows in a lifetime. The knowledge that one is being tried by a real scale and not by shifting revery is like having land underfoot after weeks at sea.

Now having examined the currents of our nature which lead us to acquiesce in failure, let us see what is operating *immediately* to keep us from the healthy efforts we must make to succeed. And here we can learn something from hypnotism. Some feats of a good hypnotist with a good subject sound utterly beyond nature. One man, ordinarily suffering from vertigo at even a slight eminence, when hypnotized can walk a very narrow plank at a great height. Another, slight and delicate, can lift a dead weight. One remarkable case is cited by F. W. H. Myers in his chapter on hypnotism in *Human Personality:* A young actress, an understudy, called upon suddenly to replace the star of her company, was paralyzed with apprehension and stage fright. Under light hypnosis she performed with brilliance and won great applause.

Now the removal of shyness (he wrote) *which hypnotic suggestion can effect is in fact a purgation of memory — inhibiting the recollection of previous failures and setting free whatever group of aptitudes is for the moment required.*

There is the clue. No sentence was ever more packed with rich implications for those who are in earnest about reorienting their lives toward success.

Ordinarily, we learn by "trial and error" — when one course of action brings failure we try again, perhaps many times, until we find the successful procedure. But meanwhile we have experienced failure, sometimes ridicule, sometimes real pain, sometimes grave humiliation, and the final success does not wipe out from our Unconscious a memory of the failures and pain.

The Unconscious dreads pain, humiliation, fatigue; it bends its efforts ceaselessly to avoid them. This fact accounts for much of the inactivity, the inertia, to which we succumb at moments when positive action would be to our advantage: rather than face the mere possibility of pain, rather than revive the memory of our early failures, we *unconsciously* decide not to act at all. Or else we choose to do something easier than we should, start on a program and carry it near the spot where we were hurt before, and there find any excuse to beat a hasty retreat. The childish Unconscious wins — and, in order to avoid a trivial discomfort, we roll up a great account of failure to wound us in the future.

Now, if all that goes before is true — and only a little self-analysis will prove that it is true — how convenient it would be if each of us could carry a hypnotist about, to cast his spell whenever we had to get to work! Yet the solution is far simpler.

All that is necessary to break the spell of inertia and frustration is this: *Act as if it were impossible to fail.*

This is the talisman, the formula, the command of right-about-face which turns us from failure toward success.

Everyone has either experienced or observed the state called the courage of desperation. In the most extreme cases, this courage arises because some catastrophe or series of misfortunes *has completely wiped out every alternative to success.* "He has nothing to lose," we say of one in this situation. Very well, then; he acts with directness and daring which he could not ordinarily command. So often that it has become legendary, this action is attended with overwhelming success. The man who is in such straits that he *dare* not fail invariably acts *as he should always act*: as if it were impossible to fail.

But desperation is not the only tool which will cut away the possibility of failure. Imagination will do the work even better and more neatly. You will find that if you can imaginatively capture the state of mind which would be yours if you knew you were going toward a prearranged and inevitable success, the first result will be a tremendous surge of vitality. It will seem as though your mind gave a great sigh of relief at the liberation and stretched itself to its fullest extent. It is not that one is suddenly given wonderful new powers but, by ceasing to let fear hold its sway, *we come into the use of already existing aptitudes which we formerly had no energy to explore.*

But how can you get into the frame of mind to act as if it were impossible to fail? Well, everyone has had a taste of success in some line, if only in a very minor matter. Think back to some such success of yours, even if it was a success of your school days. What you want to recapture is the *state of mind* — the steady, confident feeling — that was yours in former moments of success.

Fix your attention on that, for that is to be your working frame of mind. Until you can reach it, refuse to begin, but *insist* to yourself on reaching it as soon as possible. When you have found the mood, hold it steadily for a while, as if waiting for a word of command. All at once you will feel a release of energy. You have received from yourself your working orders, and you can begin. You will see that you no longer have to *push yourself to do the work;* all your energy is free to *push the work alone.*

But, having achieved the proper mood for successful action, there are still two mental qualities to be acquired. We must make our minds both keener and more flexible. We all tend to find a routine which gets our day's tasks done with a minimum of effort, a fact which might have no unfortunate effects if we used the time we save to good purpose. But the cold truth is that we apply the routine-observing tendency to our whole lives, growing mentally and spiritually more flaccid, more timorous, less experimental with every day we spend supported by the rigidity of habit. Indeed we have so far allowed ourselves to soften, to abandon our ingenuity, to escape responsibility whenever possible, that we have grown to abhor the very word "discipline."

Yet discipline is essential if we are to develop the qualities necessary for a full life. Mental discipline should connote the equivalent in the sphere of the mind which the athlete undertakes for perfecting his body. We should first take stock of our minds and then put them through their paces so that we can get the maximum use from them.

Not all of the disciplines suggested here will be equally valuable to all cases, but, before rejecting any one of them, examine yourself to discover if you are not possibly throwing it aside simply because it *does* ask you to put a little more restraint on yourself than you find pleasurable.

1. *The first exercise is to spend an hour every day without saying anything except in answer to direct questions.* This should be done without giving anyone the impression that you are sulking or suffering from a bad headache. Present as ordinary an appearance as possible; simply do not speak. Answer questions just to their limit, and no further, and do not attempt in any way to draw another question.

One thing which soon becomes apparent to many who try this is that we usually rush into speech, see by the expression on another's face that we have not made ourselves entirely clear or have misspoken in some way, and try again. This likewise may not make our intention understood; we try again. We pause a moment, think the matter over, issue a clearer statement. But in the meanwhile there are those three earlier attempts still remaining in our hearers' minds, beclouding the issue, making us seem ineffectual.

And all who have experimented with it agree that, while the silence lasted, a sense of mastery grew in them. When they resumed speech it was with the sense of using speech definitely and purposefully.

2. *Learn to think for half an hour a day exclusively on one subject.* Simple as this sounds, it is at first ludicrously hard to do. The novice should begin by thinking on his solitary subject for five minutes a day at first, increasing the period daily till the half hour has been attained. To begin with, a concrete object should be chosen: say a flower. Do not have it before you; build it up in your mind. Describe it to yourself as each of the senses would report it. When that is done, go on to how it grows and where; what it symbolizes, if anything; what uses are made of it. From this simple beginning, work up to considering a concrete problem and, finally, to an abstraction. Start with subjects which really interest you, but when you have taught your mind not to wander even for a moment, begin

choosing a subject by putting your finger at random on a newspaper or the page of a book and think on the first idea suggested by the lines you have touched.

You will find it revealing to start this exercise with a pencil and pad, making a slight check on the paper whenever you find your attention slipping. You will find your paper full for the first few days. Fortunately, improvement in this is fairly rapid. At the end of a week, at the end of a month in refractory cases, the pad will be found nearly blank at the end of your half hour.

This, of course, is simply the "concentration" which was often so vainly preached to every one of us in our school days. Once it is learned, it is of immense benefit. Anyone who is capable of it can, for instance, pick up a foreign language in very short order. The accent may be barbarous unless one has learned phonetics early, but books and newspapers can be easily read, and enough of a vocabulary to get around in the strange land can be acquired in less than a month.

Moreover, in any competitive performance, the one who has trained himself to think steadily, without deflection, will arive at his conclusions first.

3. *Write a letter without once using the following words: I, me, my, mine.** Make it smooth and keep it interesting. If the recipient notices there is something odd about it, the exercise has failed.

This practice allows us to see ourselves in perspective. In order to write a good letter of the sort, it is necessary to turn the mind outward — to give up, for a while, obsessions with our own affairs. We come back to our own lives refreshed.

4. *Talk for 15 minutes a day without using I, me, my, mine.*

5. *Write a letter in a "successful" or placid tone.* No actual misstatements are allowed. No posing as successful, no lying. Simply look for aspects or activities which *can* be honestly reported in this way and confine your letter to them. Indicate by the letter's tone that you are, at the moment of writing, not discouraged in any way.

---

* In my innocence, I believed this exercise was wholly mine. I recently came across it, and similar exercises, in Alys Bentley's *The Dance of the Mind.*

The purpose here is to turn yourself from a negative and discouraging attitude toward a positive and healthy one. However unpromising the prospect for finding enough good items for a letter may appear at first, one soon discovers that a number of matters are going smoothly and well, but that they have been ignored while one centers on disappointment and frustration. A complete holiday from self-pity and depression is necessary to success.

6. *Keep a new acquaintance talking about himself without allowing him to become conscious of what you are doing.* Turn back, at first, any courteous reciprocal questions in such a way that your auditor does not feel rebuffed. You will find a genuine interest rising in you for your companion; soon, if you are at all kindly or imaginative, you will find yourself engrossed. The last lingering trace of self-consciousness will drop from you. At the very least you will have extended your horizon and learned a little more about how the world looks to another.

7. (The exact opposite of the above exercise, and infinitely harder to do with intention): *Talk exclusively about yourself and your interests without complaining, boasting, or (if possible) boring your companion.* Make yourself and your activities as interesting as you can to the person to whom you are talking.

This, paradoxically, is an excellent discipline for those who ordinarily talk too much about themselves. When concentrated talking about one's own interests is undertaken consciously, every sign of indifference, of boredom, of impatience, which may ordinarily escape us, is only too plainly seen. It soon becomes apparent that talking about the trivial, the commonplace, the recurring incidents of one's life leads to certain ennui in our hearers. If, on the other hand, we have had genuinely interesting experiences, have been more imaginative in a situation than usual, are undertaking something new, we are likely to hold our audience. The conclusion that perhaps we might profit by extending our interests, undertaking new adventures, or bringing more imagination to our everyday lives can hardly be escaped.

8. *Plan two hours of a day and live according to the plan.* Make a schedule for reading the paper, opening mail, writing letters, filing papers, etc., and turn from one activity to the next, not at the approximate minute of your schedule, but on the exact moment. If you are only halfway through the newspaper, that's very sad. But down it must go, and you open your mail — hitherto disregarded. Wherever you are at 8:20 with your correspondence, you stop and turn to the arranging of your papers.

One purpose of this discipline is to demonstrate how badly we lose our sense of the time necessary to accomplish any stipulated activity. We will nonchalantly plan to cram the work of half a day into a couple of hours after lunch. It is possible to learn — by planning, first, two hours of a day, then three, then four, and so on till we have planned and lived an effective, eight-hour day (at the least) — to use time to the best advantage. Rigid scheduling of a whole day is not always possible or desirable, but a few days lived by timetable now and again will refresh our sense of the value of time and teach us what we can expect of ourselves when we do not waste it.

9. (This is the most difficult of all. It will seem so arbitrary to many readers that they will not even try to apply it. It *is* arbitrary; that is its very essence.): *Arrange to put yourself into situations where you must act nonhabitually, where you must adapt yourself.* It is not easy to get resiliency into our lives, but it is a quality too valuable to be lost. If the following recommendation seems somewhat too dramatic, almost too ridiculous, be assured that the results will show the worth of the discipline.

On a number of slips of paper — 12 will do to start with — write instructions like these:

"Go 20 miles from home, using ordinary conveyance." (In other words, streetcars, buses, ferries, subways.)

"Go 12 hours without food."

"Eat a meal in the unlikeliest place you can find." A restaurant in a totally foreign quarter of a city is good here.

"Say nothing all day except in answer to questions."

"Stay up all night and work."

And this, by the way, is the most valuable order of them all. You must plan to work steadily and quietly, resisting every temptation to lie down for a few moments, but relaxing very slightly against the chair-back every hour or so, bracing yourself to your work again the moment lassitude threatens to overcome you. Only those who have actually done this realize that there are depths to our minds which we seldom plumb, accustomed as we are to succumb to the first attack of fatigue or to stay awake only so long as we have outer stimulation.

Seal these slips of paper in 12 envelopes, shuffle them thoroughly, and put them in a drawer. Every other week, or on a given day of each month, pick one of the envelopes, open it, and perform your own command. It may be raining pitchforks on the day you command yourself to travel 20 miles by common carrier; nevertheless, unless your state of health absolutely forbids it, you go. The oftener you can be arbitrary with yourself — without turning into a restless jumping jack, it goes without saying — the better for your character eventually!

10. (An alternative to the above): *From time to time give yourself a day on which you say "Yes" to every request made of you which is at all reasonable.* The more you tend to retire from society in your leisure, the more valuable this will be. You may find yourself invited to go sleigh riding in your 24 hours; you may be invited to change your job. The sleigh ride should certainly be accepted, however much you may hate straw and cold weather. The job changing, fortunately, can be submitted to examination, since it is only "reasonable" activities which you are to undertake. Don't be afraid nothing will occur on that day; it is astonishing how many small requests we can turn aside daily rather than interrupt our even course. The consequences may be wide-reaching, often educative, sometimes extremely advantageous.

The first time I put this discipline into practice, for example, I was asked, for the first time in years, to teach a class in fiction writing. Now I had always said that I abhorred teaching and that most courses in fiction writing did almost nothing for the pupils. Under my own orders, I had to accept. I took the class, listened to the questions my students asked me, discovered that no book I knew of answered them fully, and was led into writing one of my own. And this present book is the result of another such "Yes-saying" day. The lecture I was asked to give came at a time when my schedule was more than full, when I would, if I had not given myself blanket instructions to accept, have begged off. Not every day of the sort has quite such consequences. But in my life they are almost always interesting, if nothing more.

Nevertheless do not jump to the conclusion that, because one day of the sort may bring many interesting possibilities to light, *every day* should be led in that manner. On the contrary, to deny oneself an opportunity now and again is fully as illuminating, particularly for those who waste too much time in party-going, theaters, and so on. Such persons should plan to refuse many invitations and spend the time in intensive self-cultivation.

Once you get the idea, you will find these disciplines not only helpful but genuinely amusing. In many cases they replace the rather haphazard puzzle-solving activities which call on somewhat the same capacities. In matching your wits against yourself you take on the shrewdest and wiliest antagonist you can have, and consequently a victorious outcome in this duel of wits brings a great feeling of triumph. At last, when one is in training, one can call at will on any of the mental traits which have been strengthened or exercised in these ways and find that it performs exactly and quickly.

Now, to consider the technique of success in these pages, we have had to sacrifice pace to slow-motion analysis. The actual tempo of success is quicker, smoother, more brisk than any book analyzing it can ever show. There is a delightful conciseness in successful action. "I know I'm doing a good picture if I'm painting just as fast as I can move," a great artist said to a group of friends recently. "The minute I dabble I know I'm stalling, that there's something I'm not seeing right; when I'm right it's almost like play."

But though purposeful action seems quicker and more enjoyable than any other, in reality you may be working more slowly and carefully than ordinarily. It is the fact that there is no confusion of issues, no part of your mind off wool-gathering as you move, which gives an unmistakable "tone" to successful work.

It is to attain this directness that we put ourselves through exercises in flexibility and restraint, learn to turn imagination away from apprehension and into useful channels, determine to act wisely in minor matters in order to store up courage for major issues. And courage is the *sine qua non* of success.

Only by acting as if it were impossible to fail can we discover the farthest reaches of what our best may offer. And success, for any sane adult, is exactly equivalent to doing his best.

How to Win an Argument

THE WAY to convince another is to state your case moderately and accurately. Then scratch your head, or shake it a little and say that is the way it seems to you, but that of course you may be mistaken about it; which causes your listener to receive what you have to say, and as like as not, turn about and try to convince you of it, since you are in doubt. But if you go at him in a tone of positiveness and arrogance you only make an opponent of him.

— Benjamin Franklin

FATHER FORGETS

Condensed from
an editorial that originally appeared in People's Home Journal
W. Livingston Larned

Listen, son: I am saying this as you lie asleep, one little paw crumpled under your cheek and the blond curls stickily wet on your damp forehead. I have stolen into your room alone. Just a few minutes ago, as I sat reading my paper in the library, a stifling wave of remorse swept over me. Guiltily I came to your bedside.

These are the things I was thinking, son: I had been cross to you. I scolded you as you were dressing for school because you gave your face merely a dab with a towel. I took you to task for not cleaning your shoes. I called out angrily when you threw some of your things on the floor.

At breakfast I found fault, too. You spilled things. You gulped down your food. You put your elbows on the table. You spread butter too thick on your bread. And as you started off to play and I made for my train, you turned and waved a hand and called, "Good-bye, Daddy!" and I frowned, and said in reply, "Hold your shoulders back!"

Then it began all over again in the late afternoon. As I came up the road I spied you, down on your knees, playing marbles. There were holes in your stockings. I humiliated you before your boy friends by marching you ahead of me to the house. Stockings were expensive — and if you had to buy them you would be more careful! Imagine that, son, from a father!

Do you remember, later, when I was reading in the library, how you came in, timidly, with a sort of hurt look in your eyes? When I glanced up over my paper, impatient at the interruption, you hesitated at the door. "What is it you want?" I snapped.

You said nothing, but ran across in one tempestuous plunge, and threw your arms around my neck and kissed me, and your small arms tightened with an affection that God had set blooming in your heart and which even neglect could not wither. And then you were gone, pattering up the stairs.

Well, son, it was shortly afterward that my paper slipped from my hands and a terrible sickening fear came over me. What has habit been doing to me? The habit of finding fault, of reprimanding — this was my reward to you for being a boy. It was not that I did not love you; it was that I expected too much of youth. It was measuring you by the yardstick of my own years.

And there was so much that was good and fine and true in your character. The little heart of you was as big as the dawn itself over the wide hills. This was shown by your spontaneous impulse to rush in and kiss me good night. Nothing else matters tonight, son. I have come to your bedside in the darkness, and I have knelt there, ashamed!

It is a feeble atonement; I know you would not understand these things if I told them to you during your waking hours. But tomorrow I will be a real daddy! I will chum with you, and suffer when you suffer, and laugh when you laugh. I will bite my tongue when impatient words come. I will keep saying as if it were a ritual: "He is nothing but a boy — a little boy!"

I am afraid I have visualized you as a man. Yet as I see you now, son, crumpled and weary in your cot, I see that you are still a baby. Yesterday you were in your mother's arms, your head on her shoulder. I have asked too much, too much.

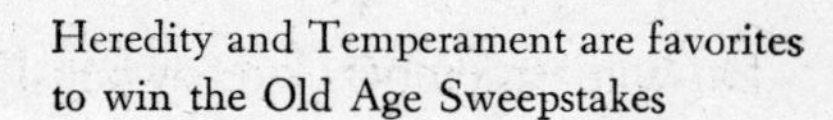

The Business of Living a Long Time

Condensed from The Forum

Raymond Pearl

NO SIBYLLINE ORACLE or scientific formula can predict how long you will or *ought* to live; all that science can do is prepare tables showing you how long human beings actually *do* live, then let you estimate your own chances. If, for example, you aspire to round out a Biblical "three-score years and ten" on earth, the tables indicate that you have slightly more than one chance in three of doing so. Life insurance statistics reveal that out of each hundred persons born in the United States over a third are alive at 72. A decade later, about 12 of the original hundred are still living. Thereafter, the odds against further longevity rise more rapidly. Only one or two of a hundred starters in life's race ever pass the 92nd milepost. As for spanning a full century — well, a genuine centenarian, you may console yourself, is exceedingly rare.

For a number of years I have kept exhaustive records of persons who have lived to be 95 or older, and from an analysis of these records — some 2000 carefully authenticated cases — it has been possible to derive a composite picture of the biologic, physical and temperamental equipment possessed by persons who might be called "practicing Methuselahs."

The first and by far the most important requisite of longevity, as these actual case histories show, is having ancestors who were long-lived. In other words, you *inherit* the biological characteristic of living a long time, just as you inherit blue eyes or red hair. If your parents and grandparents lived to a ripe old age, you probably will in some degree inherit this same biological trait. Let us take an example from our records — Case P 191. Mrs. P 191 is a hale and hearty nonagenarian. Her father died at 78 years of age and her mother at 91. Her paternal grandfather reluctantly left this vale of tears after a sojourn of 99 years and 6 months; his wife, P 191's grandmother, died at the respectable, if not particularly extraordinary, age of 78. But the grandmother on the mother's side did better. She stayed around for 94 years. Her husband unfortunately died of typhoid infection at 35 years of age. But anyone whose parents and grandparents together lived over 475 years has a sound background of family longevity.

Actuarial studies we have made show that the contribution of heredity to longevity can be precisely measured. As an example, consider two groups of baby boys. The fathers of all the boys in one group all died before reaching 50 years of age; the fathers of the other group all lived to be over 80. The average duration of life of the babies in the second group was 22 percent greater than in the first group; more than ten years per person, on the average, of longer living.

Next to heredity in insuring long life seems to be the matter of temperament. Are you naturally tranquil-hearted and does your temper ride an even saddle? Let us hope so, for the calm and contented type seems to have a very important advantage in the Old Age Sweepstakes over the person who is fretful, irritable, and inclined to worry.

The evidence also tends to show that persons who avoid too strenuous exercise after 40, and do not engage in heavy muscular labor, have a much better chance of long life than the misguided chap who overtaxes his middle-aged boilers with a freshman head of steam.

One of the commonest myths about longevity is the notion that dietary coddling and abstinence from alcohol and tobacco will guarantee a full harvest of years. In the records there appears to be little to support this admirable but deluded point of view. Some of the persons on the list of nonagenarians have been lifelong teetotalers and abstemious eaters; others have habitually tamped home vast cargos of food, and quaffed Olympian draughts of malt and vinous liquors whenever thirst so dictated. Many of them smoked cigars, pipes and cigarettes; others abhorred tobacco in any form. Some lived amid toxic urban fumes, others inhaled nothing but pure country air. None of these things appeared to affect longevity either favorably or unfavorably. Obviously abuse can wreck a sturdy frame, but it is also true that no amount of dietary solicitude and no heroic devotion to a "daily dozen" will carry an individual into advanced old age if he has a constitution biologically inadequate for the journey. To put it another way: it makes less difference what you *do* than what you biologically *are*.

A thing that is noticeable in the old age records generally is that few persons who live past 90 have ever had a surgical operation, or if they have, the surgery has been of a minor character. There is nothing mysterious about this fact; it merely means that people who live to be 90 or more are the kind of people who constitutionally are not susceptible to surgical diseases. Major surgery, in a broad sense, is the branch of the science of medicine which devotes itself primarily to the correction of innate, constitutional biological defects of the individual. Nonagenarians, by and large, have no such defects.

This leads to another odd paradox. No small number of the persons in our collection of cases have "enjoyed poor health," as the phrase goes, throughout the greater part of their long lives. The reports say that they have "always been sickly," or "frail," or "semi-invalid." This is really not surprising. It has long been known, from a variety of evidence, that morbidity and mortality do not connote the same things biologically. A person may have a great deal of sickness, continued intermittently over many years, and yet live to a ripe old age.

What kills nonagenarians and centenarians in the end? Comprehensive studies indicate that heart diseases are responsible for roughly 24 percent of all deaths at ages of 90 years and above; diseases of the arteries (hardening, etc.) account for approximately ten percent of such deaths; breakdown of our breathing apparatus, the respiratory system, accounts for 12 to 13 percent; failure of the kidneys to perform their function takes off roughly 12 percent of the males and nine percent of the females. About seven percent in each sex die because their alimentary tracts (stomach, intestines, etc.) fail. Roughly three quarters of all the deaths of nonagenarians and centenarians occur simply because these four systems — circulatory, respiratory, excretory and alimentary — finally wear out.

The whole subject of longevity boils down to this: Persons who spring from long-lived ancestors and thereby inherit a toughly constructed, infection-resisting, soundly functioning constitution are likely to live to an unusual old age. Medical science has done much, and will do more, to prevent what might be termed "premature mortality" — that is, death before 50, especially from infections; but persons in the extreme old age group will continue to live because heredity and temperament have given them a physical organization capable of resisting the noxious forces that cause death to their less sturdily constructed fellow men.

We should be careful to get out of an experience only the wisdom that is in it — and stop there; lest we be like the cat that sits down on the hot stove-lid. She will never sit down on a hot stove-lid again — and that is well; but also she will never sit down on a cold one any more.

— Mark Twain, *Following the Equator* (Harper)

He Brought Them Back to Health

Condensed from
The American Magazine
By M. K. Wisehart

At 79, William Muldoon, the world's most famous trainer of men, was, except for his white hair, a marvelously young man. He had the spring of youth, the grace of long-accustomed self-control, which are as much a quality of mind and of character as of physique. He rehabilitated thousands — rich and poor, industrial leaders and financiers, statesmen, generals, playwrights, college professors, athletes — more than 18,000 in all!

What had Muldoon learned which the average man can apply in his own life? His recipe may be put in one word — self-control. We *know* pretty definitely what we ought to do. Doctors have laid down the fundamental rules of diet, exercise, work, recreation — all the principles of right living. The trouble is, we don't follow them. Health is ours, to have and to keep, if we will have the mental and moral backbone to stand up and take it.

"I can honestly assert," Muldoon said to me, "that my mind is the master and my body is its slave. I simply do not do anything I think I ought not to do — whether it is taking more than one cup of coffee in the morning, or staying up late when I am tired, and know I ought to go to bed.

"I have found that a man's bad physical condition usually comes from a bad mental condition. My first effort is to reach his mind. For the time being I supply the element of control which he himself lacks. The part that exercise plays in the daily routine must not be overemphasized. It is important and necessary; but the real problem is always one of mind-building. The rapidity with which a man improves when he has the right living conditions and the right habits is astonishing.

"If a man is going to accomplish anything, if he is going to have a character that is worth the name, he must practice self-discipline. Remember this! Any man can save himself from most of the ills and unhappiness of life if he will live according to the right principles and will guard himself against the habits that weaken his will.

"What most people fail to realize is that nerve energy is the motive power of the body. The bad habits most of us acquire are a tax on this supply of nerve energy. If you don't arrange your work, diet, sleep, and recreation so that you are regularly renewing your supply of nerve energy in every period of 24 hours, you are bound to suffer serious consequences. Without a good supply of nervous energy none of the organs can function properly. The heart action and the circulation are disturbed. The stomach and the entire gastro-intestinal tract lose tone.

"When your way of living keeps you near nervous exhaustion, your judgment becomes impaired. You make mistakes, and so begin to lose confidence in yourself. You are fretful and easily irritated. You become careless about your appearance. Such symptoms come on gradually, as one harmful habit leads to another.

"One of the most destructive things a man can do is to follow the easy way in little things. He grows careless about his table manners, instead of making a decent ceremony of a meal, as a man should. Or take a little thing like getting up in the morning. Perhaps this man ought to get up at seven o'clock. But he regularly turns over for another nap, so that when he finally gets up he must make up for his tardiness.

"He hurries into his bath. But the water, instead of being cold or lukewarm, is hot. He dawdles, instead of making his bath a smart exercise with a brisk rubbing afterward. Then he dresses hastily, slighting small but important details of dress. A day begun thus, on the plane of self-indulgence, will continue on that plane. Weakness in little things is a moral gangrene, which slowly destroys the will.

"The man who lacks a true conception of self-mastery doesn't even walk, stand, and sit properly. You see him slouching in a chair with his legs crossed. Has he ever stopped to think that all the main blood vessels that supply the extremities run down the back of the legs; that when he crosses his legs he shuts off the arteries and puts an unnecessary strain on the heart, by increasing the amount of nerve energy required to send the blood through the body?

"He knows that the digestion of a hearty meal requires a tremendous amount of nervous energy. Yet he takes the attitude that a heavy meal won't hurt him, just this once.

"Perhaps the time comes when this man thinks he is breaking down from overwork. But I've never known a man to break down from overwork alone! The work would have been only a stimulus to him had all his other living conditions been wholesome and normal.

"Let me emphasize this point! The mind, or the body, that is forced beyond itself by artificial stimulants inevitably suffers injury. In my opinion, the habit which most commonly brings a man to the verge of disaster is overeating. The next most common cause is the use of narcotics — smoking and drinking.

"So far as smoking is concerned, it is excess that does the harm, not one cigar or a pipe after a meal. However, the man who never indulges in narcotics will stand up under a test that tries him mentally and physically where the other man will fail.

"When a man is mentally tired by honest work, he ought to seek relaxation in solitude. Don't do anything! Just relax.

"I believe that the greatest happiness on earth is to have health and that sense of triumph which comes from being your own master, able to do the things, big and little, which you know you ought to do and can do. But this joy of living will come only to the man who has learned self-discipline. In nine cases out of ten, physical breakdowns are due to lack of self-control! Watch yourself for one single day. See how often you transgress what you *know* to be the principles of health. There lies the secret of physical well-being."

Pointers on cultivation of new interests, and on getting along with one's in-laws

I Am the Mother-in-Law in the Home

Condensed from The Saturday Evening Post

Anonymous

As far back as I can remember I have had a horror of being dependent upon my children in my old age. I had planned in every possible way to insure my independence. When declining health and declining finances left me no alternative but to live with my daughter, my first feeling was one of bitterness.

In the seven years since my husband's death I had lived alone. Would I be able, at my age, to give up this accustomed freedom and adapt myself to the ways of another home? My daughter and I are both positive characters, and before her marriage we were often at odds. And her husband, a high-strung businessman, is not the easiest nature to live with. I had seen too many elderly women in the situation upon which I was about to enter to contemplate my fate with anything but foreboding.

I said to myself: "You are tackling the hardest job you ever had. Hitherto your difficult problems have come when your vitality and adaptive qualities were better than today. But you have won before. If you win this time, the reward will be a peaceful old age near those you love best."

First, I told myself that, for the fact of my having brought her into the world and reared her, my daughter owed me nothing. I therefore had no right to demand from her any particular kind of conduct toward me. If I could live fully up to this conviction I would never have occasion to feel hurt or neglected — a common failing among elderly women.

For the same reason I must not forget that the owner of a home has the right of way in it. When my daughter lived in my home she yielded the right of way to me. Now that right belonged to her, and I must make her feel that I understood the rules. It is not always easy.

I recall my experience with a friend shortly after I entered my new home. Alice was a young woman whose kindnesses I wished to return. But complications arose. I tried asking Alice to visit me at times when my son-in-law and daughter planned to be out. But Alice had the failing of never knowing when to leave, and was usually here when Don and Katherine came in. Obviously, they were becoming tired of her; soon she might become an issue.

My first impulse was to state my case — that I made few demands in my daughter's home, that I had few contacts, and should not be denied this small pleasure. But such a course would have left a basis for irritation. I decided to give Alice up. Moreover I would not feel abused nor mention the fact that I missed her.

Then there was the matter of housework. Too often I have heard daughters say, "I let Mother help as much as I can stand it, because she needs something to do. But how her way of doing things irritates me!" I decided not to be too insistent about helping. I believed my daughter knew me well enough to ask for whatever she needed and thought I could do. And I wanted her to feel under no necessity to provide me with occupation at the expense of her own nerves. This meant that I must not be around when she was getting her work done, or when she had her friends in. I must ask no questions and give no unasked advice. I resolved to spend the greater part of each day alone in my room.

If there is one outstanding thing which makes old people a problem in their children's homes, it is that their lives are too empty. They have so few outside interests that they look to their families constantly for pleasure and work. I made up my mind to become absorbed in something quite apart from my daughter's life.

To find that thing did not seem easy. My life had been devoted almost exclusively to home and family. What was there for me now? All occupations involving any but the lightest physical exertion were closed to me. I had once wanted to learn golf, to drive a car, to swim, to climb mountains, to learn amateur photography. What good were those wishes now? But many years ago I had wanted to play the piano. As a girl I had taken a few lessons, and I had always loved piano music. Why not learn to play now?

When I broached the subject, my daughter looked at me as if her worst fears concerning my senility had been confirmed. But she assented and offered to pay for my lessons. Knowing that she needed the money for other things, I refused. I would teach myself.

I obtained a good instruction book and went over each lesson carefully. I longed for the nimbleness my fingers had once had, and it seemed that my mind creaked as did my joints. But I refused to become discouraged. When, after a few weeks, I could read a little music I was positively elated! Was it possible, too, that my fingers were a bit more flexible?

When my daughter realized that I was actually learning to play a little, and, incidentally, was having genuine fun, she was delighted. And for the first time since I had come to her home, I noticed in her attitude toward me a sense of relaxation, as though she need no longer have me on her mind.

At Christmas Katherine and Don gave me a small piano which fitted into my room, and my joy knew no bounds! Now I could play to my heart's content, with no fear of bothering my hearers.

I am still far from being a pianist, but some time ago, at the mid-week meeting in our church, the young woman who plays the piano sent word at the last minute that she was unable to come. I volunteered to take the pianist's place, and got through all the music of the evening without faltering. Since then I have been called upon extemporaneously many times for simple music, and just now I have charge of the music for a children's program.

I am particularly happy when I can thus help others. But most of all I have helped my own self-confidence. The value to me in finding that, at an age when most people consider their lives over, I can still learn something new, has been inestimable.

My next undertaking was learning to use the typewriter. Again I procured a book and set out to give myself a course in touch typing. My slowness, due to age, was balanced by having far more practice time than the average younger person. I now use the typewriter for all my letters, and when my son-in-law occasionally asks me to do some typing for him, I swell with professional pride, for his standards are high.

I had always wanted to go to college. This was impossible now, but I might read some of the books which would be given me if I went to college. My first choice was English literature, and from a number of college catalogues I made a list of the required readings. With this I treated myself to a course in reading which has proved one of the most delightful experiences of my life, and has led me to the belief that most such reading is required of students who are far too young to appreciate it.

In the same way I studied art history, and learned what I should look for in paintings. I formed the habit of visiting the gallery whenever I felt equal to it, looking at only one or two pictures each time, studying each in detail, and trying to carry away a living memory. I venture to say that today I have a better knowledge of the things in that gallery than the average educated citizen in our town.

Also the small radio in my room has opened up many entirely new interests for me. Among these are sports, about which I had previously known nothing.

As Don and Katherine are not particularly interested in sports, I had not mentioned my latest hobby. But one evening, contrary to my usual custom when there are guests, I was present when Don brought a business prospect home for dinner. The conversation was lagging noticeably, till a chance remark revealed that our guest was tremendously interested in horses. Katherine and Don made a few perfunctory remarks on the subject. Then I entered the conversation, mentioning the names of horses and riders with an easy familiarity which evoked gasps from my astonished children. But the evening was saved! From that moment the visitor came to life and talked with boyish enthusiasm of sports in general, and then of other things. I felt that I had scored.

Of course old age is a disease which we can escape no more than any other illness. When I feel it getting the better of me I fight for all I am worth. One of its signs is a tendency to self-pity. Try as I will to conquer it, I cannot help thinking of myself, at times, as a pathetic old woman. This state of mind seems to go with waning vitality. When I feel these attacks coming on I try to keep Katherine from detecting them. On those days I stay more closely in my room than usual. Or, if possible, I go out for a walk. Above all, I refrain from talking of the possible proximity of my death. I have known old people who cast a constant gloom over those around them by habitual references to this sinister subject.

It is now eight years since I came here to live, and I recently passed my 73rd birthday. I am sure, now, that I have become a welcome member of the household. For, a few weeks ago, I overheard a friend telling Katherine about her difficulties with her mother. It was the usual story of the older woman who did not fit into a home not her own — of slights, jealousies, moods. Then, fearfully, I heard my daughter speak.

"When Mother came here to live," she said, "no one will ever know how I dreaded it. But now I can truthfully say that Don and I both love having her here."

"You're lucky," said the friend.

"Indeed I am," said my daughter. "In fact, Mother has made me dread old age less than I did. I am going to try, when I am old, to be just like her."

Tears of gratitude came into my eyes, and I felt repaid a thousandfold for my efforts.

IT'S MORE FUN TO BE FIT

By Gene Tunney

Lieut.-Commander, U. S. N. R.; author of "Arms for Living"

PHYSICAL flabbiness has always seemed to me a criminal, even sacrilegious abuse of that wonderful instrument, the human body. Ever since boyhood I've made a religion of keeping in shape by regular, conscientious exercise. Adhering to a high ideal of stamina and endurance has paid me dividends not only in the prize ring but in the almost equally grueling struggle of everyday life.

To enjoy the glow of good health, you must exercise. I don't recommend that you develop bulging biceps or go in for exhausting roadwork and bag-punching. But I do say that, if you will regularly devote 15 minutes a day, preferably before breakfast, for 60 days to the simple set of exercises that I devised for conditioning men in the navy, I guarantee that you will enjoy increased physical buoyancy and mental vigor. Perform them faithfully and you can take puffy inches off your waistline, recondition unused muscles, feel better, work better and live longer.

The man who has allowed his body to deteriorate cuts a pitiful figure — chest collapsed, stomach protruding. His sagging diaphragm forces his visceral apparatus out of place, hindering digestive and eliminative processes. He tires easily and complains that he feels like the breaking up of a hard winter.

The first thing this human mealsack must learn is proper posture, the basis of all physical conditioning. "Head up, chin in, chest out, stomach in." Proper body-carriage conserves the energy that postural defects drain away.

The worst of these defects is the protruding paunch caused by abdominal muscles that have become flabby through disuse. There are broad bands of muscle-like cinch-straps around our waistline, whose job is to hold the stomach, intestines and liver in place. When these muscles lose their firmness or "tone," they allow the intestines to sink down and become impaired in function. Indigestion, headache, constipation and chronic fatigue follow.

To toughen the abdominal muscles, I developed exercise No. 1. If you perform it 20 times every morning, gradually working up to 50, you'll get rid of

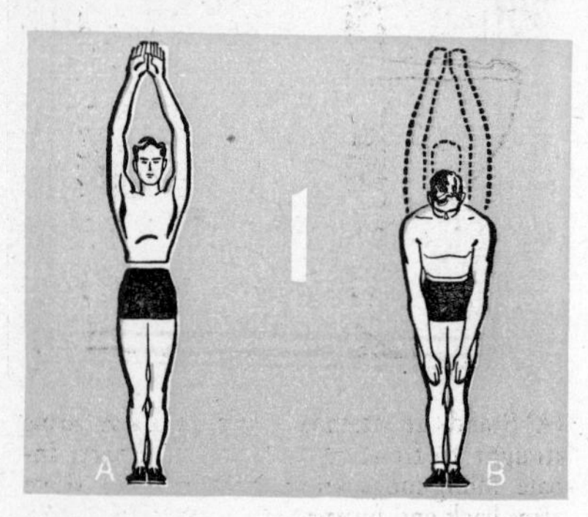

(A) Raise arms to front and above head, inhaling deeply. (B) Lower arms, keeping them stiff and straight, until hands touch knees, with head dropped until chin touches collarbone. Bend at diaphragm, not at waist. Draw stomach up as far as possible. As hands touch knees, exhale. Do 20 times.

(A) Clasp hands behind head, heels 5 inches apart. (B) With diaphragm drawn up and shoulder muscles relaxed, swing upper body in circle, ending at original position. Exhale on way down, inhale on way up. Circle to left 10 times, then to right 10 times.

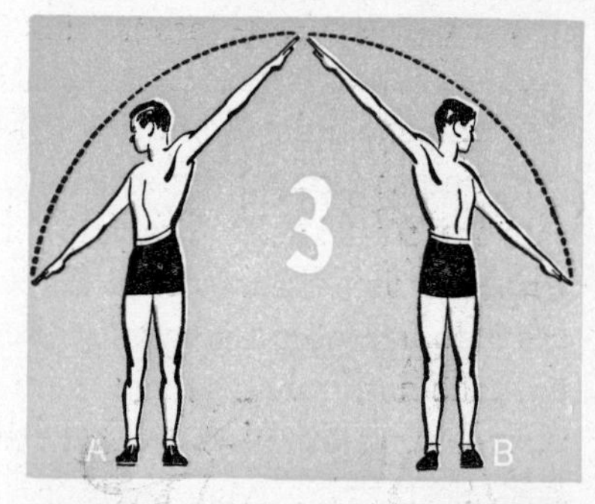

(A) Extend arms sidewise at shoulder level. Drop right hand 10 inches, raise left 10 inches. Draw stomach up; hold hips stationary. Swing right hand behind and down, the left going forward and up. Keep arms in straight line. Pivot from diaphragm, eyes and head following hand that goes back and down. Inhale as head comes up. (B) With stomach drawn up, exhale as head follows left hand around and down. Do 20 times to each side.

that paunch and the evils that accompany it. Remember that it's never too late to start rehabilitating broken-down muscles. The material is there, waiting for you to begin working on it.

Another deformity of posture is the flat, sunken chest, which occurs when we persistently neglect to use full lung capacity. We can get along on only 20 percent of our lung capacity, but that dragging sort of existence is a poor substitute for the vitality we enjoy when the twin bellows of our lungs are taking in great drafts of oxygen. As Dr. George Crile said, "Oxidization is the only source of animal energy. We *live* in proportion to the amount of oxygen we get into our lungs."

A concave chest means that

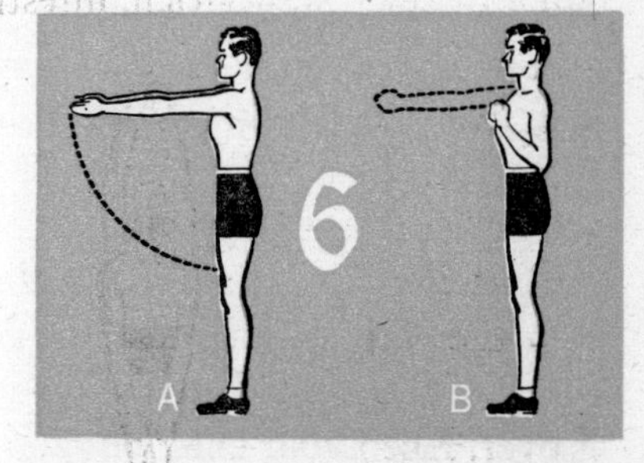

(A) Stand at attention; slowly raise arms straight to front, shoulder width apart. Inhale, filling lungs, and clench fists. (B) Move arms back and forward as vigorously as possible 6 times, holding breath. On 6th stroke, exhale and return to attention. Do this 6 times.

(A) Stand with heels 15 inches apart. Inhale while rising on toes and reaching arms overhead. (B) Bring arms down stiff and straight between legs, exhaling and bending knees and touching floor with backs of hands as far behind heels as possible, to stretch back, hips and abdominal muscles. Repeat 20 times.

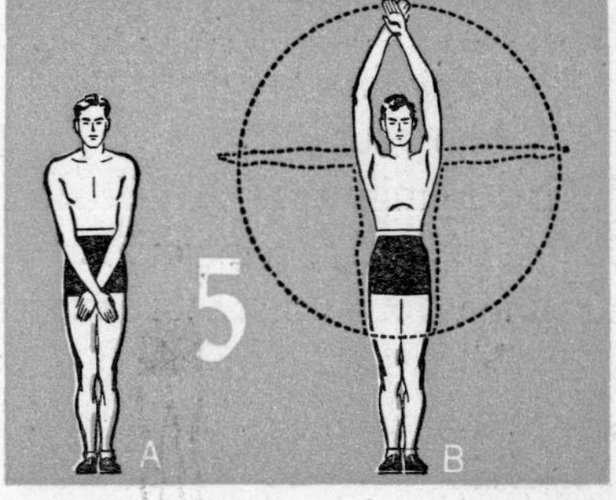

(A) Stand at attention; cross hands. (B) On count of 1, slowly raise arms in semicircle to front and overhead, rising on toes and inhaling steadily. Hands cross each other before reaching top position. On count 2, bring arms in semicircle slowly down to sides, holding breath until they reach original position. On count 3, exhale completely. Do 6 times vigorously.

your diaphragm is sagging. This elastic wall of muscle, the partition between your abdomen and chest, forms the major part of the bellows mechanism that we use in breathing. If the diaphragm sags, the bellows won't work properly; you can't breathe deeply and therefore don't get as much oxygen as you need. According to Dr. Herman N. Bundesen of Chicago, a sagging diaphragm may lead to a stroke of coronary thrombosis. He explains that an insufficient supply of oxygen slows down heart action; the blood flow becomes sluggish; a blood clot may form and clog the coronary artery of the heart, stoppering it like a cork.

Exercises Nos. 1, 2 and 3 will strengthen and put new resiliency into the diaphragm, and draw blood-purifying oxygen into every recess of the lungs. But the job isn't done when the exercise period is over. Keep your chest out and keep your stomach in, until it becomes a habit. At the end of a month you will have doubled your lung capacity, and thereby benefited every cell of your body.

Many people complain of a chronic weariness that sleep will not banish. Their trouble is that too little blood is pumped through the body per minute; this sluggishness, permitting poisonous waste matter to accumulate in every cell, clogs the channels of energy.

Sinking into an overstuffed armchair is not the cure. You must speed up your circulation. The only way to do this is to exercise. A brisk 20-minute walk will send 25 to 30 quarts of blood coursing vigorously through your arteries every 60 seconds — blood that contains four times more oxygen than when you loll in a chair.

While walking, inhale deeply for six paces, holding the breath, then exhale slowly. Do this ten or 15 times during your walk. Like a cleansing torrent, the increased circulation and fresh oxygen will sweep away stagnant, toxic impurities — and your tired feeling.

In youth, we get plenty of exercise through games and running around, but as middle life approaches, we settle down, literally and *figuratively*. Muscles that formerly were lean and resilient become slack and overlaid with fat. Fat is one of the chief enemies of the heart because it has to be plentifully supplied with blood and thus needlessly increases the pumping load that the heart must sustain. The less superfluous lard that you carry around with you, the easier job your heart has. The useless burden carried to a degree by every overweight man and woman is recognized as one of the principal factors in premature death.

If you are accumulating pads of fat around hips and abdomen, or if your once-lean arm and leg muscles are becoming suety, you must decrease your intake of starches and fats, and take regular exercise. Not violent week-ends of golf and tennis or sporadic outbursts of squash, but a daily drill that becomes as much a part of your life as brushing your teeth. The six exercises shown here, if performed every morning on rising, will not only strengthen the diaphragm and lungs but will also take off a pound a week.

Exercise should be regarded as tribute to the heart. This marvelous organ — which is a tough bundle of muscles — thrives on a good workout, and no person free of organic heart trouble need fear that exercise will strain it. More hearts have failed from flabby degeneration than from overexercise. If you're in doubt about the advisability of exercising regularly, see your family doctor and have him check you over.

You can buy substitutes for exercise in any drugstore — headache powders, antacids, laxatives, pick-me-ups — which promise to confer priceless blessings. But you need never buy them again. You will not need the false stimulation of benzedrine or the pain-killing effects of aspirin; you can shake off your dependence on habit-forming laxatives and overcome the acid torments of heartburn if you spend 15 minutes every day in exercise.

Today exercise is a voluntary effort that all civilized men and women should make toward physical perfection — a quickening, cleansing discipline that does for the body what prayer does for the spirit. Stimulated by it, our life-flame burns with a clearer ray; nothing seems hopeless or impossible, and we are charged with the joy of being wholly alive.

THE WORTH OF *Beauty*

Condensed from Good Housekeeping

James C. Derieux

THERE IS not anywhere, so far as I can learn, a monument to the Rev. John Grimké-Drayton. Yet Mr. Drayton did one of the remarkable bits of work that has been done in this world. About his country home, Magnolia Gardens, near Charleston, S. C., he brought into being such beauty as perhaps no other individual in America has been able to achieve.

Each spring thousands of persons travel hundreds of miles to see the work of this modest clergyman. In a prewar edition of his famous travel guide, Baedeker marked but three places in the United States with the double star: the Grand Canyon, Niagara Falls and Mr. Drayton's garden.

Said John Galsworthy: "Nothing so lovely and wistful, nothing so richly colored, yet so ghostlike, exists, planted by the sons of men. Beyond anything I have ever seen, it is other-worldly. To this day I have seen no garden so beautiful as Magnolia Gardens."

I shall not even attempt to tell of the millions of azalea blooms of many hues; of the stately camellias, a single bush yielding blooms of many colors; of the white and bluish wisteria climbing to the very tops of mighty trees; the roses; the *Magnolia grandiflora;* the live oaks with their eerie draperies of gray moss; the mirroring pools. Acre after acre of rapturous beauty, changing from hour to hour as the sun's angle alters, from week to week as the season advances. There seems no end to the clergyman's desire to make manifest here on earth some hint of the heavenly glimpses that came to his heart.

Last summer an elderly woman leaving Magnolia Gardens said,

"This is my fortieth visit here. I come each spring to South Carolina to see Magnolia. It restores my soul."

Another woman said to Mr. C. Norwood Hastie, present owner of the garden and grandson of Mr. Drayton: "My husband, a clergyman, was on the edge of losing his reason when he first came here. Day after day he returned. In the end, his faith returned to him, and his poise. This garden saved him, made it possible for him to continue in his pastorate."

Innumerable persons, afflicted with grief too heavy for them, go to Magnolia to find peace. A man stood looking across one of the small lakes at banks of color, at the clear reflections of that color beneath water. Softly he spoke to the woman with him.

"I know now what Heaven is like, and I am content for my child to be there."

There is no record of any person's ever having been ejected from the garden for misconduct. Rarely does one hear loud talking or noisy laughter — no more than in a cathedral. As many as 12,000 persons have entered the garden within a single day — and when night came on, no flowers were missing, no damage of any kind had been done, no litter left. Yet there never are guards on duty.

One day Mr. Hastie himself went out to gather flowers. Twenty persons started toward him. "Stop that!" they demanded. Now when he wishes flowers for his own use, he gathers them before the gates have been opened.

Many a garden within 50 miles of Magnolia has been despoiled by visitors, but there is something about Magnolia that puts thievery and all other low conduct out of one's mind. "Dis gyrden ain't fo' sin," is the way an old Negro explains it. "Gawd, He done walk here."

In the heart of every imaginative person resides a desire to be of lasting worth. But what can he do that will survive him? If he has access to a bit of earth, this he can make lovely, and so add immensely to his own satisfaction with life and to the joy of others.

The village in which I live, Summerville, S. C., is one of several established by the rice planters of the early 19th century. Most of these settlements have pined away, some have disappeared, but Summerville is living merrily, though it has no industry to speak of, and is not a trading center. Why did Summerville survive? Because many years ago it had intelligence enough to prohibit the cutting of trees, and its home owners esthetic sense enough to plant wisteria, roses, tea olives, magnolias, azaleas, camellias, and innumerable other flowering trees, vines and bushes. To this day one may not cut a tree in Summerville, though it is in his own yard, without permission of the town authorities. Now the huge wisteria vines spread over the tops of tall trees, roofing the village with heavenly blueness, while the floor of the forest flames in many flower colors.

It is beauty that sustains the community, that brings to it annually hundreds of winter residents, some of whom, having traveled widely, declare it to be America's loveliest forest village.

In a Carolina valley an old woman lives in a small, unpainted house. There is no sign to tell passers-by that here he can buy eggs, butter, milk and vegetables, yet the old woman rarely can supply the demand for them.

"How do people know you have them for sale?" I asked her.

"Well, sir, mostly they don't know right off. But when they're drivin' by, they sees my flowers, and they stop. Then they come in to ask questions, and I tell 'em what I've got."

And so, with the most remarkable front yard within 20 miles as her advertisement, the old woman gets along. The beauty she developed by transplanting flowers from the mountainsides and glens and by obtaining cuttings and bulbs from friends is her sales agent. More, her yard is a contagious beauty spot. Other women are getting flowers from her, and inspiration. Her presence is transforming that whole valley into a more pleasing, more civilized place.

If we ever should attain to universal enthusiasm for beauty, many of our sorest economic problems would dissolve. We then would find more of the satisfaction in activities that are not costly. We would have a standard of living, as distinguished from the standard of spending. And that may be what we must have before we can climb toward the heights of satisfying life. On those heights dwells serenity, and serenity and beauty are sisters.

The Minor Pleasures of Life

THERE never was a golden world, and I don't suppose there ever will be, yet now and then — in moments of delight — we catch the glint and gleam of it. I don't mean lumps of glittering happiness, but moments brought by little things. There's delight in city streets — the smell of roasting coffee alone might stop a desperate man from suicide. I once stood several minutes outside a fishmonger's in an ecstatic marine reverie, because I had caught sight of a noble, rich-looking fish, and it had set me thinking about the sea — all the oceans in the world, their vast extent, their strength and mystery, the incredible variety of life in them.

Do you remember the enchantment, when you were a child, of waking in a strange, muffled world, to find snow blanketing everything? I still feel the magic of that. The beginnings of journeys are delightful: settling down in a railway carriage, or having a preliminary prowl over the ship. But better still is coming home after a long absence, the moment you open your own front door.

Think of the tiny things that bring delight: a child laughing, somebody playing the piano well in a strange house, the smell after a shower. How one of these things can light up and change a whole day!

— J. B. Priestley in *The Listener*

What Makes a Husband Easy to Live With?

Condensed from Woman's Home Companion

The Testimony of Nine Wives

My Soul Is My Own

MY HUSBAND — and he's a Scotchman too — is easy to live with because he's generous. He likes detective stories; I enjoy Russian literature. He likes golf; I like the movies. He likes fishing; I like dancing. What do we both like? Each other! Never in the nine years of our married life has he attempted to impose a detective story or a golf club on me. Never has he tried to choose my friends, my clothes, my amusements. Never has he pawed over the grocery bill — liberal in everything from his ideas to his checking account.

He drops cigarette ashes in all the vases, brings guests home without forewarning and forgets our wedding anniversary, but every fault is erased by his liberality of spirit. Easy to live with because my soul and mind are my own: he may explore them but he never attempts complete ownership!

Freedom from Curiosity

I have been married nearly 40 years and my husband has many qualities that make him easy to live with. But the outstanding one is his freedom from curiosity. I have a very generous allowance but am never questioned as to how I spend it or whether or not I am saving any of it. I can be out late, have unexpected callers, without tiresome explanations. It isn't that he isn't interested but he trusts me to take care of my affairs as he does his, without questions. To me it means peace and happiness.

A Peaceful Husband

My husband is easy to live with because he is not faultfinding. In the five years of our married life I do not recall a single meal made unpleasant by disagreeable comments upon the food or a single night's rest interrupted by useless arguments and recriminations. I am ready and willing to admit that my husband is not perfect, but who wants a perfect husband anyway? As for me, I say, "Thank God for a peaceful husband."

He Covers His Tracks

I have chosen "picking up after himself" as the best among my husband's many easy-to-live-with qualities. If there's anything that makes a tired mother desperate it's to try to teach her children to hang up their hats, put their shoes in the closet and their soiled clothes in the hamper, in the face of the living example of a husband and father who casts off clothing and all responsibility for it in the general direction of the nearest chair. Any woman will seethe with resentment if she has to follow in the tracks of a man picking up the collars, newspapers, shoes and shirts he sheds. From my heart I thank my mother-in-law, who taught her son to "cover his tracks" in the house.

Words of Praise

My husband never forgets that besides being a wife I am also a Feminine Person and as such love to hear that my dress was the prettiest there, that my nose never shines except in the privacy of my boudoir and that no other lemon meringue pie can equal mine. Such honeyed words, not to say downright blarney, make my husband a mighty easy man to live with.

When to Be Quiet

I very much appreciate my husband's quiet way when I am struggling to make a train, or to get to some place on time. He may look at his watch and ask, "Do you think you can make the 2:15 bus?" And I make it, unruffled and unflurried. Whereas should he hustle me and become impatient I lose my equilibrium and probably the bus as well.

And I'm thankful for his quiet help in getting the last-minute things ready for the picnic and his quiet manner of taking the responsibility of fixing windows and shades, and seeing that wraps and luggage are all together and doors locked when we are leaving home for a vacation.

I think a husband who knows the times when it helps most to be quiet is an easy man to live with.

Martin the Approachable

Martin, my husband, has a close friend, John, married to Kate. Kate said to me the other day, "I wish you'd ask Martin how John feels about us all going camping together."

Ask Martin? Why not ask John direct? I did not put this question to Kate, but in my heart I sang paeans of praise of Martin the approachable, the responsive.

Here I had been blissfully ignorant of a remarkable quality that makes life with Martin as comfortable as an old shoe. Anything from dollars to doughnuts I can broach. No reticence, no explosion; just response, fair and frank. We can disagree with zest but somehow no debris from the past encounter clutters up the future approach.

He Argues with Me

Bless my husband — he argues with me! He considers my opinions worthy of refutation. Dick will listen attentively to my reasons why the mountains are the only sensible place to spend the summer vacation, and then ever so courteously he begins to pick my logic apart, to show me, with infinite patience, meticulous care and flattering seriousness, where I'm wrong. My, but it's easy to live with a man who takes the trouble to argue matters out with one!

Something to Say

A gift of gab helps a lot. What a difference it makes to a wife who has been in the house all day occupied with seemingly petty and certainly irritating duties to have her husband come home with something to say — interesting news or trifling gossip, thoughts, impressions, anything at all but that stony silence that makes one want to scream: "Talk, talk, for heaven's sake, talk!"

We often hear of the wife who talks too much but don't forget to be sorry for the wife of the husband who talks too little.

Mary White

A famous little classic from the Emporia Gazette

William Allen White

One of America's best known and best loved editors, William Allen White wrote for his Emporia Gazette the following tribute to his daughter on the day of her funeral

THE PRESS REPORTS carrying the news of Mary White's death declared that it was the result of a fall from a horse. How she would have hooted at that! She never fell from a horse in her life. Horses have fallen on her and with her — "I'm always trying to hold 'em in my lap," she used to say. She could ride anything that had four legs and hair. Her death resulted not from a fall but from a fractured skull, and the blow came from the limb of an overhanging tree.

The last hour of her life was typical of its happiness. She came home from school, and felt that a ride would refresh her. She climbed into khakis, chattering to her mother, and hurried to get her horse and be out. As she rode through the town on an easy gallop she kept waving at passers-by. She knew everyone. For a decade the little figure with the long pigtail and the red hair-ribbon has been familiar in Emporia. She passed the Kerrs, and waved at them; passed another friend farther on, and waved at her. As she turned into Merchant Street the horse swung into a lope. She passed a school boy friend and she waved at him, but with her bridle hand; the horse veered quickly, plunged into the parking where the low-hanging limb faced her, and, while she still looked back waving, the blow came. But she did not fall from the horse; she slipped off, staggered and fell in a faint. She never recovered consciousness.

But she did not fall from the horse, neither was she riding fast. A year ago she used to go like the wind; but that habit was broken, and she used the horse to get fresh, hard exercise. Need for that has kept the dauntless little brown-clad figure on the country roads of this community; it built into a strong, muscular body what had been a frail and sickly frame. But the riding gave her more than a body; it released a gay and hardy soul. She was the happiest thing in the world. And she was happy because she was enlarging her horizon.

She came to know all sorts and conditions of men; Charley O'Brien, the traffic cop; and all the girls, black and white, above the track and below the track, were among her acquaintances. She brought home riotous stories of her adventures. She loved to rollick; persiflage was her natural expression at home; her humor was a continual bubble of joy. She was mischievous without malice, as full of faults as an old shoe. No angel was Mary White, but an easy girl to live with, for she never nursed a grouch five minutes in her life.

With all her eagerness for the out-of-doors, she loved books. On her table when she left her room were a book by Conrad, one by Galsworthy, and a Kipling. She read Mark Twain, Dickens and Kipling before she was ten. Within the last two years she had begun to draw. She began as most children do by scribbling in her schoolbooks funny pictures. She took a course — rather casually, naturally, for she was, after all, a child with no strong purposes — and she tasted success by having her pictures accepted by the high school Annual. But her delight when asked to do cartoons for the Normal Annual was too beautiful for words. The drawings accepted, her pride — always repressed by a sense of the ridiculous — was a gorgeous thing to see. In her glory, she almost forgot her horse — but never her car.

She used the car as a jitney bus. It was her social life. She never had a "party" in all her nearly 17 years — wouldn't have one; but she never drove a block in the car in her life that she didn't fill it with pick-ups! Everybody rode with Mary White — white and black, old and young. She liked nothing better than to fill the car full of long-legged high school boys and an occasional girl, and parade the town. She never had a "date," nor went to a dance, except once with her brother, Bill, and the "boy proposition" didn't interest her — yet. But great spring-breaking carloads of "kids" gave her great pleasure. Her zests were keen.

The poor she had always with her, and was glad of it. The last engagement she tried to make was to take the poor folks at the county home out for a car ride. And the last endeavor of her life was to try to get a rest room for colored girls in the high school. She found one girl reading in the toilet, because there was no better place for a colored girl to loaf, and it inflamed her sense of injustice and she became a nagging harpie to those who, she thought, could remedy the evil.

She hungered and thirsted for righteousness; and was the most impious creature in the world. She joined the church because she felt the church was an agency for helping people, and she wanted to help. She never wanted help for herself. Clothes meant little to her; she never wore a jewel and never asked for anything but a wristwatch. She refused to have her hair up, though she was nearly 17. Above every other passion of her life was her passion not to grow up, to be a child. The tomboy in her seemed to loathe to be put away forever in skirts. She was a Peter Pan, who refused to grow up.

Her funeral was as she would have wished it; no singing, no flowers save the big bunch of red roses from her Brother Bill's Harvard classmen — Heavens, how proud that would have made her! and the red roses from the *Gazette* force — in vases at her head and feet. A short prayer, Paul's beautiful essay on "Love" from First Corinthians, some remarks about her democratic spirit by her friend the pastor (which she would have deprecated if she could), a prayer, and opening the service, the slow, poignant movement from Beethoven's Moonlight Sonata, which she loved, and closing the service the joyously melancholy first movement of Tschaikowsky's Pathetic Symphony, which she liked on the phonograph; then the Lord's Prayer by her friends.

That was all.

It would have made her smile to know that Charley O'Brien, the traffic cop, had been transferred to the corner near the church to direct her friends who came to bid her good-bye.

A rift in the gray clouds threw a shaft of sunlight upon her coffin as her energetic little body sank to its last sleep. But the soul of her, the glowing, fervent soul of her, surely was flaming in eager joy upon some other dawn.

The Art of Evasion

An actress was testifying in New York in a suit for damages, and the cross-examiner plotted to discredit all her testimony by proving that she consistently lied about her age. She was 52, but posed as being about 40. She didn't want to lie under oath.

"How old are you?" the cross-examiner asked.

"I don't know," she said promptly.

"What! You don't know?"

"No. I have never had a birth certificate. I have never looked up the record of my birth."

"But, miss —" the cross-examiner protested suavely, "surely your parents told you how old you are. When did they say you were born?"

"That," said the actress firmly, "is hearsay evidence and I am sure you would not ask that it be admitted."

"But . . . but . . ." the cross-examiner sputtered.

The actress turned to the judge. "Am I right or wrong, Your Honor?"

The judge grinned. "You are correct," he said.

— J. B. Griswold in *The American Magazine*

"Inferiority complexes are seldom more than senseless timidities that rob courage, sap ambition and retard enterprise"

Do the Thing You Fear

By Henry C. Link, Ph.D.

Director of the Psychological Service Center, New York City, and author of "The Return to Religion"

It is with some hesitancy that I write on the subject of fears because, unquestionably, many of the fears from which people now suffer are due to the voluminous writings on this subject. I wish, for example, that the term *inferiority complex* had never been printed, because then millions of people would not even know they had an inferiority complex. There would be one less idea for them to fear.

Most fears are actually generated by too much reading, thinking and talking. They do not, as a rule, just happen. We nurse them and feed them until, from an inconsequential trifle, they have grown to monstrous proportions. The mother who avidly reads the extensive literature on bringing up children becomes increasingly fearful of how to deal with them, and well she may. The young woman too fussy about her appearance soon worries too much over what people will think of her. Groups of people who learnedly discuss the state of the country often turn pessimism into fear.

Before me as I write is a letter from a young woman, beginning: "Ever since I was 16 years old I have been afraid to converse in a strange group." The letter goes on to enumerate other fears — fear of her employer, fear of losing her job, a fear of men, fear of driving a car, fear to make a report at a girls' club, and others to the total of 11. All of them are fears on a common level, experienced by millions of people. In almost every case, the result of these fears is the same — a sort of creeping paralysis, a feeling of misery, of suffocation, of panic, of defeat.

A young man told me that he could not sleep. He gave me a long psychological explanation of how this had come about. "Can you help me get rid of this obsession?" he asked. "No," was my reply. "Then what can I do?" he implored. "Run around the block at night until you are ready to drop. What you need is exertion. You have put too much of your physical energies into imagining things. If you run hard enough, you will automatically relax and go to sleep. You have thought yourself into this fear with your mind, you can run yourself out of it with your legs" — and he did.

A mother not long ago gave this significant summary of her life: "As a young woman I was troubled with many fears, one of which was the fear of insanity. After my marriage these fears still persisted. However, we soon had a child, and ended by having six. Whenever I started to worry, the baby would cry or the children would quarrel and I would have to straighten them out. Or I would suddenly remember that it was time to start dinner, or that the ironing had to be done. My fears about myself were being continually interrupted by family duties, and gradually they disappeared. Now I look back on them with amusement."

The moral of this episode may not be to have six children, but it is true that the smaller families and increased leisure of our time are conducive to the generation of fears. It is equally true that many people who are obsessed by nagging fears might find a new interest in life if they became concerned *about other people* through participation in community activities.

You don't like such activities? Then you must remember that every step in the conquest of fear requires, at the outset, an act of will. Those who have learned to dive remember the process. You got yourself poised, then leaned forward, hesitated, and drew back in fear. Again you made the attempt and withdrew. With each hesitation your fears mounted. Finally, in angry disgust with yourself, you plunged in, arms and legs askew, and with a terrific flop. You came up chagrined and embarrassed, the laughter of your friends making you feel still worse. If, at this point, your fears had prevented you from making further attempts, you might never have learned to dive; your fears might have become insurmountable. If, however, you persisted, and continued to make awkward and painful dives, you finally went in smoothly and came up feeling pleased. You were on the way to becoming an expert.

This is the basic psychology of overcoming fear and gaining confidence in every phase of life, *and there is no escape from this process.* Again and again we must plunge into the stream of life, adding one conquest to another, overcoming first this fear and then that. As Emerson said, do the thing you fear and the death of fear is certain. Actually our fears are the forces that make us, when dealt with by decisive action, or that break us if dealt with by indecision, procrastination and ratiocination.

A young man not long ago asked me to suggest some difficult things for him to do. "Your book recommends," he said, "such activities as dancing, basketball or some competitive sport, bridge, parties and games. It says a person should do such things even though he dislikes them. I not only disliked but was afraid to do these things. However, I made up my mind to try them. For a while I had a terrible time, I was miserable. But before long I lost my fears and actually began to like these new activities. In fact, I am enjoying my new life so much that I am in danger of getting soft. I wish you would tell me some things to do which I would really find difficult."

This young man had learned the lesson of using his fears as a means to conquest and livelier enjoyment. He was headed for a fuller and more effective life, both socially and intellectually.

The first step in overcoming fear is sometimes a very elementary process. I remember a certain young man so overwhelmed with various fears that he could scarcely talk audibly. He worked in a large bank and knew a dozen men in his department, but as he went to his desk in the morning he greeted no one. We suggested that he begin by saying a hearty "Good morning, Frank! Hello, Keating! Good morning, Mr. Eaton," to the men as he passed.

He tried it with such gratifying results that he was encouraged to try more difficult tasks, one conquest leading to another.

The more general fears — of insanity, of persecution, of strangers, of inferiority, are usually the result of one's failure to conquer enough minor fears by such practice. Sometimes, however, they are due to the fact that a person for some reason — disappointment in love, the death of a dear relative, financial reverses, loss of a job — withdraws from his accustomed activities. After a catastrophe, especially, one should not only keep up old activities but bend his will and energies toward beginning some new and preferably strenuous pursuit. After losing his position, a man of 56 who had been with one company for 30 years began to mope and to withdraw from all contacts with his former friends. Within six months he had become a bundle of fears, both small and great. Finally he was persuaded to visit a relative living on a farm. Soon he was drawn into the routine of the establishment. In six months he was himself again.

Although generalizations are dangerous, I venture to say that at the bottom of most fears, both mild and severe, will be found an overactive mind and an underactive body. Hence, I have advised many people, in their quest for happiness, to use their heads less and their arms and legs more — in useful work or play. We generate fears while we sit; we overcome them by action. Fear is nature's warning signal to get busy.

In its mild and initial stages, fear takes the form of aversion to, or criticism of, certain activities and people, constituting an alibi by which the individual justifies his continued inaction. The world is full of malcontents, parlor communists and social theorists who, because they will not change themselves, talk about changing the entire system. Many of them do not seem to realize that in any social order whatsoever there would still be misfits. Through conversation they rationalize their anger with the world, instead of becoming enraged with themselves and flying into worth-while action.

A tie that binds the family together and all to God

We Teach Our Children to Pray

Condensed from Better Homes & Gardens

O. K. Armstrong

A SMALL phonograph and a Bible rest on the buffet of our dining room. They are our "props" for family prayers. They help make possible what the children call "God's minutes."

Those minutes are not long — seldom more than five. But they are important. They stand for daily recognition that there is a Power greater than we, a heavenly Father who is kind and good to His children.

My wife and I both were reared in homes where prayers were said. When the children came along we thought prayers would be a good thing for them, too, but we couldn't find the right routine. My work at first was teaching and writing, then holding public office. There was always something to do at night — meetings to attend, work to finish, social engagements. We taught our children the "Now I lay me" prayer and let it go at that.

The first two boys grew into husky lads. The little girl, Sister, was progressing in school. The last two boys were ready for kindergarten. All were dutifully enrolled in Sunday school. Still we weren't getting anywhere with their spiritual training. Half-heartedly we experimented with prayers at various times of the day. It was difficult to find a time when the family was all together. Before school there was the rush of brushing teeth and gathering up books; after school there were music lessons, games and what not. We gave up.

Then a bolt of lightning brought us suddenly to an intense appreciation of our blessings. The two older boys were doing summer work, packing blackberries in a small community cannery. A storm came up. Lightning struck the building and stunned everyone there. Although no one was seriously injured, the realization of how close the boys had come to death brought to my wife and me an overwhelming sense of thanksgiving that they were spared. Perhaps it was just the workings of chance; we found it easier to believe in the hand of Providence. We said some extra thanks at our evening meal and next day decided to add a bit of Scripture reading.

"We sing at church. Why not sing before our prayers?" Sister asked. Good idea. I dug out some old Homer Rodeheaver records. We added other transcriptions. "I need Thee every hour" and "Blest be the tie that binds" are favorites.

After the song, comes the Scripture. Maybe it's only a verse, perhaps a short chapter. Then the prayer. Sometimes it's the Lord's prayer, all together. Sometimes an older boy will lead. Or the tiny treble of one of the little boys will startle us into hidden smiles as he thanks God for "the wienies and taters we got for supper." Whatever the prayer, it's spontaneous, and it makes God a sort of partner for the household. It breaks down barriers that so often keep a father or mother from mentioning the most fundamental fact in any child's life: the existence of a Creator.

God's minutes take only a tiny fraction of the busy day, but they have brought us a new sense of family closeness. Troubles seem easier to forget. Anger cannot outlive a verse of song. Worry fades when we come upon the lines "Seek ye first the kingdom of God, and His righteousness; and all these things shall be added unto you."

We've passed on the idea to numerous friends. Professor and Mrs. Blank over at the college, with two girls in high school, find breakfast-time the best. Mike, widower nightwatchman, has a good-night prayer with his six children before he goes to work. We'll never know how many have copied our plan. A visiting minister was so impressed he went back to his home parish and started a crusade for family devotions.

At first we felt some embarrassment when we held prayers with guests present. Now it seems like an added note of hospitality. Politicians, businessmen, teachers — all pause with us while we recognize the presence of the constant Guest. As the phonograph began the hymn "Beulah Land" one evening, our dinner visitor, a noted manufacturer, burst into a roaring baritone. "Sing it again!" he shouted on the last note. "I haven't heard that since I was a boy!" A criminal-court judge seriously told us, "If all families had prayers I wouldn't have much to do."

The brief Scripture reading, we've found, adds up to a lot of Bible knowledge as the days merge into months and years. We've learned many favorite passages "by heart" — the first Psalm, the shepherd Psalm, the Beatitudes, the eighth chapter of Romans, and St. Paul's marvelously beautiful words on faith, hope and charity in First Corinthians. Children, we have discovered, are just as interested in Bible stories, with their deep spiritual meanings, as in any others. David and Goliath, Joseph and his brothers, feeding the five thousand, the lame man at the beautiful gate — all have new significance for us.

Several publishers have brought out helps for family prayers, such as "The Upper Room" with its daily Scripture lesson, comments and prayer, all requiring only a few minutes. The Catholic Church has long provided helps for private devotions. A rabbi assured us that Jewish families could secure similar guiding pamphlets. Thus prayer becomes our spiritual common denominator.

Our young people face a future sure to be hard and trying. Great problems will rest upon their shoulders. Not employment alone, nor liberty nor opportunity alone, will see them through. The character and moral strength that are built by communion with God will be essential for the supreme test.

Most of us read badly. Here's how to test your reading ability and how to improve it

How Well Do You Read?

Condensed from Liberty

Ruth McCoy Harris

WOULD YOU like to know how fast you read? Then get a pencil and a watch. When you come to the end of this paragraph, write down the exact time. Continue reading at your regular speed. Questions at the end of the article will test your understanding of what you have read. Are you ready?

"Slow readers are poor readers," says Norman Lewis, author of *How to Read Better and Faster*. "A person reads fast because he thinks fast, has good eyesight, a good vocabulary, and a wide background of information. Most persons who read ten times as fast as the plodder absorb much more of what they read than he does."

Lewis, who teaches remedial reading to adults at the College of the City of New York, points out that reading is perhaps the most important skill we ever learn. There is hardly a job that does not require reading. And while less than four percent of American adults cannot read at all, at least 60 percent do not read well.

Millions who read nothing but the comics would fine pleasure and stimulation in magazines and books if their reading habits were improved. A child who does not read reasonably well is doomed to failure in school. Most delinquents have a long record of school failures, beginning with reading troubles.

Exercise is an important part of trying to improve your reading. For a certain time every day make a conscious effort to read a little faster and to see more at each glance. Your eyes see nothing as they are moving along a line of print; it is during the brief pauses they make that they read. The wider your eyes span, the more words you see at once and the faster you read. A good reader makes only two or three stops on an ordinary line of print; a poor reader stops for nearly every word. An excellent reader will see an entire line at once, so that he can read *down* a narrow column of type without moving his eyes from left to right. That is how Theodore Roosevelt got the reputation of reading a whole page at a glance — an obvious impossibility. He read rapidly down the page, and he knew how to skim, often reading only the key words.

According to Dr. Stella S. Center, head of the New York University Reading Clinic, the chief reading faults are reading one word at a time and turning back to reread. Many of those who read slowly pronounce each word, either aloud or mentally. If you want to find out whether you are vocalizing, touch your lips lightly as you read. If they do not move, try touching your throat over your vocal cords. If they vibrate slightly, you are vocalizing. To keep from vocalizing, try to read easy material faster, so that there is no time to pronounce and, most important, try to keep your mind focused on the author's thought. This is also the best way to keep from regressing. We read efficiently when our minds and imaginations are captured by what we read.

All reading experts agree that a poor vocabulary is a drawback to rapid reading. But don't stop to look up every new word in a dictionary. Keep going, at least to the end of the paragraph. Often the meaning of the word is made clear by the way it is used. If not, it may become clear if you try to figure it out before looking it up. "A large vocabulary," says Norman Lewis, "does not come from looking up long lists of words in a dictionary. It comes from wide reading, from being alert and curious."

The books Lewis recommends for his students' outside reading seem heavy going for slow readers: history and biography, psychology and physiology, mathematics, sociology. "If my students also read whodunits and boy-meets-girl stories, that's fine. It will help them speed up. But one trouble with slow readers is a narrow background of information. Since they have never enjoyed reading, some of them haven't opened a book since their school days. They've missed a lot of facts that other people know. Reading a few solid, factual books will give them a background to build on. The more you know, the faster you read."

Adapting your reading speed to your material is important. If you are studying directions for making a cake or building a shelf, you will take your time in order to be sure you have every step clearly in mind. On the other hand, if you are reading a "western," it's no crime to skip elaborate descriptions of mountain scenery and get on with the story. Skimming is not the same as skipping. Skimming — glancing rapidly over a paragraph and picking out the key words — is the secret that enables many professional people to keep up with everything published in their field.

How fast should you read? If you read 225 words a minute, you are reading at about the national average and as well as a sixth-grade child is expected to read his school books. That is not fast enough to make newspaper or magazine reading enjoyable. High school students get into difficulties if they cannot read 300 words a minute, and college students who read below 350 words will find the going tough. In some jobs even 600 words a minute is too slow, and Dr. Center has had men come to her clinic to improve that rate. They did it too. Lewis reads faster than 800 words a minute, and is still improving. Apparently you can always read faster and better, no matter how well you read. To many of us, it will be challenging to learn that most adults can improve their reading rate at least 35 percent — by their own efforts.

Now look at the time. Divide the number of minutes into 920, the number of words you have read, and you'll know your rate per minute.

To test how well you absorbed what you read answer the following questions without looking back at the article. Count ten for each correct answer. If you score 80 or higher, you have grasped the main points.

1. Fast readers miss a lot of what they read. True? False?

2. A poor vocabulary slows up your reading. True? False?

3. If you pronounce each word, you will understand what you read better and build up your vocabulary. True? False?

4. Theodore Roosevelt read a whole page at once. True? False?

5. Reading is more important than any other school subject. True? False?

6. The number of adults who have reading troubles is probably about (a) 5 percent; (b) 25 percent; (c) 60 percent.

7. Most adults can increase their reading speed at least by (a) 10 percent; (b) 35 percent; (c) 100 percent.

8. (Two answers are wrong. Cross them out.) The commonest reading faults are (a) reading word by word; (b) reading comics; (c) rereading or regression; (d) pronouncing the words; (e) going to the movies.

9. Anyone who reads very fast can learn to read even faster. True? False?

10. Using a dictionary to look up each new word immediately will improve your reading rate. True? False?

Answers to questions on reading: 1. False. 2. True. 3. False. 4. False. 5. True. 6. 60 percent. 7. 35 percent. 8. Wrong answers are (b) and (e). 9. True. 10. False.

When two men in a business always agree, one of them is unnecessary.
— William Wrigley, Jr.

A baby malformed at birth — and choice of life or death in the doctor's hands

Who Shall Be the Judge?

Condensed from "Consultation Room"
Frederic Loomis, M.D.
Well-known gynecologist and obstetrician

HOWEVER they may feel about it in individual instances, doctors rightly resent and resist the persistent effort to make them the judges of life and death. Our load of responsibility is enough without that. So far as I am concerned, my duty, as I see it, is to preserve life, to fight for a patient's life with every resource at my command, remembering always that "a man's never licked till he's licked." But, like other doctors, I have not escaped the problem — or the temptation.

There came to my office one day a fragile young woman, expecting her first baby. Her emotional history was not good, though she came from a fine family. I built her up as well as I could and as time went on, I could not but admire the effort she made to be calm and patient and to keep her nervous reactions under control.

One month before her baby was due, her routine examination showed that it was in a breech position. As a rule, the baby's head is in the lower part of the uterus for months before delivery. The occasional baby found in a breech position in the last month not infrequently changes to the normal position with the head down by the time it is ready to be born, so that only about one baby in 25 is born in the breech position.

This is fortunate, as the death rate of breech babies is comparatively high because of the difficulty in delivering the aftercoming head, and the imperative need of delivering it quickly after the body is born. At that moment the cord becomes compressed between the baby's hard little head and the mother's bony pelvis. When no oxygen reaches the baby's blood stream, it inevitably dies in a few short minutes. And if it is a first baby, the difficulty is even greater.

In this case it was a "complete" breech — the baby's legs and feet being folded under it, tailor-fashion. The hardest thing for the doctor in breech delivery is to keep his hands away until the natural forces of expulsion have thoroughly dilated the firm maternal structures which delay progress. I waited as patiently as I could, sending frequent messages to the excited family in the corridor outside.

At last the time had come, and I gently drew down one little foot. I grasped the other but, for some reason I could not understand, it would not come down beside the first one. I pulled again, gently, with light pressure on the abdomen from above by my assisting nurse; the baby's body moved down a little and, to my consternation, I saw that the other foot would *never* be beside the first one. The entire thigh from the hip to the knee was missing and the foot never could reach below the opposite knee. And a baby girl was to suffer this, a curious defect that I had never seen before, nor have I since!

There followed the hardest struggle I have ever had with myself. I knew what a dreadful effect it would have upon the unstable nervous system of the mother. I felt sure that the family would impoverish itself in taking the child to every famous orthopedist whose achievements might offer a ray of hope.

Most of all, I saw this little girl sitting sadly by herself while other girls laughed and danced and ran and played — and then I suddenly realized that there was something that would save every pang but one, and that thing was in my power to do.

One breech baby in ten dies in delivery because it is not delivered rapidly enough, and now — if only I did not hurry! If I could slow my hand, if I could make myself delay those few short moments. It would not be an easy delivery, anyway. No one would ever know. The mother, after the first shock of grief, would probably be glad she had lost a child so sadly handicapped.

"*Don't bring this suffering upon them,*" the small voice within me said. "This baby has never taken a breath — don't let her ever take one . . . you probably can't get it out in time anyway . . . *don't hurry!*"

I motioned to the nurse for the warm sterile towel which is always ready for me in a breech delivery to wrap around the baby's body so that the stimulation of the cold air may not induce a sudden expansion of the baby's chest, causing the breathing in of fluid or mucus which might bring death.

But this time the towel was only to conceal that which my eyes alone had seen. My decision was made.

I glanced at the clock. Three of the allotted seven or eight minutes had already gone. Every eye in the room was upon me. These nurses had seen me deliver dozens of breech babies successfully — yes, and they had seen me fail, too. Now they were going to see me fail again. For the first time in my medical life I was deliberately discarding what I had been taught was right for something that I felt sure was better.

I slipped my hand beneath the towel to feel the pulsations of the baby's cord, a certain index of its condition. Two or three minutes more would be enough. So that I might seem to be doing something, I drew the baby down a little lower to "splint out" the arms, the usual next step, and as I did so the little pink foot on the good side bobbed out from its protecting towel and pressed firmly against my hand, the hand into whose keeping the safety of the mother and the baby had been entrusted. There was a sudden convulsive movement of the baby's body, an actual feeling of strength and life.

It was too much. I couldn't do it. I delivered the baby with her pitiful little leg. I told the family and the next day, with a catch in my voice, I told the mother.

Every foreboding came true. The mother was in a hospital for several months. She looked like a wraith. After that I heard of the family indirectly from time to time. They had been to Rochester, Minnesota, to Chicago, to Boston. Finally I lost track of them.

As the years went on, I blamed myself bitterly for not having had the strength to yield to my temptation.

FOR MANY YEARS our hospital has staged an elaborate Christmas party for the employes, nurses and doctors of the staff. This past year the service was unusually impressive.

As the organ began the opening notes of an ancient carol, slowly down the aisle, from the back of the auditorium, came 20 nurses in full uniform, each holding high a lighted candle, and singing softly the familiar strains of *Holy Night*.

And then a great blue floodlight was turned on the stage, gradually covering the silvered tree with increasing splendor — brighter and brighter until every ornament was aflame. On the opposite side of the stage a curtain was drawn and we saw three lovely young musicians, all in shimmering white. They played softly in unison with the organ — a harp, a cello and a violin. I am quite sure I was not the only old sissy there whose eyes filled with tears.

I have always liked the harp and I love to watch the grace of a skillful player. I was especially fascinated by this young harpist. She played extraordinarily well, as if she loved it. Her slender fingers flickered across the strings, and as the nurses sang, her face, made beautiful by a mass of auburn hair, was upturned as if the world that moment were a wonderful and holy place.

I waited, when the short program was over, to congratulate the chief nurse on its effectiveness. And as I sat alone, there came running down the aisle a woman whom I did not know. She came to me with arms outstretched.

"Oh, you saw her," she cried. "You must have recognized your baby. That was my daughter who played the harp and I saw you watching her. Don't you remember me? Don't you remember the little girl who was born with only one good leg 17 years ago? We tried everything else first, but now she has a whole artificial leg on that side — but you would never know it, would you? She can walk, she can swim, and she can almost dance.

"But, best of all, through all those years when she couldn't do those things, she learned to use her hands so wonderfully. She is going to be a great harpist. She enters the university this year at 17. She is my whole life and now she is so happy. And here she is!"

As we spoke, this sweet young girl had quietly approached, her eyes glowing.

"This is your first doctor, my dear — our doctor," her mother said. Her voice trembled. I could see her literally swept back, as I was, through all the years of heartache to the day when I told her what she had to face.

Impulsively I took the child in my arms. Across her warm young shoulder I saw the creeping clock of the delivery room of 17 years before. I lived again those awful moments when her life was in my hand, when I had decided on deliberate infanticide.

I held her away from me and looked at her.

"You never will know, my dear," I said, "nor will anyone else in all the world, just what tonight has meant to me. Go back to your harp for a moment, please — and play *Holy Night* for me alone. I have a load on my shoulders that no one has ever seen, a load that only you can take away."

Her mother sat beside me and quietly took my hand as her daughter played. Perhaps she knew what was in my mind. And as the last strains of *Holy Night* faded again, I think I found the answer, and the comfort, I had waited for so long.

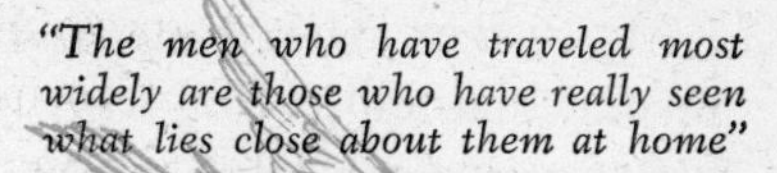

"The men who have traveled most widely are those who have really seen what lies close about them at home"

Every Man His Own Naturalist

Condensed from Natural History

Donald Culross Peattie *Naturalist; author of "Green Laurels," "Singing in the Wilderness," "An Almanac for Moderns," etc.*

YEARS AGO when I was jobless I walked into a newspaper office and asked to be allowed to write a nature column. The editor, in a welter of next Sunday's pictures, told me wearily that I might try — but he'd have to drop it if readers did not respond.

The day came when I had to have a secretary to battle with their response. I don't attribute this to any popularity of mine, but to the popularity of nature. The column was only a daily jotting of the things I saw that everybody may see. But when the readers began to help me write it, they showed me more than I could show them. They showed me that nature belongs to everyone. That nobody hungers for it like the city dweller. That the young need little help to turn their interest into this widest and healthiest field. That the mature are not too old to want to learn, and find in nature pleasures of which neither years nor adversity can deprive them.

Most of the people who wrote me had never had formal training in natural science. But they heard the beguiling whistles of the birds; they glimpsed from the commuters' train window the fields filling up with wild flowers; they saw the wheeling of the unknown constellations over their suburban roofs. And they saw that human life is short; the years rush down the stream and do not return; and all about is a greater life, zestful, enchanting and deeply significant. And they wanted to learn.

My readers showed me, too, that this vast army of intelligent amateur naturalists can, with their enthusiasm and curiosity, ably assist the professional scientists. A Chicago doctor, for example, who has only a small back yard in the city, has become a leader in bird-banding. To his metropolitan station have come bobwhite and saw-whet owl, Wilson's thrush and Montana junco — 90 kinds of birds and many hundreds of individuals. Every one of these he has banded, and he finds that certain birds return year after year. Birds banded by other workers, in Canada, in South America, come to his harmless trap, and so he helps map their mysterious sky-roads.

A New York businessman, with only his Sundays free, has become an authority on that fascinating bird, the osprey. A Massachusetts judge found that his collection of flowers from all over the world was eagerly studied by scientists. A Pennsylvania mine owner, after 30 years at his desk, began to study fungi and became, when past 60, an expert consulted by professionals. A Manhattan advertising man has just had a brilliant success with his book of insect photographs, taken in that unknown jungle that is the vacant lot next to yours.

These amateurs all won names for themselves. Some of the greatest naturalists were likewise amateurs. Fabre taught school, Audubon kept a store, Alexander Wilson was a weaver. But a big reputation is not the goal; it is an incidental award. A love and a knowledge of nature can mean in any life a happiness comparable with that which religion brings. If you want to find divinity in nature, you will perceive it there. Or if it is enough for you just to find out something you did not know before, there will be no end to your fun.

And there is no telling what you may turn up that will be new to everybody. A boy of ten who had read the greatest authority on ants in his age discovered, by watching them in his own garden, things that were not in his book. He decided to become the historian of the ants; and while engaged in important medical work during his maturity, he also made himself the greatest formicologist of his time — Auguste Forel.

The wonders of nature exist for everyone, and are found in all places. On the flat roofs of the city, unknown to the sleepers below, nest the nighthawks. To the puddles in an excavation may come flocks of sandpipers, ruddy turnstones and black-bellied plovers. The whole mystery of life is in the inky clouds of frogs' eggs in a ditch, and the riddle of instinct is to be studied in the pavement ants.

People often ask me how to learn — what to look for, and how to understand what they see. Few wish to spend much money on technical equipment, but fortunately no other hobby requires so little outlay. John Muir, when asked how he prepared for an expedition, said: "I put a loaf of bread and a pound of tea in an old sack, and jump over the back fence."

However, I disagree with the logical-sounding maxim that you should study nature, not books. You should study both; a good book will unriddle nature faster than a beginner could hope to do it. As a rule, the books you need are in your public library.* Probably you will soon find that some books are so good you want to own them; if so, buy those which look just a little hard, for you will soon catch up with them.

The pocket guide is very helpful in beginning field work, but is usually so general that it doesn't tell enough about the region in which you live. Your state museum or natural history survey has published local studies that are twice as interesting, and are either free or sell at a nominal price.

Every community has in it at least one person who knows a great deal about natural science. High school biology teachers, state and federal foresters and park guides can often help you to just what you need to know. And it is inspiring to see how everyone in this freemasonry of natural science is eager to share his knowledge.

---

* Among the books which will tell you what to look for, and help you identify what you see, are the following: *Birds of America*, by T. Gilbert Pearson; *Field Book of Insects*, by Frank Lutz; *The Reptile Book*, by Raymond Ditmars; *American Animals*, by W. Stone and W. Cram; *The Butterfly Book*, by W. J. Holland; *The Shell Book*, by Julia E. Rogers; *The Stars in Their Courses*, by Sir James Jeans; *Field Book of American Wild Flowers*, by F. S. Mathews; *Field Book of Western Wild Flowers*, by M. N. Armstrong and J. J. Thornber; and *Southern Wild Flowers and Trees*, by Alice Lounsberry.

Some people think of nature only as something to collect. Alas for the butterflies, birds' eggs, ferns and orchids! A collection, of course, can be scientifically valuable, but the collecting mania is not related to science or to the enjoyment of nature; the urge to have something nobody else has breaks the first rule of honest science.

Nevertheless, you can make collections that museums themselves may envy. Herbaria are overflowing with specimens of flowers, but are weak on fruits and seeds; a correlated collection of the fruits and seeds the local birds eat would be well worth while.

Many beginners sweat needlessly after the rare. Common objects have the widest and deepest significance, and there is never any end to what you can learn about them. Instead of the rare, go after what is new to *you;* you get the same thrill.

Accurate reports of the birds' first coming in the spring are valuable to science. Still more important will your nature diary be if it records the little-known autumn migrations, or the departure dates. The Audubon Society has amateur observers all over the country who count the birds during Christmas week and the nestings in June. Science is also on the lookout for sudden changes in the population of rabbits, field mice, squirrels, chipmunks and tree rats, which give other animals serious trouble.

Not enough has been said about the rapid rise in importance of animal motion pictures, and what the camera fan can do with films of birds and quadrupeds and reptiles living their own private lives.

The men who have traveled most widely are those who have really seen what lies close about them at home. Even a little knowledge puts tremendous new interest into every familiar scene. We behold nature as something more than a beautiful picture. It becomes peopled with friends whom we call by name. And in this newly revealed world we may walk, happy in the mastery that is ours at the price of just a little curiosity and effort.

Making Habits Work for You

Condensed from "Psychology: Briefer Course"

William James

"HABIT a second nature? Habit is ten times nature," the Duke of Wellington exclaimed; and the degree to which this is true no one can appreciate as well as a veteran soldier. Daily drill and years of discipline make a man over in most of his conduct.

Habit is the flywheel of society, its most precious conserving agent. The great thing, then, is to make our nervous system our ally instead of our enemy. We must make automatic and habitual, as early as possible, as many useful actions as we can, and guard against growing into ways that are disadvantageous as we guard against the plague. The more of the details of our daily life we can hand over to the effortless custody of automatism, the more our higher powers of mind will be set free for their proper work. There is no more miserable person than one in whom nothing is habitual but indecision, and for whom the lighting of every cigar, the drinking of every cup, the time of rising and going to bed every day, and the beginning of every bit of work are subjects of deliberation. Half the time of such a man goes to deciding or regretting matters which ought to be so ingrained in him as practically not to exist for his consciousness at all.

In the acquisition of a new habit, or the leaving off of an old one, there are four great maxims to remember: First, *we must take care to launch ourselves with as strong an initiative as possible.* Accumulate all possible circumstances which reinforce the right motives; make engagements incompatible with the old way; take a public pledge, if the case allows; in short, envelop your resolution with every aid you know. This will give your new beginning such momentum that the temptation to break down will not occur as soon as it otherwise might; and every day a breakdown is postponed adds to the chances of its not occurring at all.

Second, *never suffer an exception to occur till the new habit is securely rooted in your life.* Each lapse is like letting fall a ball of string which one is carefully winding up; a single slip undoes more than a great many turns will wind up again. Continuity of training is the great means of making the nervous system act infallibly right.

Success at the outset is imperative. Failure is apt to dampen the energy of all future attempts, whereas past successes nerve one to future vigor. Goethe says to a man who consulted him about an enterprise but mistrusted his own powers: "Ach! You need only blow on your hands!" And the remark illustrates the effect on Goethe's spirits of his own habitually successful career.

The question of tapering off in abandoning such habits as drink comes under this head, and is a question about which experts differ in individual cases. In the main, however, all expert opinion would agree that abrupt acquisition of the new habit is the best way, *if there be a real possibility of carrying it out.* We must be careful not to give the will so stiff a task as to insure its defeat at the outset; but *provided one can stand it*, a sharp period of suffering and then a free time is the best thing to aim at, whether in giving up a habit like drinking, or in simply changing one's hours of rising or of work. It is surprising how soon a desire will die if it be *never* fed.

"One must first learn to proceed firmly before one can begin to make oneself over again," writes Dr. Bahnsen. "He who every day makes a fresh resolve is like one who, arriving at the edge of the ditch he is to leap, forever stops and returns for a fresh run. Without *unbroken* advance there is no such thing as *accumulation* of positive forces."

The third maxim is: *Seize the first possible opportunity to act on every resolution you make.* It is not in the moment of their forming, but in the moment of their producing *motor effects* that resolutions communicate the new "set" to the brain. No matter how full a reservoir of *maxims* one may possess, and no matter how good one's *sentiments* may be, if one has not taken advantage of every concrete opportunity to *act*, one's character may remain entirely unaffected for the better. With mere good intentions hell is proverbially paved. And this is an obvious consequence of the principles we have laid down. A "character," as J. S. Mill says, "is a completely fashioned will"; and a will, in the sense in which he means it, is an aggregate of tendencies to act in a firm, prompt and definite way upon all the principal emergencies of life.

A tendency to act becomes effectively ingrained in us only in proportion to the frequency with which the actions actually occur, and the brain "grows" to their use. When a resolve or a fine glow of feeling is allowed to evaporate without bearing practical fruit it is worse than a chance lost; it works so as positively to hinder the discharge of future resolutions and emotions. There is no more contemptible human character than that of the nerveless sentimentalist and dreamer, who spends his life in a weltering sea of sensibility and emotion, but who never does a manly concrete deed. Never should we suffer ourselves to have an emotion at a play, concert, or upon reading a book, without expressing it afterward in some active way. Let the expression be the least thing in the world — speaking genially to one's grandmother, or giving up one's seat in a car, if nothing more heroic offers — but let it not fail to take place.

If we let our emotions evaporate, they get into a way of evaporating. Similarly, if we often flinch from making an effort, before we know it the effort-making capacity is gone; and if we suffer the wandering of our attention, presently it will wander all the time. As the fourth practical maxim, we may, then, offer something like this: *Keep the faculty of effort alive in you by a little gratuitous exercise every day*. That is, be systematically ascetic or heroic in little unnecessary points, do every day or two something for no other reason than that you would rather not do it, so that when the hour of dire need draws nigh it may find you nerved and trained to stand the test. Asceticism of this sort is like the insurance a man pays on his house.

The tax does him no good at the time and possibly may never bring him a return. But if the fire does come, his having paid it will be his salvation from ruin. So with the man who has daily inured himself to habits of concentrated attention, energetic volition, and self-denial in unnecessary things. He will stand like a tower when everything rocks around him, and when his softer fellow mortals are winnowed like chaff in the blast.

The hell to be endured hereafter, of which theology tells, is no worse than the hell we make for ourselves in this world by habitually fashioning our characters in the wrong way. If we realize the extent to which we are mere walking bundles of habits, we would give more heed to their formation. We are spinning our own fates, good or evil, and never to be undone. Every smallest stroke of virtue or of vice leaves its never so little scar. The drunken Rip van Winkle in Jefferson's play excuses himself for every fresh dereliction by saying, "I won't count this time!" Well! he may not count it, and a kind Heaven may not count it; but it is being counted none the less. Down among his nerve cells and fibers the molecules are counting it, registering it and storing it up to be used against him when the next temptation comes. Nothing we ever do is, in strict scientific literalness, wiped out. Of course this has its good side as well as its bad one. As we become permanent drunkards by so many separate drinks, so we become saints in the moral, and experts in the practical and scientific spheres, by so many separate acts and hours of work. Let no one have anxiety about the upshot of his education, whatever its line may be. If he keep faithfully busy each hour of the working day, he may safely leave the final result to itself. He can with perfect certainty count on waking up some fine morning, to find himself one of the competent ones of his generation, in whatever pursuit he may have singled out.

Savings of a Lifetime

Condensed from The Saturday Evening Post

Margaret Culkin Banning

WE WERE TALKING of a man we all knew, and someone remarked, in the customary tones of horror, that the savings of his lifetime had all been swept away. Perhaps the lady who answered back had heard those words once too often. She said sharply, "You mean that he lost his money."

The mourner nodded. "That's what I said."

"No," said the lady, "you didn't say that. You told us that the savings of his lifetime were gone, which is not true. He has a mind stored full of knowledge and experience. He has made large investments in charities and educations for other people — investments which haven't depreciated and are yielding a return to society today. He's saved his simple habits and his pleasure in living. You don't have to worry about him. Worry about yourself if the savings of your lifetime are all the kind that can be swept away in a depression."

I know a woman who has saved more responsibilities than anything else during the seven decades of her life. She has seen more family troubles than most of us could endure. She has watched money come and go. Now her income must be no more than a wisp, and her responsibilities are bountiful. She always has relatives who need to have things done for them. They come to her, as do her friends, because she has saved so much human warmth and courage. If she were like the people of her own age, she would be old and tired. But during her lifetime she has saved enough competence and energy to keep herself going.

It is illuminating to make a mental list of the people you know who could stand up under poverty. Miss M. couldn't. She diminished under it. She seemed to have saved nothing with which to meet the emergencies of life except money, and when that was gone she was desperately afraid of existence.

There are two predominant reasons why we save money at all! The first reason is that other people are dependent on us. The second reason we save is for that state called an independent old age.

My savings for my children are to a considerable extent expenditures. I do not mean that I would like to leave them penniless, especially during their dependent years. But if I had to make a choice, I would prefer to leave my children well-filled minds and many happy experiences of childhood and youth rather than money. It seems to me that we can be perfectly sure of one thing. Money that is put into a good education isn't going to be lost by any economic changes. I do not mean only four years in college; education begins early, and only a part of it is housed on campuses. Yet parents will save almost hysterically and actually neglect the culture of their children's habits and minds, in the name of providing for a higher education that the child is sometimes incompetent to appreciate when he is offered it.

Often you save what you spend. The saving may be by spending money on a home which the children will remember with such affection that it becomes a permanent incentive to decent living. Tuition paid to good schools and colleges is a saving; money put into travel, or casual equipment, like tennis rackets or skates or riding habits, may be money saved; money given away is often the best saving. These same things may be extravagances or losses, I know. The test comes in the contribution that such expenditures make to an individual's development and whether the individual is what may be called a going concern.

If one can leave an estate to his children, it is a satisfaction to the testator. But it is always debatable as to whether it is good for the ones who receive it. One simply doesn't know in advance. A legacy in trust for a daughter may save her from an unhappy marriage. Or push her into one. A fortune for a son may thwart his natural ability. For myself, I never can understand why any person who has known the joy of earning should want to deny it to anyone else, particularly to those dear to him. Money spent in bringing children up to be strong, intelligent and resourceful is the best saving, both for the individual and for civilization. As far as my children are concerned, there will be a modest competence, if possible. Even that competence might be swept away. Well, then, they will still have what is being saved for them every day, what goes not into banks or bonds but into mind, and facility of body, and happiness.

There remains the other problem — that of saving for myself; for my own old age. I must admit that I find this much less interesting. That independent old lady sketched by the insurance agents isn't nearly the incentive the children are. She may never exist. But still I suppose I must take some thought for the care of her, if only to keep her from being a nuisance to other people. Here again expenditures and savings dovetail. Much of the money put into experiences that are apparently transient I consider savings. The concert, the voyage, the visit with friends — I'm putting by a few of those things as I go along. What does one save for, anyhow? For a few tired hours at the end of life when one sits and counts dollars? Or do we save so that those last years will not be mentally barren or esthetically shabby? I try to save a few things to furnish my mind decently, on the theory that no auctioneer can get in there to sell off all the furniture.

Still, one must be practical. So I ought to save some money. Probably I can save enough for a small income unless things change too radically. But I must be able and content to live on a small income. That means that I had better save all the simple tastes I have. It is a comfort to me that I really enjoy a boiled egg, a cup of tea and a piece of toast. I'm often extravagant about clothes. But I have some historic garments — a blue bathrobe and a tweed suit — that prove that I can wear things threadbare. I like possessions, but I mean to keep from being dependent on them. I'll scrap the expensive tastes, if I must, and save the frugal ones. And if, in the end, I go over the hill to the poorhouse, I'll go in no slinking spirit. My tax receipts will be clasped to my bosom, and I'll feel that at last I'm getting my money's worth!

We worry too much about money and possessions; without them most of us feel helpless. Is it because we forget that the only thing each man is required to save — the only thing he secretly wants to save, no matter what his philosophy or method — is his own soul?

I Got a Glory

ON A DAY memorable to me, I boarded a tiny tugboat I used often on a southern river and saw that we had a new Negro engineer. He sat in the doorway of the engine room reading the Bible; he was fat, and black, but immaculate and in his eyes was the splendor of ancient wisdom and peace with the world. I noticed that the characteristic odors that had always emanated from the engine room were no longer there. And the engine! It gleamed and shone; from beneath its seat all the bilge-water was gone. Instead of grime and filth and stench I found beauty and order. When I asked the engineer how in the world he had managed to clean up the old room and the old engine, he answered in words that would go far toward solving life's main problems for many people.

"Cap'n," he said, nodding fondly in the direction of the engine, "it's just this way: I got a glory."

Making that engine the best on the river was his glory in life, and having a glory he had everything. The only sure way out of suffering that I know is to find a glory, and to give to it the strength we might otherwise spend in despair.

— Archibald Rutledge, *It Will Be Daybreak Soon* (Revell)

"Human Engineering" may help you fit your aptitudes into the right job

What Are You REALLY Fitted For?

Condensed from Nation's Business

Edwin Muller

TWENTY YEARS ago it occurred to a young engineer of the General Electric Company that far too many persons are in jobs not best suited to their talents. He was appalled by the enormous wastage of human material. Why couldn't human beings — like materials — be analyzed by laboratory methods? He went to work on employes of General Electric, and eventually evolved a series of aptitude tests.

Then he started his own organization, the Human Engineering Laboratory. The engineer was Johnson O'Connor. Under his direction — at laboratories in New York, Boston, Chicago and Philadelphia — more than 70,000 persons have had their aptitudes appraised. His testing staff frequently visits schools and business houses, for the usual fee of $10 per test plus expenses.

In taking the test, you sit facing a competent young woman with a stop watch. First she hands you the "wiggly block," which is like a three-dimensional picture puzzle, a cube that has been carved into a number of irregular pieces. She lets you look at it assembled for a few moments, then scatters the pieces and tells you to put them together — as fast as you can.

At once you fall into one of two classes of human beings. Either you reach for the pieces and slip them quickly into the right places in something over 30 seconds, or you start fumbling and try to force the pieces into place — taking as long as half an hour to get it done.

O'Connor calls the fundamental aptitude tested by the wiggly block "structural visualization," or "structure" for short. It is the most essential quality of engineers, architects, those who deal with machines. Successful engineers given the test always rate far above average. One engineering class at Stevens Institute of Technology which took this test was canvassed ten years later. Those who had been good with the wiggly block had, nearly without exception, attained well-paying positions in engineering. Among those who rated low, about the only successful members were those who had left engineering and gone into other activities.

For the next aptitude — creative imagination — the young woman gives you paper and pencil. "Suppose," she says soberly, "the earth were suddenly to stop turning on its axis. What ideas does that suggest to you? Write them down as fast as you can."

You scribble furiously — or, you stare alternately at the paper and the stop watch. After five minutes your score is recorded.

Creative imagination, O'Connor says, is essential not only to writers but to salesmen, teachers, store managers, research workers — a score of others. It isn't essential — indeed may be a detriment — to foremen and accountants.

Other tests determine whether you have accounting aptitude — speed and accuracy in handling figures. Finger dexterity is measured by picking up tiny pegs, three at a time, and fitting them as quickly as possible into holes just large enough for them. To test "tweezer dexterity" you do the same sort of thing with tweezers. Oddly enough, these two aptitudes are not necessarily related.

By the end of three hours the young woman is through with you for the day. Next day you have another three-hour session. You have then been measured for 13 separate aptitudes.

Aptitudes are inherent, not acquired. In three months' practice with the little pegs you might improve your performance by about ten percent. But if you were given a different dexterity test you would revert to your old score. If you lack the musical aptitudes — "tonal memory" and "pitch discrimination" — no amount of musical training will give them to you.

The all-important thing is to find out which aptitudes you have and what they are good for. All jobs, save those of the simplest manual nature, require more than one aptitude, but there's no advantage in having an unusually large number. Nine out of ten people have at least four aptitudes — plenty to win with if they are played right. The Laboratory has found that there are few jobs, if any, that a woman can't do as well as a man.

An unused aptitude, according to O'Connor, can do harm. A man doing a job for which he has the needed aptitudes may feel a nagging dissatisfaction because he also has another aptitude which the job doesn't use.

This fact is important to employers as well as their men. Often the best answer is to shift jobs around, to find men with unsuspected abilities. Instead of discharging a bookkeeper who had gone sour on his job, a manufacturer of machine tools sent him to the Laboratory. The man scored high in accounting aptitude, but he also scored high in structure. The unused aptitude had rankled in him. On the Laboratory's advice he was shifted to a job in the cost accounting department, which brought him in direct contact with the tools. In the new job he was a success.

O'Connor gives positive vocational advice only when the pattern is obvious. Usually a person is shown the aptitudes he has and then makes his own decision. And the chances are that a man can get more out of the job he is in if he knows his aptitudes and makes judicious use of them.

The Laboratory encourages parents to have their children tested. O'Connor thinks it is a mistake for parents to advise their children to postpone thinking about their careers until they grow up. He gave the tests to his own son when the boy was 11. The youngster ranked exceptionally high in structure, so O'Connor set about in every way he could to encourage him toward engineering. In particular, he provided him with a good library — one considerably beyond his years at that time. Today young O'Connor is in charge of tool design for a large aircraft concern.

Of course success in any field involves more than aptitudes. A man may be determined enough to overcome even marked deficiencies. And it is a mistake for any man to assume that aptitudes alone are enough. He must not exaggerate their importance to the neglect of knowledge and skill — the qualities that can be acquired as against the aptitudes that can't. A boy entering medical school may have tweezer dexterity, structural visualization, subjectivity — the ideal pattern for a surgeon. But unless an inward urge drives him to learn surgery's vast accumulation of facts and theory, and to translate his dexterity into its specific manual skills, he'll get nowhere in his profession.

O'Connor's formula for success is: Find out early in life your pattern of aptitudes, and what sort of work it fits you for. Then work unremittingly to acquire the particular body of knowledge and skill that goes with that pattern.

Original Article — Published by The Chamber of Commerce o fthe United States, 1615 H St., N. W., Washington, D. C. (Nation's Business, August, '43)

Intimation of Immortality

A VETERAN NURSE (quoted in *The American Magazine*): It has always seemed to me a major tragedy that so many people go through life haunted by the fear of death — only to find when it comes that it's as natural as life itself. For very few are afraid to die when they get to the very end. In all my experience only one seemed to feel any terror — a woman who had done her sister a wrong which it was too late to right.

Something strange and beautiful happens to men and women when they come to the end of the road. All fear, all horror disappears. I have often watched a look of happy wonder dawn in their eyes when they realized this was true. It is all part of the goodness of nature and, I believe, of the illimitable goodness of God.

Why be a victim of your own emotional cycles?
Here's a way to turn them to advantage

Why We All Have "Ups and Downs"

Condensed from Redbook Myron Stearns

FOR years psychologists have known — as you know yourself — that people react differently, on different days, to the same things. One day the Boss is genial; his secretary's small mistakes don't bother him. On other days her work must be letter-perfect or he'll bite her head off. Every mother knows that on some days her youngster is affectionate and obedient, while on others he seems "possessed." On some mornings your husband sings in his shower: on others he is glum.

"Ups and downs" are commonplace. You take it for granted that a run of bad luck will get you "down." Good news, on the other hand, raises you to the top of the world. You're sure of it.

Now along comes science to tell you you're wrong. Dr. Rexford B. Hersey of the University of Pennsylvania, who has been studying the rise and fall of human emotions for more than 17 years, has found that with all of us high and low spirits follow each other with a regularity almost as dependable as that of the tides. Outside circumstances merely advance or postpone slightly our regular periods of elation or depression. Instead of lifting you out of a slump, good news will give your spirits only a brief boost. And, conversely, bad news is less depressing when you're in an emotional "high." About 33 days after your particularly low or high spots, you're likely to find yourself feeling the same way again, for that is the normal length of the human "emotional cycle."

Research into the best working conditions for railroad repair-shop men led to Hersey's discovery of emotional cycles in 1927. Checking 25 repair-shop men every day, four times a day for more than a year, he made charts based on what they said, how they acted, their physical condition and state of mind.

Presently, to his astonishment, he found that all the charts fell into a fairly regular pattern. For each worker one week in every period was much lower than the rest, and the intervals were remarkably steady. Between the low points there was a rise to relatively high spirits.

One man lost an arm in an auto accident. It occurred during his high period, and for the first weeks of his stay at the hospital he remained cheerful. "You can't keep a good man down!" he'd say. "Maybe I'll get me a better job!"

It worked out exactly that way. Returning to work, he was given a job as a minor supervisor, with more authority and pay than he'd ever had. But by that time he was in a low period; instead of being elated, he became so depressed that he broke off his engagement to an attractive girl who was genuinely in love with him. "She'd regret it," he said. "She's just being sorry for me."

An elderly mechanic claimed he was not subject to ups and downs of any sort. "I'm always cheerful," he said. But Hersey's chart showed that about every fifth week he became much more critical of his superiors, refused to joke with his companions, and didn't want to talk with anybody.

Almost without exception, the men failed to recognize any particular changes within themselves. Outside conditions, they felt, were responsible. The reason for feeling poorly was always immediate and plausible: a man hadn't slept well, or he'd had a spat with his wife, or it was the nasty weather.

Wanting more information as to *why* our spirits go up and down and how we can use the constant ebb and flow of well-being more efficiently, Hersey made a detailed investigation of his own ups and downs.

In his low periods, he soon learned, he became more critical than at other times, and more irritable. He didn't want to be bothered by talking to people. He planned his schedule so that during his periods of depression he could devote himself to research, avoiding anything that required much self-confidence. During his high periods he scheduled his consultations and lectures.

Then he made a long-drawn-out investigation of his own internal processes to ascertain the physiological basis for his emotional changes. Joining forces with Dr. Michael J. Bennett, endocrinologist of the Doctor's Hospital in Philadelphia, he underwent every week, for over a year, a searching physical examination.

He found that the work and output of his thyroid glands, his pituitary glands, his liver and other internal production plants varied markedly from week to week. The number of his red blood corpuscles, his blood cholesterol, each had — as with all of us — its own particular rhythm. The thyroid output, which to a greater extent than any other single factor determines the total "emotional cycle" rhythm, usually makes a round trip from low to high and back in from four to five weeks. Together, Hersey and Bennett decided, all the different factors work out to a "normal" cycle length of between 33 and 36 days.

Basically this emotional cycle consists of an over-all upbuilding and giving-out of energy. But the production and use of energy do not parallel each other quite evenly. First, we gradually build up more energy than we use. That makes us feel better and better, and we become more and more active and high-spirited. So we begin to use more energy than our system is producing. This keeps on until exhaustion of our surplus energy induces a reaction. We slump, often quite sharply, into feeling tired, depressed, discouraged.

We feel on top of the world for some time after our store of energy created for best conditions has begun to diminish. And conversely we feel low for some time after the rebuilding process has started up again. When everything seems hopeless we have already turned the corner.

Bringing more and more people under observation, Drs. Hersey and Bennett concluded that variations from the 33-day cycle are largely caused by unusual thyroid activity. If you are a hyperthyroid case, your cycle may be as short as three weeks. If you have a low, or hypothyroid, output, your cycle may be several weeks longer than average. Hersey has noticed that his own emotional cycles have a tendency to lengthen as he gets older. They are now, he says, about three days longer than they were ten years ago.

There seems to be no difference in cycle length between men and women. With women, however, the results are confused by the menstrual cycle, which has its own ups and downs. When the emotional low of the menstrual cycle and the low of the basic emotional cycle coincide, an abnormally bad state of nervousness or anxiety may develop. Many unnecessary marital separations have unquestionably, Hersey and Bennett believe, been started at such a time.

You can see at once how tremendously important these findings can be to you personally. First of all, you can lessen any discouragement you may feel from temporary setbacks, any worry or anxiety about the future you experience when you are blue, by the realization that your depression may be a perfectly natural phase of living, soon to be followed by days or weeks of greater strength, assurance and optimism. No matter how dismal the outlook may seem to be, you simply won't be able to avoid feeling better presently.

Next, you can keep track of your emotional cycles, so you will know when to expect a high or a low period. Simply mark on a calendar the days when you feel unusually discouraged or depressed. Your low days give you more accurate dates to go by than your high periods, because the "happiness" portions of your curve are usually more long-drawn-out; low periods seldom run more than a few days or a week and usually occur with regularity.

After you have found when to expect your high and low emotional tides, you can take advantage of both by planning your work intelligently. In high periods you are likely to be stimulated by difficult tasks. In low periods you are likely to be defeated by them. With a little experimenting you may find yourself able to plan the tough, constructive jobs, which require energy and confidence, for your high periods. At the bottom of your cycle, your powers of observation, coördination and memory seem less acute; you are more likely to make mistakes or have accidents. Hence that is the period to reserve for easy but tiresome routine.

One great danger is that during low periods minor crises or mishaps seem unduly important.

"Be sure," Dr. Hersey advises, "not to let unimportant troubles be magnified just because you are 'down.'"

In the Province of Prayer

IN THE FOOTHILLS of the Himalayas, among the Khonds of North India, one hears the prayer: "Oh, Lord, we know not what is good for us. Thou knowest what it is. For it we pray."

— Dr. Harry Emerson Fosdick, *The Meaning of Prayer*

ONE DAY Robert Louis Stevenson read us a prayer he had just written. In it were words none of us ever forgot: "When the day returns, call us up with morning faces and with morning hearts, eager to labor, happy if happiness be our portion, and if the day be marked for sorrow, strong to endure."

We waked on the morrow with happy morning faces; only Louis' wife was troubled with a premonition that the day was marked for sorrow. That day, at the height of his fame, in the best health he had ever enjoyed, Louis went out of this life suddenly, quietly, painlessly.

— Isobel Field (R. L. S.'s stepdaughter), *This Life I've Loved* (Longmans, Green)

HOW TO TAKE A WALK

Condensed from Coronet

Alan Devoe

WE ARE an ingenious and highly educated people, uniquely proficient in designing automobiles, decorating night clubs, staging World Fairs, and other intricate crafts. Unhappily, however, we have been so engrossed in mastering these techniques that we have largely forgotten older, more basic lore.

It is a lamentable fact that walking as an art, as a performance involving subtle spiritual values, is today nearly extinct. The thing that William Wordsworth meant when he spoke of taking a walk — or that Lao-tse meant, or John Burroughs or Henry Wadsworth Longfellow or Marcus Aurelius meant — is almost totally unknown. It is too bad.

Consider briefly those ingredients which can make a walk a surpassing joy to the walker and an enrichment to his soul.

In the first place, a walk should never have an objective. If you have it firmly fixed in your mind that you are on your way to Cousin Ella's or that you are going to the A & P, the awareness of this objective will gnaw constantly at your subconscious, like a maggot in a walnut. It will tinge your sensibilities and irritate your psyche. Do not, therefore, have an objective. Just go for a walk.

In the second place, a walk must never be a premeditated ritual, like a bridge party or an application for a bank loan. It must be as spontaneous as a sudden smile. One of these days, while quietly reading, or doing the housework, you will suddenly and unaccountably get the notion that it would be pleasant to take a walk. Act upon it instantly. Just open the door and go out.

The third and most important of all requirements for successful walking is also the most difficult. You must learn to expunge from your mind every single one of your usual worriments and vexations. Until you have learned to do this, walking is worse than useless. If you start out with a mind overloaded with worry about (for example) your mortgage, the rhythmic motion of your legs will resolve into a kind of ghastly refrain, dinning into your inner ear, "The mortgage is due, the mortgage is due, the mortgage is due." You have doubtless experienced something of this sort while listening to the clickety-click of train wheels or the ticking of a clock. If you start out on a walk with a bad worry in your mind, by the time you get home again the worry will be infinitely more deep-rooted. It is therefore a cardinal rule that with the first step you take you must deliberately and resolutely cast off your everyday preoccupations as a serpent sheds its skin. This is not so difficult as it seems, and you will soon get the hang of it. Say to yourself, "Now, for a few magical minutes, I am going to step out of my usual universe, and into a different and wonderful one. In due course, no doubt, I shall have to return to my old universe, but now, for these few minutes, I am going to escape into an enchanted otherworld."

Neither hurry on rushing feet nor idle along so slowly that your circulation stays unstimulated. Set a normal, moderate, free-swinging pace. Fall into a pattern of rhythm. Our modern lives suffer from a jerky instability and lack of balance — and the rhythmic swing of a correctly calculated walk takes the cramps out of a man's muscles and loosens the tight little inhibitions of his mind.

Do not (and there is no more vital walking rule than this) let your attention be arrested by *people*. In our sardine-packed modern lives we are daily reduced to wretchedness by the too-close and too-continuous proximity of our fellow men. Forget people; ignore them; leave them out of your consciousness, as you have left out the mortgage and the rest. Open your awareness, instead, to the wonderworld of the things which in your everyday life you never have time to see. Look at leaves if it is summer, or at the bare bark of winter-stripped trees. Look at the reflections in puddles of rain water; stare up at the shapes and patterns of cumulus and cirrus clouds; open your consciousness to tactile perceptions, and feel the sensation of grass or loam or stones against your soles.

Twenty-four hours a day, most days, your ears are shut. They have been rendered unhearing, in self-defense, by the clatter of traffic and typewriters and telephones. Open your ears. Let them be attentive to the tiny sounds that underlie the roar of our civilization — the soft sibilance of dead leaves whisking in the wind, the small songs of sparrows. No city is so urban that the sky has been blotted out, that no grass-blade grows, or that the subtle scent of earth does not now and again drift along the wind. Attend these things! Remark (if it is winter) the dry Promethea cocoons that rattle on high frozen twigs even in the heart of New York or Chicago; let your nostrils be receptive to the water smells that blow from lake or river; ponder upon the way a dandelion thrusts up between paving stones, upon the light of afternoon shadows, the feel of the wind against your flesh, and the Providence of God.

The world, after all, is not so unendurable, when a man gets a chance to look at it and smell it and feel its texture and be alone with it. This acquaintance with the world — this renewal of the magical happiness and wonderment which you felt when you were a child — such is the purpose of taking walks. To see things clearly — to set aside for a little while the raucousness and the clangor and the worried preoccupations which confuse you, and to come to grips with the realities which underlie the fret and stress — such has ever been the core of the art of walking. Happy walking!

A RELIGION That Does Things

Condensed from "Forty Years for Labrador"

Sir Wilfred Grenfell
World-famous medical missionary

LOOKING BACK over my 40 years' work for Labrador, I see more clearly now than ever that a man's religion must be measured by what it enables him to do. One bitter morning my host for the night had gone when I rose for breakfast. I found that he had taken the road which I had intended to travel to the next village, some 14 miles distant, just to break a trail for us, as we did not know the way; and secondly, to carry some milk and sugar to "save the face" of my prospective host for the next night. The man who walked to the village 14 miles distant was a Roman Catholic, and the neighbor to whom he carried the milk and sugar was a Methodist.

Another day that winter the father of eight children sent in from a nearby island for immediate help. His gun had gone off while his hand was on the muzzle and practically blown it to pieces. To stop the bleeding he had plunged his hand into a barrel of flour and tied it up in a bag, and as a result the wounded arm was poisoned way up to the elbow. He preferred death to losing his right arm. Slowly his fine constitution brought him through, and at last an operation for repair became possible. We took chances on bone-grafting to form a hand; and he was left with a flipper like a seal's. But there was no skin for it. So my colleague and I shared the honors of supplying some. He had English Episcopal skin on the palm of his hand

and Scotch Presbyterian skin on the back, but the rest of him has still remained a devout Roman Catholic.

After all, it is impertinent on the part of any individual to criticize how another keeps in touch with God; and if I am not religious in the way I deal with my fellow men, the fact that I accept all the theology we were taught does not make me so. There is no way to judge the value of religion except by what it *does*.

Any druggist's shelves are full of patent medicines that testify to the fact that men will always be interested in anything they believe "does things." Though I am a perfectly orthodox physician, I have known osteopaths and bone-setters help to make new men out of old. I once asked two of the best-known surgeons in the world what was the secret that brought hundreds of doctors from all over the earth, when they were in need of help, to a village in a western state to get it. One reason was my friends' plain common sense. They went everywhere, studying what methods made men new, and when they found anything that seemed helpful they tried it out, and if it worked better for the patient than their own old one they threw the old methods out of the window. What a lot of time would be saved, now wasted in criticizing and arguing about sects and creeds, what strength and money would be released for better work, instead of being dissipated in bolstering up outworn "religious" institutions and superstitions, if that plan were followed. There is no way to judge the value of religion other than the way we judge the value of surgery or of navigation. The only gauge is what it does.

To love one's neighbor as one's self is not a mere pious sentiment. It is every whit as much a law of life as fresh air is to the body. To live to one's self only is never to live at all. Once, when in need of nurses, I went to the Massachusetts General Hospital, with many qualms as to what success I should have in luring them away from so attractive an environment. I told them the following story of one of their own nurses who had been serving with us in Labrador.

One spring, a telegram came from a hamlet about 60 miles to the south, asking me to come at once, as there was an outbreak in the village of a fatal type of influenza. Unfortunately, I could not leave the hospital. However, one of my nurses offered to make the attempt. So we wired the village to send a team of dogs for her. A fortnight later an urgent telegram came from her asking for help. One of the fishermen, delirious from high fever, had escaped from his cottage in the night and gone down to his fishstage. There he got hold of a fish-splitting knife, and had ripped himself open. Then he had walked to the nurse's cottage carrying his intestines, none of which he had injured.

Meantime, dog-team travel had become impossible, while the sea-ice was so broken that no one could make the journey from the hospital to her by water. All one could do was to wire her simple instructions. Six weeks later we saw a trap boat forging its way into the harbor, covered by a tent with a funnel through it. Out of it onto the ice climbed the nurse, followed by her patient, who was by that time on the road to recovery.

She told us that the priest had consented to help her operate, provided he gave the patient the Viaticum first. As soon as this last rite was administered, the little nurse produced the chloroform from her maternity kit-bag. The good priest, who had never been present at an operation before, then gave the patient the anesthetic, while the nurse, who, in her turn, had never performed an operation of any kind, washed out the abdominal cavity with buckets of boiled water, and having rearranged the insides as best she could, sewed the wound partially up to prevent infection. . . . When I had finished recounting this story, half the nurses in the hospital wanted to go to Labrador on the next boat. Experience convinces me that never in the world's history has youth been so chivalrous as it is today. Why worry overmuch if young people express their attitude to God or their neighbors by preferring to pay the bill for a down-and-out brother to eat, rather than by hurrying to a church service?

Why is it that the very term "religious life" has come to voice the popular idea that religion is altogether divorced from ordinary life? That conception is the exact opposite of Christ's teachings. Faith, "reason grown courageous," as someone has called it, has become assurance to me now, not because the fight is easy and we are never worsted but because it has made life infinitely worth while, so that I want to get all I can out of it, every hour.

God help us not to neglect the use of a thing — like faith — because we do not know how it works. It would be a criminal offense in a doctor not to use the X ray even if he does not know how barium chloride makes Gamma rays visible. We must know that our opinions are not a matter of very great moment, except in so far as in what they lead us to do. I see no reason whatever to suppose that the Creator lays any stress on them either. Experience answers our problems — experience of faith and common sense. For faith and common sense, taken together, make reasonable service, which ends by giving us the light of life.

The Discipline of Sport

Real sport is an antidote to fatalism; the deep objective of games is really to train one's reflex of purpose, to develop a habit of keeping steadily at something you want to do until it is done. The rules of the game and the opposition of other players are devices to put obstacles in your way. The winner must keep everlastingly after his objective with intensity and continuity of purpose.

Wilfred Trotter, the famous English surgeon and philosopher, once remarked: "I think the great contribution the English have made to the valuable things of world culture is this: an interest in struggling for an unpredictable goal. As you go eastward from the British Isles, you run into cultures of gradually increasing susceptibility to fatalism. The Englishman's games have made him less fatalistic, and as a result of the discipline of sport he will keep struggling even though his intellect would indicate his cause to be lost."

— John R. Tunis, *Democracy and Sport* (Barnes)

HOW TO WIN FRIENDS *and* INFLUENCE PEOPLE

A condensation from the book by

DALE CARNEGIE

President of the Carnegie Institute of Effective Speaking and Human Relations, New York City; author of "Public Speaking," "Little Known Facts About Well Known People," etc.

FOR more than 30 years Dale Carnegie has been training business and professional men, including some of the most famous, in public speaking and in the technique of handling people. His courses have proved so valuable in business relationships that such organizations as the Westinghouse Electric and Manufacturing Company, McGraw-Hill Publishing Company, American Institute of Electrical Engineers, and the New York Telephone Company have had this training conducted in their own offices for their members and executives.

"This book," the author says, "wasn't written in the usual sense of the word. It grew and developed out of the experiences of thousands of adults in my classes." And from this extensive reservoir of experience has come the wealth of anecdote and common-sense lessons in human relationships in which *How to Win Friends and Influence People* abounds.

HOW TO WIN FRIENDS
AND
INFLUENCE PEOPLE

Criticism Is Futile

In May 1931, when "Two Gun" Crowley was captured — after being besieged by 150 policemen with machine guns and tear gas — Police Commissioner Mulrooney declared that this desperado was one of the most dangerous criminals in the history of New York. "He will kill," said the Commissioner, "at the drop of a feather."

But how did "Two Gun" Crowley regard himself? While the police were firing into his apartment, he wrote a letter addressed "To Whom It May Concern." In this letter he said: "Under my coat is a weary heart, but a kind one — one that would do nobody any harm."

A short time before this, Crowley had been having a necking party on a country road out on Long Island. Suddenly a policeman walked up to the parked car and said: "Let me see your license."

Without saying a word, Crowley drew his gun, and shot the policeman dead.

Crowley was sentenced to the electric chair. When he arrived at the death house at Sing Sing, did he say, "This is what I get for killing people"? No, he said: "This is what I get for defending myself."

The point of the story is this: "Two Gun" Crowley didn't blame himself for anything.

Is this an unusual attitude among criminals? If you think so, listen to Warden Lawes of Sing Sing: "Few criminals regard themselves as bad men. Most of them attempt to justify their anti-social acts even to themselves, consequently stoutly maintaining that they should never have been imprisoned at all."

If the desperate men behind prison walls don't blame themselves for anything — what about the people with whom you and I come in contact?

Personally I had to blunder through a third of a century before it even began to dawn upon me that, 99 times out of a hundred, no man ever criticizes himself for anything, no matter how wrong he may be; and that criticism is futile because it puts a man on the defensive, and usually makes him strive to justify himself.

Criticism is also dangerous, because it wounds a man's precious pride, hurts his sense of importance, and arouses his resentment.

When I was very young and trying hard to impress people, I wrote a foolish letter to Richard Harding Davis. I was preparing a magazine article about authors; and I asked Davis to tell me about his method of work. I had just received a letter with this notation at the bottom: "Dictated but not read." I was quite impressed. I felt the writer must be very busy and important. And as I was eager to make an impression on Richard Harding Davis, I ended my own short note, "Dictated but not read."

He never troubled to answer the letter. He simply returned it with this scribbled comment: "Your bad manners are exceeded only by your bad manners." True, I deserved his rebuke. But, being human, I resented it. I resented it so sharply that when I read of the death of Richard Harding Davis ten years later the one thought that still persisted in my mind — I am ashamed to admit — was the hurt he had given me.

When dealing with people, remember you are not dealing with creatures of logic, but with creatures of emotion, creatures bristling with prejudices and motivated by pride and vanity. And if you want to stir up a resentment tomorrow that may rankle across the decades and endure until death, just indulge in a little stinging criticism — no matter how certain you are that it is justified.

Benjamin Franklin, tactless in his youth, became so diplomatic, so adroit at handling people that he was made American Ambassador to France. The secret of his success? "I will speak ill of no man," he said, "and speak all the good I know of everybody."

As Dr. Johnson said: "God Himself, sir, does not propose to judge man until the end of his days."

Why should you and I?

We Want to Be Important

PROFESSOR John Dewey, America's most profound philosopher, says the deepest urge in human nature is the "desire to be important." Remember that phrase, "the desire to be important." It is a gnawing and unfaltering human hunger. It was this desire that led the uneducated, poverty-stricken grocery clerk, Abraham Lincoln, to study law; that inspired Dickens to write his immortal novels. It makes you want to wear the latest styles, drive the latest car, and talk about your brilliant children.

People sometimes become invalids in order to win sympathy and attention, and get a feeling of importance. Some authorities declare that people may actually go insane in order to find, in the dream-land of insanity, the feeling of importance that has been denied them in the harsh world of reality.

If people are so hungry for a feeling of importance, imagine what miracles you and I can achieve by giving them honest appreciation. The rare individual who honestly satisfies this heart hunger will hold people in the palm of his hand.

Andrew Carnegie paid Charles Schwab the unprecedented salary of a million dollars a year. Because Schwab knew more about the manufacture of steel than other people? Nonsense. Schwab told me himself that he had many men working for him who knew more about steel than he did, and that he was paid this salary largely because of his ability to deal with people. And what is his secret?

"I consider my ability to arouse enthusiasm among the men," he said, "the greatest asset I possess, and the way to develop the best that is in a man is by appreciation. There is nothing that so kills the ambitions of a man as criticism from his superiors. So I am anxious to praise but loath to find fault. I have yet to find the man, however exalted his station, who did not do better work and put forth greater effort under a spirit of approval than under a spirit of criticism."

Sincere appreciation was one of the secrets of Rockefeller's success in handling men. For example, when one of his partners, Edward T. Bedford, lost the firm a million dollars by a bad buy in South America, John D. might have criticized; but he knew Bedford had done his best. So Rockefeller found something to praise; he congratulated Bedford because he had been able to save 60 percent of the money he had invested. "That's splendid," said Rockefeller. "We don't always do as well as that upstairs."

Almost everyone considers himself important. So does every nation. Do you consider yourself superior to the Hindus in India? That is your privilege; but a million Hindus wouldn't befoul themselves by touching the food your heathen shadow has fallen across. Do you feel superior to the Eskimos? Again, that is your privilege; but would you really like to know what the Eskimo thinks of you? Well, there are a few native hoboes among the Eskimos, worthless bums who refuse to work. The Eskimos call them "white men" — that being their utmost term of contempt.

The truth is that almost every man you meet feels himself superior to you in some way; and a sure way to his heart is to let him realize that you recognize his importance. A line in *Reunion in Vienna* runs, "There is nothing I need so much as nourishment for my self-esteem." We nourish the bodies of our children and friends; but how seldom do we nourish their self-esteem!

No! I am not suggesting flattery. Flattery ought to fail and usually does. But flattery is from the teeth out. Sincere appreciation is from the heart out.

Let's cease thinking of our own accomplishments, our wants. Let's try to figure out the other man's good points. Give him honest, sincere appreciation for them and he will cherish your words years after you have forgotten them.

Emerson said: "Every man I meet is my superior in some way. In that, I learn of him."

What the Other Fellow Wants

TOMORROW you will want to persuade somebody to do something. Before you speak, remember there is only one way under high Heaven to get anybody to do anything. And that is by making them *want* to do it.

Andrew Carnegie was a past master at influencing people by talking in terms of what the other person wants. To illustrate: His sister-in-law was worried sick over her two boys at Yale, who neglected to write home and paid no attention to their mother's letters. Carnegie offered to wager a hundred dollars that he could get an answer by return mail, without even asking for it. Someone called his bet; so he wrote his nephews a chatty letter, mentioning casually in a postscript that he was sending each a five-dollar bill.

He neglected, however, to enclose the money.

Back came replies by return mail.

This strategy appealed, of course, to a relatively low motive; but it is often possible to influence people by appealing to the highest motive possible to the situation. When the late Lord Northcliffe found a newspaper using a picture of himself which he didn't want published, he wrote the editor a letter. But did he say, "Please do not publish that picture of me any more; I don't like it"? No, he appealed to the respect all of us have for motherhood. He wrote, "Please do not publish that picture of me any more. My mother doesn't like it."

When John D. Rockefeller, Jr., wished to stop newspaper photographers from snapping pictures of his children, he didn't say: "I don't want their pictures published." No, he appealed to the desire, deep in all of us, to refrain from harming children. He said: "You know how it is, boys. You've got children yourselves. And you know it's not good for youngsters to get too much publicity."

Charles Schwab had a mill manager whose men weren't producing their quota of work. "How is it," Schwab asked, "that a man as capable as you can't make this mill turn out what it should?"

"I don't know," the man replied, "I've coaxed the men; I've pushed them; I've sworn and cussed. They just won't produce." It happened to be the end of the day, just before the night shift came on.

"Give me a piece of chalk," Schwab said. Then, turning to the nearest man: "How many heats did your shift make today?"

"Six." Without another word, Schwab chalked a big figure six on the floor and walked away. When the night shift came in, they saw the "6" and asked what it meant. "The big boss was in here today," the day men said. "He asked us how many heats we made, and we told him six. He chalked it down on the floor." The next morning Schwab walked through the mill again. The night shift had rubbed out "6," and replaced it with a big "7."

When the day shift reported for work, they saw a big "7" on the floor. So the night shift thought they were better than the day shift, did they? Well, they would show the night shift a thing or two. They pitched in with enthusiasm and when they quit that night, they left behind them an enormous, swaggering "10." Shortly this mill, that had been lagging way behind in production, was turning out more work than any other mill in the plant.

The principle? "The way to get things done," says Schwab, "is to stimulate competition. I do not mean in a sordid, money-getting way, but in the desire to excel."

Back in 1915 when Woodrow Wilson determined to send a peace emissary to counsel with the war lords of Europe, William Jennings Bryan, Secretary of State, the peace advocate, longed to go. He saw a chance to make his name immortal. But Wilson appointed Colonel House, and it was House's thorny task to break the news to Bryan. "Bryan was distinctly disappointed," Colonel House records in his diary, "but I explained that the President thought it would be bad for anyone to do this officially, and that his going would attract a great deal of attention and people would wonder why he was there."

You see the intimation? House practically tells Bryan that he is too important for the job — and Bryan is satisfied. Colonel House, adroit, experienced in the ways of the world, was following one of the important rules of human relations: Always make the other man happy about doing the thing you suggest.

Don't Argue

AT A BANQUET one night the man next to me told a story in which he used the quotation, "There's a divinity that shapes our ends, rough-hew them how we will," and attributed it to the Bible. He was wrong. And to display my superiority, I corrected him. He stuck to his guns. From Shakespeare? Absurd! That quotation was from the Bible. An old friend of mine, seated at my left, was a Shakespearean scholar. The story-teller and I agreed to submit the question to him. My friend listened, kicked me under the table and said: "Dale, you are wrong. The gentleman is right. It is from the Bible."

On our way home that night, my friend explained: "Of course that quotation is from Shakespeare, Dale; but we were guests at a festive occasion. Why prove to a man he is wrong? Is that going to make him like you? Why not let him save his face? He didn't ask for your opinion. Why argue with him? Always avoid the acute angle."

"*Always avoid the acute angle.*" I sorely needed that lesson because I had been an inveterate arguer. During my youth, I had argued with my brother about everything under the Milky Way. In college I studied logic and argumentation, and later taught them in New York. As a result of it all, I have come to the conclusion that there is only one way to get the best of an argument — and that is to avoid it. Nine times out of ten, an argument ends with each of the contestants being more firmly convinced than ever that he is absolutely right. You can't win an argument. You can't win because even if you win it, you lose it, for you will never get your opponent's good will.

Moreover, my experience has been that it is all but impossible to make *any* man — regardless of his I.Q. rating — change his mind by a verbal joust. For example, Frederick S. Parsons, an income-tax consultant, had been disputing and wrangling for an hour with a government tax inspector. An item of $9000 was at stake. Mr. Parsons claimed that this $9000 was a bad debt, the inspector that it must be taxed.

"This inspector was cold, arrogant and stubborn," Mr. Parsons said. "The longer we argued, the more stubborn he became. Finally I said, 'I suppose that this is a very petty matter in comparison with the really important and difficult decisions you are required to make. I've made a study of taxation myself. But I've had to get my knowledge from books. You are getting yours from the firing line of experience. I sometimes wish I had a job like yours. It would teach me a lot.' I meant every word I said. Well, the inspector straightened up in his chair, leaned back, and talked for a long time about his work, telling me of the clever frauds he had uncovered. His tone gradually became friendly; and presently he was telling me about his children. As he left, he advised me that he would consider my problem further, and give me his decision in a few days. He called at my office three days later and informed me that he had decided to leave the tax return exactly as it was filed."

This tax inspector was demonstrating one of the most common of human frailties. He wanted a feeling of importance; and as long as Mr. Parsons argued with him, he got his feeling of importance by loudly asserting his authority. But as soon as his importance was admitted, and the argument stopped, and he was permitted to expand his ego, he became a sympathetic and kindly human being.

I have quit telling people they are wrong. And I find it pays. Few people are logical. Most of us are prejudiced, blighted with preconceived notions. When we are wrong, we may admit it to ourselves. And if we are handled gently and tactfully, we may admit it to others and even take pride in our frankness. But not if someone else is trying to ram the unpalatable fact down our esophagus.

In his biography, Ben Franklin tells how he conquered the iniquitous habit of argument and made himself one of the most able diplomats in American history. One day, when Franklin was a blundering youth, an old Quaker friend took him aside and lashed him with a few stinging truths: "Ben, your opinions have a slap in them for everyone who differs with you. Your friends find they enjoy themselves better when you are not around. You know so much that no man can tell you anything. Indeed no man is going to try, for the effort would lead only to discomfort. So you are not likely ever to know any more than you do now, which is very little."

Ben Franklin was wise enough to realize that this was true, and he made a right-about-face. "I made it a rule," said Franklin, "to forbear all direct contradiction to the sentiments of others, and all positive assertion of my own. I even forbade myself the use of every expression that imported a fix'd opinion, such as 'certainly,' 'undoubtedly,' etc., and I adopted, instead, 'I conceive,' a thing to be so; or 'it so appears to me at present.' When another asserted something that I thought an error, I deny'd myself the pleasure of contradicting him abruptly, and of showing immediately some absurdity in his proposition: and in answering I began by observing that in certain cases or circumstances his opinion would be right, but in the present case there seem'd to me some difference.

"And this became at length so habitual that perhaps for these 50 years past no one has ever heard a dogmatical expression escape me. And to this habit (after my character of integrity) I think it principally owing that I had early so much weight with my fellow citizens when I proposed new institutions, or alterations in the old, and so much influence in public councils."

When You're in the Wrong

WHEN one is at fault, it is frequently disarming to admit it quickly. Ferdinand E. Warren, a commercial artist, used this technique to win the good will of a petulant art director. "Recently I delivered him a rush job," Mr. Warren told me, "and he phoned me to call at his office immediately. When I arrived, I found just what I had anticipated — he was hostile, gloating over his chance to criticize. He demanded with heat why I had done so and so. Trying a new strategy, I simply said, 'I am at fault and there is absolutely no excuse for my blunder. I have been doing drawings for you long enough to know better. I'm ashamed of myself.'

"Immediately he started to defend me. 'Yes, you're right, but after all, this isn't a serious mistake —'

"I interrupted him. 'Any mistake may be costly. I should have been more careful. I'm going to do this drawing over.'

" 'No! No!' he protested. 'I wouldn't think of putting you to all that trouble.' He praised my work, assured me that he wanted only a minor change, a mere detail — not worth worrying about. My eagerness to criticize myself took all the fight out of him. Before we parted, he gave me a check and another commission."

The First Person Singular

MANY OF the sweetest memories of my childhood cluster around a little yellow-haired dog with a stub tail. Tippy never read a book on psychology. He didn't need to. He had a perfect technique for making people like him. He liked people himself — and his interest in me was so sincere and genuine that I could not keep from loving him in return.

Do you want to make friends? Then take a tip from Tippy. Be friendly. Forget yourself. People are not interested in you. They are interested in themselves — morning, noon, and after dinner. The New York Telephone Company made a detailed study of telephone conversations to find out which word is the most frequently used. It is the personal pronoun "I." It was used 3900 times in 500 telephone conversations. "I," "I," "I," "I," "I."

That is why you can make more friends in two months by becoming interested in other people than you can in two years by trying to get other people interested in you.

This was one of the secrets of Theodore Roosevelt's astonishing popularity. Roosevelt called at the White House one day when the President and Mrs. Taft were away. His honest liking for humble people was shown by the fact that he greeted all the old White House servants by name, even the scullery maids.

"When he saw Alice, the kitchen maid," writes Archie Butt, "he asked her if she still made corn bread. Alice told him that she sometimes made it for the servants, but no one ate it upstairs.

" 'They show bad taste,' Roosevelt boomed, 'and I'll tell the President so when I see him.'

"Alice brought a piece to him on a plate, and he went over to the office eating it as he went and greeting gardeners and laborers as he passed. They still whisper about it to each other, and Ike Hoover said with tears in his eyes: 'It is the happiest day we have had in nearly two years.' "

It was this same intense interest in the problems of other people that made Dr. Charles W. Eliot of Harvard one of the most successful presidents who ever directed a university. One day a freshman, L. R. G. Crandon, went to the president's office to borrow $50 from the Students' Loan Fund. The loan was granted. "Then" — I am quoting Crandon — "President Eliot said, 'Pray be seated.' To my amazement, he continued, 'I am told that you cook and eat in your room. Now I don't think that is at all bad for you if you get the right food and enough of it. When I was in college I did the same. Did you ever make veal loaf? That, if made from sufficiently mature and sufficiently cooked veal, is one of the best things you could have, because there is no waste. This is the way I used to make it.' He then told me how to pick the veal, how to cook it slowly, with such evaporation that the soup would turn into jelly later, then how to cut it up and press it with one pan inside another and eat it cold."

Does this attitude work in business? Does it? I could cite scores of illustrations.

Charles R. Walters, of one of the large banks in New York City, was assigned to prepare a confidential report on a certain corporation. He knew of only one man who possessed the facts, the president. As Mr. Walters was ushered into his office, a young woman stuck her head through a door and told the president that she didn't have any stamps for him that day.

"I am collecting stamps for my 12-year-old son," the president explained.

Mr. Walters stated his mission, and began asking questions. The president was vague, general, nebulous. The interview was brief and barren. Mr. Walters didn't know what to do. Then he remembered that the foreign department of his bank collected stamps, taken from letters pouring in from every continent.

"The next afternoon I called on this man again," said Mr. Walters, "and sent in word that I had some stamps for his boy. He greeted me radiating smiles. 'My George will love this one,' he kept saying as he fondled the stamps. 'And look at this. This is a treasure.'

"We spent half an hour talking stamps, and then he devoted more than an hour of his time to giving me every bit of information I wanted — without my even suggesting it."

If we want to make friends, let's put ourselves out to do things for other people — things that require time, energy and thoughtfulness.

Be a Good Listener

I RECENTLY MET a distinguished botanist at a dinner party. I had never talked to a botanist before, and I literally sat on the edge of my chair the whole evening while he spoke of hashish and potatoes and Luther Burbank and indoor gardens. Midnight came. I said good night and departed. The botanist then turned to our host and paid me some very flattering compliments. I was "most stimulating," a "most interesting conversationalist."

An interesting conversationalist? I had said hardly anything at all. I couldn't have said anything if I had wanted to without changing the subject, for I know nothing about botany. But I had done this: I had listened intently, because I was genuinely interested. And he felt it. Naturally that pleased him. That kind of listening is one of the highest compliments we can pay.

And that is the secret of success alike in social conversation and in a business interview. Remember that the man you are talking to is a hundred times more interested in himself and his wants and problems than he is in you and your problems. His toothache means more to him than a famine in China. Think of that the next time you start a conversation. And if you want people to like you, be a good listener. Encourage them to talk about themselves.

The Magic of Names

I ONCE ASKED Jim Farley the secret of his success. He said, "Hard work," and I said, "Don't be funny."

He then inquired what *I* thought was the reason for his success. I replied: "I understand you can call 10,000 people by their first names."

"No. You are wrong," he said. "I can call 50,000 people by their first names."

Make no mistake about it. That ability helped Mr. Farley put Franklin D. Roosevelt in the White House. During the years that Jim Farley traveled as a salesman for a gypsum concern, he built up a system for remembering names. Whenever he met a new acquaintance, he found out his complete name, the size of his family, the nature of his business, and the color of his political opinions. He got all these facts well in mind, and the next time he met that man, he was able to slap him on the back, inquire after the wife and kids, and ask him about the hollyhocks in the back yard. No wonder he developed a following!

He had discovered early in life that the average man is more interested in his own name than in all the other names on earth put together. Remember that name and call it easily, and you have paid him a subtle and very effective compliment. But forget it or misspell it — and you have placed yourself at a sharp disadvantage.

Andrew Carnegie, by the time he was ten years old, had discovered the astonishing importance people place on their own names. And he used that discovery to win coöperation. He had a nest of little rabbits, but nothing to feed them. Then he had a brilliant idea. He told the boys in the neighborhood that if they would pull enough clover and dandelions to feed the rabbits he would name the bunnies in their honor.

The plan worked like magic; and Carnegie never forgot it. When Carnegie and George Pullman were battling each other for supremacy in the sleeping-car business, the Steel King again remembered the lesson of the rabbits.

The Central Transportation Company, which Andrew Carnegie controlled, was fighting with the company Pullman owned. Both were struggling to get the sleeping-car business of the Union Pacific Railroad, bucking each other, slashing prices, and destroying all chance of profit. Both Carnegie and Pullman had gone to New York to see the board of directors of the Union Pacific. Meeting Mr. Pullman one evening in the St. Nicholas Hotel, Carnegie suggested a merger of the two companies. He pictured in glowing terms the mutual advantages of working with, instead of against, each other. Pullman listened attentively, but was not wholly convinced. Finally he asked, "What would you call the new company?" and Carnegie replied promptly: "Why, the Pullman Palace Car Company, of course."

Pullman's face brightened. "Come into my room," he said. "Let's talk it over." That talk made industrial history.

Men are so proud of their names that they strive to perpetuate them at any cost. Two hundred years ago, rich men used to pay authors to dedicate their books to them. Our millionaires helped finance Admiral Byrd's expedition to the Antarctic with the understanding that ranges of icy mountains would be named after them. Even blustering, hard-boiled old P. T. Barnum, disappointed because he had no sons to carry on his name, offered his grandson, C. H. Seeley, $25,000 if he would call himself "Barnum" Seeley.

One of the simplest, most obvious, and most important ways of gaining good will and making people feel important is by remembering names. Yet how many of us do it? Half the time we are introduced to a stranger, chat a few minutes, and can't even remember his name when we say good-bye. Most people don't remember names for the simple reason that they don't take the time and energy necessary to concentrate and repeat and fix names indelibly in their minds.

Napoleon III of France boasted that he could remember the name of every person he met. His technique? If he didn't hear the name distinctly, he said, "So sorry. I didn't get the name clearly." Then, if it was an unusual name, he would say, "How is it spelled?"

During the conversation, he took the trouble to repeat the name several times, and tried to associate it in his mind with the man's features, expression, and general appearance. If the man were someone of importance, Napoleon went to even further pains. As soon as he was alone, he wrote the man's name down on a piece of paper, looked at it, concentrated on it, fixed it securely in his mind, and then tore up the paper. In this way, he gained an eye impression of the name as well as an ear impression.

All this takes time, but "good manners," said Emerson, "are made up of petty sacrifices."

Remember that a man's name is to him the sweetest and most important sound in the English language.

Why must we have enough memory to recall to the tiniest detail what has happened to us, and not have enough to remember how many times we have told it to the same person? — La Rochefoucauld

The tragic end of America's best-loved baseball player who, doomed by infantile paralysis, devoted his last days to public service

LOU GEHRIG'S *Epic of Courage*

Condensed from Cosmopolitan

Paul Gallico

Former sports writer: author of "Secret Front," "Farewell to Sport," etc.

I REMEMBER writing years ago: "There is no greater inspiration to any American boy than Lou Gehrig. For if the awkward, inept and downright clumsy player that I knew in the beginning could through sheer drive and determination turn himself into the finest first-base-covering machine in all baseball, then nothing is impossible to any man or boy in this country."

The last chapter in the life of this baseball hero put a big exclamation point after that statement. Gehrig was at the height of his career. From the press box, sports writers looked down with honest affection at the piano legs, the broad rear porch which had earned him the name of Biscuit Pants, the powerful shoulders and the pleasant face of "that big dumb Dutchman."

In 1936–7–8, with Gehrig as captain, the Yankees won three World Series in a row. In 1936, Lou was for the second time named the most valuable player in the American League, nine years after he had first achieved this honor. And his consecutive-games record went on and on. Sick or well, he never missed a game. Lou played in spite of colds, in spite of fevers. He played so doubled over with lumbago that he couldn't straighten up — and, though bent over at the plate, he still got himself a single.

One year he fractured a toe. He played on. Knocked unconscious by a wild pitch and suffering from a concussion that would hospitalize the average man for two weeks, he was at his position the next day *and collected four hits.* When, late in his career, his hands were X-rayed, they found 17 assorted fractures that had healed by themselves. He had broken every finger on both hands and some twice, and hadn't even mentioned it to anyone.

The fantastic thing about all this is not that Lou was able to endure the pain of breaks, sprains and torn tendons, but that it failed to impair his efficiency. If he had something the matter with him he tried all the harder.

The slow tragedy of disintegration began in the winter of 1938–39 when Lou, a fine skater, fell repeatedly on the ice. The following spring, finding himself slow in training, he began to drive his body harder to make up for its mysterious failure. When the symptoms of his slowing up were obvious at St. Petersburg training quarters, the sports writers sadly wrote that the old Iron Horse was running down. But the players on the Yankee ball club knew that a ballplayer slows up gradually — he doesn't come apart all at once.

There are grim tales of things that happened in the locker room. One tells of Gehrig leaning over to lace his shoes and falling forward to the floor, to lie helpless; and of tough men with the fine instinct to look away and not to hurt him by offering help as he struggled painfully to his feet.

Among the elements that go to make up a hero is the capacity for quiet, uncomplaining suffering. This was Lou Gehrig. Not even his wife, Eleanor, knew how terribly he suffered during those days when his speed and skill were deserting him, when he found, to his bewilderment, that he could not bat, could not run, could not field. The nightmare strain and terror of it lined his face in a few short months and brought gray to his hair. But it could not force a complaint from his lips.

When it became apparent that there was something wrong, Lou drove himself still more relentlessly. It never occurred to him to blame something beyond his control. His performance during the early part of 1939 was pitiful. And yet, so great was the spell cast by his honest attempts to please and his service over the long years that the worst-mannered individual in the world, the baseball fan, forebore to heckle him.

On Sunday, April 30, 1939, the Yankees played the Senators. At first, Lou muffed an easy throw; he came to bat four times with runners on base, failed even to meet the ball, and the Yankees lost.

Monday was an off day. Gehrig did a lot of thinking. He had the toughest decision of his life to make. Tuesday the team played the Tigers. Lou went to Manager McCarthy in the dugout. "Joe," he said slowly, "I always said that when I felt I couldn't help the team any more I would take myself out of the line-up. I guess that time has come."

"When do you want to quit, Lou?" asked McCarthy.

Gehrig looked at him steadily and said, "Now."

His consecutive-games record ended at 2130 games.

Lou went to the Mayo Clinic for a checkup. The Yankees released the doctors' diagnosis: it was a form of infantile paralysis. The cause of the sudden, mysterious decline of Henry Louis Gehrig was solved. Before Gehrig came home from the Mayos', his wife went to their family physician, told him the name of the disease and asked the truth. He told her that her husband could not live more than two years. Eleanor telephoned the Clinic. She learned that the doctors had not had the heart to tell Lou. "Please promise me that you never will let him know," she begged.

Lou came home full of smiles and jokes, and the girl who met him was gay too, though neither noticed that in the laughter of the other there was something feverish. They were too busy with their magnificent deception of each other. Eleanor fought a constant fight to keep the truth from Lou. As to what Lou knew, he never told anybody.

On July 4, 1939, there took place the most tragic and poignant scene ever enacted on a baseball diamond — the funeral services for Henry Louis Gehrig.

Lou attended them in person.

Lou Gehrig Appreciation Day, it was called, a gesture of love and appreciation, a spontaneous reaching out to a man who had been good and kind and decent, to thank him for having been so.

The most touching demonstration was the coming from the ends of the country of Gehrig's former teammates, the famous Yankees of 1927.

And there was George Herman Ruth. The Babe and Lou hadn't got along very well in the last years they played together. But despite their childish feud, the Babe was here now with an arm around Lou and a whispered pleasantry that came at a time when Gehrig was very near collapse from the emotions that turmoiled within him.

The principal speakers were Postmaster General Jim Farley and Mayor La Guardia; 61,808 were in the stands. It was what was known as a Great Day.

To Lou Gehrig it was good-bye to everything that he had known and loved.

In a box in the stands were those he held dear: his mother and father, unaware of his doom, and his wife. Lifelong friends were there, and as Lou observed them gathered in his honor, he knew he was seeing them thus for the last time.

Gifts piled up for him from the Yankees; from their great rivals, the Giants; from the baseball writers; even from the ushers and peanut boys in the stadium. The warmth of the feeling that prompted their presentation melted the iron reserve in Lou and broke him down.

It was so human and so heroic that Gehrig should have wept there in public — not for the pity of himself, nor for the beauty and sweetness of the world he would soon leave, but because the boy who all his life had convinced himself that he had no worth now understood for the first time how much people loved him.

Not only were his immediate family, his adored wife, and his personal friends broadcasting their warmth to him, but a great throng of plain, simple people with whom he felt a deep kinship. To tune in suddenly upon so much love was nearly too much for him.

The speeches were ended at last and the stadium rocked with wave after wave of cheers. Lou stood with head bowed to the tumult and pressed a handkerchief to his eyes. Then he lifted his head and spoke his epitaph:

"For the past two weeks you have been reading about a bad break I got. Yet today I consider myself the luckiest man on the face of the earth. . . ."

ALTHOUGH the tale of Lou Gehrig really ends above, perhaps in the simple story of how he lived what time was left to him is to be found his greatest gallantry. Those two years called for the most difficult heroism of all — the heroism of the laugh that covers pain, the light phrase that denies hopelessness and a sinking heart.

Lou chose to spend his last days not in one final feverish attempt to suck from life in two years all that he might have had in 40, but in work and service.

Mayor La Guardia appointed him a city parole commissioner. And so for the next months, as long as he was able to walk even with the assistance of others, Gehrig went daily to his office. He listened to cases, studied them; he brought to the job his thoroughness and his innate kindness and understanding.

He sat at his desk even when no longer able to move his arms. When he wanted a cigarette, his wife or secretary lit it for him and put it between his lips, removed it to shake the ash.

He listened to thief, vagabond, narcotic addict and prostitute. When there was help to be given he gave it unstintingly from what strength there was left to him. He would not give in.

On June 2, 1941, Lou Gehrig died in the arms of his wife in their home in Riverdale, N. Y.

Parents can shape the destiny of tomorrow's world – it's the biggest job of all time

EDUCATION BEGINS AT HOME

Condensed from School and Society

Charles F. Kettering

Research director of General Motors

"IT'S A lovely day tomorrow," I heard a youngster hum as I passed him this morning while he was waiting for a school bus. I thought: If tomorrow *is* a lovely day, it will be because you and millions like you make it so. You have the biggest job of all time on your hands. The job of rebuilding America. Of putting new and stronger foundations under our way of life.

Lincoln Steffens used to tell young people that nothing in life has been done the way it should be; that the world was full of all sorts of things to do over — and do right. That statement will be even truer in the world of tomorrow.

We oldsters know that we've only scratched the surface of knowledge, of accomplishment. Tomorrow's inventions will make our present ones look as elementary as a safety pin. But if our children are going to improve on our performance, they must get off to a better start than we did, and head into the future with less fear, fumbling and blind-alleying. The world makes way for a youth who knows *where* he is going.

The best way we can help our young folks — we who are turning over to them so much unfinished business — is to make sure that they have every chance to develop the three qualities they'll need most as creative pioneers. These are vision, imagination and courage. Through *vision* they will see things as they really are. Through *imagination* they will dream greatly of things that may be. Through *courage* they will act boldly to make their dreams come true.

To see clearly, children must first learn to think for themselves. Unless they start learning that in the home, they'll never really learn it. Yet many parents insist on handing down prejudices, conclusions and rules of conduct as antiquated as the family furniture. Stuffing a child with mental heirlooms is no way to make him think for himself, or think at all.

Youngsters naturally have exploring minds. Parents must keep them exploring; every incident of the day should be an expedition into the familiar unknown. Children should be encouraged to probe for cause and effect of everything that happens around them. A roller skate casts a wheel. A cake "falls" in the oven. A bicycle breaks down. What made it do that? How can one keep it from happening again? Boys and girls who through quest and question find out these answers for themselves are acquiring a habit worth more than all the roller skates, cakes and bicycles that can be bought.

What's more, children must be permitted to do creative things in their own way rather than ours. As I get nearer 70, I realize that there's always another perfectly good way to do almost anything. A dog scratches himself with his hind legs; a pig does it by rubbing against a post — but they're both good scratchers. If your child insists that he can make better mud pies with hot water than with cold, for heaven's sake let him boil some water and find out whether he is right.

Our youngsters are already habituated, as we are, to pushing buttons and throwing switches in order to obtain light, heat, water and other necessities of life. But let's make sure they don't take too much for granted. When they look out on the earth, sea and sky, these bright elements seem wonderful to them. So we must remind them how little we have actually brought the world under our control. Floods let loose their water, great winds blow, the sun shines too much or too little — and straightway millions of human beings hunger, go homeless, die.

As we turn a child's attention to the things undone or done badly, the riddles of waste and want yet to be solved, the discoveries yet to be made, the symphonies yet to be written, we must make him feel that in the world of tomorrow there'll be plenty of opportunity for *him* to do these things, or other things which are just as important. But it must be emphasized that the right to exercise his highest faculties in changing the world must be won by a thorough and driving preparation.

Men who came up "the hard way" usually try to make things as easy as possible for their children, thus denying them the discipline of struggle and self-establishment that worked so well in their own cases. Such parents remind me of the kindhearted amateur who raised butterflies as a hobby. He was so touched by the difficulties they had in emerging from the cocoon that once, out of mistaken kindness, he split a cocoon with his thumbnail so that the tiny inmate could escape without a struggle. That butterfly was never able to use its wings.

Every time a youngster has to face a first-class difficulty and masters it, his wings become that much stronger. Every time he makes a choice and acts on it, boldly and decisively, he is girding himself anew with confidence and courage.

There are two kinds of courage. One is a spontaneous explosion of aroused instincts to meet some sudden emergency; the other is steadfast and enduring against repeated failures and rebuffs. It's what boxers call "the fighting heart," the will to come bouncing back every time one is knocked down. All pioneers need that kind of courage, and our youngsters will need plenty of it when they plunge into the world of tomorrow.

We are prone to toss at our children the finished products of man's achievements — the radio, telephone, a lifesaving medicine — without telling them about the painful processes by which these miracles came into being. We seldom take the trouble to explain that every great improvement in aviation, communication, engineering or public health has come after repeated failures. We should emphasize that virtually nothing comes out right the first time.

Failures, *repeated* failures, are finger posts on the road to achievement. The only time you don't fail is the *last* time you try something, and it works. One *fails forward* toward success.

Even after you've succeeded, the worst stretch often begins. Westinghouse perfected his air brake before he was 30, but had to fight desperately, far into middle age, before he saw it recognized as one of the most important inventions of his time. No one can say how many discoveries have been lost because the discoverers weren't tough enough to stick to their guns and make the world believe.

Young folks must realize that when a pioneer, through toil, thought and sweat, finds out how to make better airplanes or houses or surgical instruments his troubles really begin. They will then be stouter of heart and firmer of purpose when they run into their own inevitable setbacks.

One final practical truth we must point out to our youngsters. All American boys and girls start off with the one real wealth there is — time on their hands. Nature demands eight hours for rest and nourishment; schools or jobs demand another eight; but the third eight hours belong to us to use as we will. Too much spare time is spent in listening to the radio, "cutting a rug," or at the movies.

The course of human events has been profoundly affected by men and women who made good use of their spare time. Anton van Leeuwenhoek, an uneducated Dutchman, cleaned the Delft city hall for a living, but in his leisure he taught himself to grind the little lenses that opened up the wonderful and terrible world of the microbes, probably the greatest discovery in the history of medicine. The Wright brothers made a meager living mending bicycles, but poured their spare time into a winged dream called an "airplane." Unless children are taught to devote some of their energies to preparation for the future and put their spare time to work along practical lines, they'll never be among tomorrow's real pioneers.

Original Article — Published by The Society for the Advancement of Education, Inc., 15 Amsterdam Ave., New York 23, N. Y. (School and Society, January 1, '44)

Confessions of a chain-smoking David who slew the nicotine Goliath

Are You a MAN or a SMOKESTACK?

Adapted from Your Life

J. P. McEvoy

I ONCE read a little story about Eamon de Valera. Arrested for taking part in the Easter Rebellion, he was being led off to jail by British soldiers. "Just a minute," said "Dev" — and he took his beloved pipe out of his mouth and dashed it to pieces on the sidewalk. "Why did you do that?" he was asked. "Because," he replied, "I wouldn't give you so-and-so's the pleasure of depriving me of smoking in jail. I have just quit."

I had been a chain-smoker for years. With chronometer precision I hammered another nail into my coffin every ten minutes. And the expense! I once tried to figure how much I was spending for smokes — the sum was so fantastic I couldn't believe it.

One day I took myself firmly in hand and said, "Look here, are you a man or a smokestack? 'Dev' did it, why can't you?" So I quit! Just like that. Friends heard about my earth-shaking decision and hurried over to warn me of the consequences. "The shock may kill you," said one. "Why don't you taper off?"

But I had seen too many nervous wrecks who had rationed themselves to one cigarette after each meal, or just one cigar after dinner. "Suppose I finally got myself tapered down to one smoke a day," I said. "All day I'd sit around thinking about that smoke after dinner. Not only would I get no work done, but by sundown I'd be in a state bordering on collapse. No, 'Dev' did it the only way it can be done."

Just to clinch it, I reminded my friend of the humane old gentleman who thought he could spare the dog's feeling by cutting off its tail a little at a time.

That was three years ago — and I haven't smoked since. For the first few months I was a great nuisance to other smokers — something like the reformed drunkard who goes around knocking glasses out of people's hands. "*You* can stop smoking," I would say, and then add with fake modesty, "*too*." I am sure my tone implied: "Fat chance, you poor flabby-willed victim of your lower instincts."

But months passed and I grew more tolerant. Of course, when friends asked me sympathetically, "Did you suffer much?" I broke down and confessed in words of my friend Adolphe Menjou when telling about his operation: "I had the greatest pain known to medical science."

Now after three years I can tell the truth. It really didn't hurt at all — and it didn't take any super exercise of will power. Anybody can do it. I say flatly: "You can stop smoking — *if you really want to*."

The first trick is to convince yourself that it is more important for you *not* to want to smoke than to smoke. It's a kind of self-hypnosis. You say to yourself, "I want to stop smoking. It's a darn nuisance — it stains my fingers and I burn holes in my clothes and I forget where I put my cigarettes down and they set fire to the furniture. Besides it isn't good for me. Here I am with a smoker's throat and a hacking cough which the ads tell me there is not one in a carload of. Look at the people who used to smoke like chimneys and have quit. They're always talking about how much better they feel and how they sleep nights and have no more sinus trouble and their eyes are clear and their breaths are pure and their wives are crazy about them because they don't mess up the rugs and smoke up the curtains and they don't smell like an old police station."

Of course you may say, "I can't stop — the habit has got me," or "My system craves nicotine — it's the only thing that soothes my nerves." Don't believe any of this defeatist pish-posh. Your system does not crave nicotine. Smoking is not an irresistible hunger (as for dope) or a consuming thirst (as for alcohol). Your system is not a slave to a drug; *you* are a slave to a habit — a major habit made up of a connected series of minor habits.

Smoking is merely a pattern of automatic acts, somewhat like driving a car. You throw out the clutch, shift gears, step on the gas. One act leads to another, and the car is in motion. Well, the smoking habit is composed of just such a series of events. Psychologist Henry C. Link calls it "a neuro-muscular chain of acts which begins with lifting the pack, extracting a cigarette, placing it between the lips, striking a match, inhaling the smoke, etc., until the stub reaches the ash tray."

All right, so the task is to prevent the pattern from getting started. The best and simplest method of attack is to dump all your smoking apparatus — pipes, humidors, cigarettes — into the ash can so they won't flag your attention at every turn.

Then, for the habit of smoking, you substitute the habit of not smoking. I began by chewing gum every time I thought of smoking, but I developed jaw muscles like a bulldog and had to go to bed early nights to rest my weary mandible. Another well-wisher said: "Substitute a piece of candy for that smoke." I had always loved candy and had never before found a good excuse for eating all I wanted. So I bought a box of chocolates and noticed to my horror that I'd eat a pound at a sitting. When I reproached my friend, he said: "I forgot to warn you against soft candy." So I went around with my pockets full of lemon drops. Every time I thought of smoking, which was practically every minute those first few days, I took a lemon drop. I got so tired of lemon drops, I got tired of thinking of smoking.

The most insidious thing about the habit of smoking is that it gets tied up with all your other habits. Do you find you must light a cigarette after breakfast? You have allowed the enjoyment of breakfast and smoking cigarettes to get so mixed up together that you can't think of one without the other. In this way smokers have linked up smoking with every waking activity, and many of them have even tied it up with going to sleep so that they have insomnia if they can't smoke in bed and set themselves on fire. Once you realize the true nature of these unholy unions, deliverance is at hand.

You'll meet temptations, of course. Not from the fellow who casually offers you a cigarette, or tries to undermine your resolve with a little well-placed kidding. You can slough this chap off in your stride. The real hazards are your dream-fantasies about the joys of smoking. You conjure up a mirage of those beautiful blue cool clouds that you used to blow from your cheery briar tamped with mellow Burley. And those delectable after-dinner Cabanas, clear Havana with their silky Sumatra wrappers. Not to mention a satisfying pull on one of the "three leading brands" of cigarettes.

Delusions all! The thing to do at this point is to look back on the years when your mouth tasted like a lime-burner's wig, and your overstuffed sinuses ached under the sledge-hammer assault of a two-pack day. Let that great biologist Raymond Pearl sustain you with figures proving that heavy smokers shorten their lives. Observe the happy expectancy in your wife's eyes as you bend over to kiss her with a breath sweet as mignonette. Yes, there are two faces to the coin of memory, and the tobacco-stained side isn't a pretty one.

I'll never forget the amazement, the thrill I experienced when I realized one evening that I hadn't even thought about smoking all that day, nor the day before for that matter. Soon it was weeks. I saw people smoking all around me, I lighted countless cigarettes for others and refused innumerable offers of smokes with complete indifference. As the months went by, the delicate taste buds of appetite began to raise their heads hopefully. I ate better, savored my food with a gourmet's relish. My nerves stopped jerking like a side-show dervish; my heart pumped quiet and serene. The faceless witch Insomnia cleared out of my bedroom, and a new buoyancy floated me through the day's work.

Today the physical benefits of a tobacco-free life are undeniable. But the mental lift and the moral glow from conquering an enslaving habit add up to the most exhilarating satisfaction in the world.

The Sexual Relationship in Marriage

Condensed from
The World Tomorrow

Frederick Harris
Former chief editor of the Association Press, official organ of the Y. M. C. A.

There are few personal problems of deeper concern to men and women today than the sexual adjustment in marriage. Marked sexual maladjustment issues frequently in profound nerve disorders, in shattered partnerships, and in pitiful spiritual degradation. But this is probably not the most significant phase of the problem. The real tragedy is that such a large number of people are muddling along so aimlessly that the sexual relationship, instead of being an enriching experience, remains a generally disappointing and recurrently a disruptive element in the partnership.

Sexual matters are not often treated rationally, even in an advanced civilization like America; and the result is that we live in a dim twilight beneath heavy clouds of prejudice. The relation of the sexual impulse to the association of a man and a woman in marriage remains confused because we do not analyze our experience. What we receive from nature is a powerful and imperious organic impulse. But we have omitted in sex education to instruct youth as to how this disturbing drive can be brought successfully into harmony with other elements in marital experience.

How can such an integration be achieved? I believe that the issue cannot be evaded by any vague "spiritualization" of sex. Shall we not rather look for our salvation in drawing the sexual relationship into the circle of true partnership by making it a genuinely shared interest? This means that, instead of seeking personal sexual satisfaction, each partner shall endeavor first to consider the other in order that perfect mutuality shall be established. The essence of mutuality is that the whole experience — from the first caress to the climax of sexual intercourse — shall mean essentially the same to both, and shall bring the same enduring satisfaction to both. I am aware that perfection is not within the range of human possibility, but *we can achieve as near an approximation here as in any other adventure in sharing*. It is proper that both partners shall understand the import of all their acts, that they shall ascend the heights of sexual emotion as nearly abreast as possible, and that each shall attain the climax which is essential to mental and physical well-being.

I have no illusions as to the difficulty of this achievement, but the only alternative is that one partner shall satisfy his or her desire at the expense of the other. It is such experiences which create that disgust of the physical act which mars the life of so many women. Buoyed up in the early days of marriage by the force of a deep love, later on such women come to feel more and more keenly a desperate bewilderment about, and a sharp recoil from, a passion which they are called upon to serve without sharing.

It is strange that in an enlightened age all this should have to be set down; but I have talked with a number of earnest and intelligent married men who do not even know whether or not their wives have ever experienced, in sexual intercourse, the climactic release of nervous tension technically known as an orgasm. With all their sincerity, such men must be set down as having little intelligent concern for the sexual interests of their partners. There is nothing really shared under such circumstances.

The ideal sexual partners are those who have sized up the character of their problem. As they are utterly frank with each other elsewhere, they are utterly frank with each other here. They have studied together the facts about each other's bodies and the characteristic psychological reactions of men and women. They understand that adjustment between their mutual moods must determine appropriate times and seasons for sexual satisfaction. They have not an atom of fear of each other. In all high emotion there must be a sense of abandonment, of perfect freedom; and such daring freedom is theirs because each understands that the other is not grasping selfishly at his own delight. There can be little danger of unserviceable sexual behavior when the sexual life of each partner is the object of the other's intelligent and affectionate concern.

There are many phases of love, but these phases come together in the purpose of affection — the desire for unity with the beloved. The sexual relationship may play its part in enriching and perfecting unity. In its due season, it may represent, above every other relationship, the most intimate and delicate sense of oneness. As a glance of the eye or a touch of the hand or the graceful homage of a kiss — sensuous things all — becomes not only a symbol but part and parcel of affectionate expression, so sexual intercourse, the most intense of all sensuous experiences, may be a most perfect expression of mutual love. Sexuality as it appears in acts whose purpose is merely to satisfy one's own demands tends to be cruel and relentless; but when it appears as a purpose of two partners to share an experience with each other, it is the handmaid of tenderness. This is the ideal experience.

The chief difficulty in realizing this sort of relationship is our curious reluctance — due to the habit of strict reticence regarding sex matters — to admit social intelligence into the case. We speak about nature showing the way. But the kind of sexual intercourse I have been discussing is not "natural" at all. It is as unnatural as streetcars or a Beethoven symphony. It is the product of human patience, intelligence, skill. The sex behavior of the lower animals and of undeveloped races is more or less casual, largely self-centered, and quite probably violent. Such behavior serves a purely procreative purpose, but it does not enrich the experience of sexual mates. This mutuality in the sexual relationship is an artistic achievement and artistic achievements do not just happen.

There are less ponderable obstacles. Wide differences in time of sexual response between man and woman, instability of emotional mood at certain times, odd little crotchets of time or place or conversation or preliminaries that, trivial enough in themselves, may grow in this particular experience into matters of extreme significance — the list could be multiplied. But such obstacles are nearly all surmountable by patience and skill. Because we insist upon exaggerated reticence, men and women bear in uneasy fortitude what could be readily removed by intelligence.

Again I repeat, this is not an instinctive procedure, but a delicate and personal adjustment as artificial as any other superior spiritual achievement of mankind. It must be learned properly: good intentions are not enough here. It is well-meaning blundering which so often produces that unfortunate conflict of experience between affectionate husband and wife which seems to separate the physical act from all spiritual context; and love is left painfully to climb up out of the pit into which it has been so heedlessly hurled.

Much has been written about the monotony of monogamy. But if the perfect sexual adjustment enshrined in the marital partnership brings a common happiness to both partners, there is insurance against monotony; for the very essence of sexuality is its tidal ebb and flow. "The first fine careless rapture" is recaptured, recaptured again and again; we celebrate once more a vital and enduring unity.

It is my conviction that the achievement of this sharing of the sexual experience tends to become so satisfying to the partners that their sex problem is settled within their partnership. Sexual irregularity for such partners no longer appears in their desires. I am told by those who have had the opportunity to examine many cases that under such circumstances sexual love may continue up to the threshold of senility. It is a beautiful idea that marital lovers far beyond middle age should be able to warm themselves in an emotional experience recalling all the fine romance of the first flush of youth. There is always a rich reward for the pains we take in trying to perfect a personal relationship.

Original Article — Published by The World Tomorrow

Even though you do the right thing, do you do it the right way?

Have You an Educated Heart?

Condensed from "The Bromide and Other Theories"

Gelett Burgess

LAST OCTOBER I sent Crystabel a book. She acknowledged it, and promptly. But two months afterward she actually wrote me another letter, telling me what she thought of that book; and she proved, moreover, that she had read it. Now, I ask you, isn't that a strange and beautiful experience in this careless world? Crystabel had the educated heart. To such as possess the educated heart thanks are something like mortgages, to be paid in installments. Why, after five years Crystabel often refers to a gift that has pleased her. It is the motive for a gift she cares for, not its value; and hence her tactful, iterated gratefulness.

Everything can be done beautifully by the educated heart, from the lacing of a shoe so that it won't come loose to passing the salt before it is asked for. If you say only "Good morning," it can be done pleasingly. Observe how the polished actor says it, with that cheerful rising inflection. But the ordinary American growls it out with surly downward emphasis. Merely to speak distinctly is a great kindness, I consider. You never have to ask, "What did you say?" of the educated heart. On the other hand, very few people ever really listen with kindly attention. They are usually merely waiting for a chance to pounce upon you with their own narrative. Or if they do listen, is your story heard with real sympathy? Does the face really glow?

Consider the usual birthday gift or Christmas present. By universal practice it is carefully wrapped in a pretty paper and tied with ribbon. That package is symbolical of what all friendly acts should be — kindness performed with style. Then what is style in giving? Ah, the educated heart makes it a business to know what his friend really wants. One friend I have to whom I can't express a taste that isn't treasured up against need. I said once that I loved watercress, and lightly wished that I might have it for every meal. Never a meal had I at his table since, without finding watercress bought specially for me.

Do you think it's easy, this business of giving? Verily, giving is as much an art as portrait painting or the making of glass flowers. And imagination can surely be brought to bear. Are you sailing for Brazil? It isn't the basket of fine fruits that brings the tears to your eyes, nor the flowers with trailing yards of red ribbon — all that's mere kindness, ordinary everyday kindness. It's that little purse full of Brazilian currency, bills and small change all ready for you when you first trip ashore at Rio.

There was old Wentrose — he understood the Fourth Dimension of kindness, all right. Never a friend of his wife's did he puffingly put aboard a streetcar, but he'd tuck apologetically into her hand the nickel to save her rummaging in her bag. Real elegance, the gesture of inherent nobility, I call that.

Is it sufficient simply to offer your seat in a streetcar to a woman? The merely kind person does that. But he does it rather sheepishly. Isn't your graciousness more cultured if you give it up with a bow, with a smile of willingness? Besides the quarter you give the beggar, can't you give a few cents' worth of yourself too? The behavior of the educated heart becomes automatic: you set it in the direction of true kindness and courtesy and after a while it will function without deliberate thought. Such thoughtfulness, such consideration is *not* merely decorative. It is the very essence and evidence of sincerity. Without it all so-called kindness is merely titular and perfunctory.

Suppose I submit your name for membership in a club. Have I done you (or my club) any real service unless I also do my best to see that you are elected? And so if I go to every member of the committee, if I urge all my friends to endorse you, that is merely the completion of my regard for you. It is like salt — "It's what makes potatoes taste bad, if you don't put it on."

Must you dance with all the wallflowers, then? I don't go so far as that, although it would prove that you had imagination enough to put yourself in another's place. All I ask is that when you try to do a favor you do it to the full length of the rope. Don't send your telegram in just ten carefully selected words. Economize elsewhere, but add those few extra phrases that make the reader perceive that you cared more for him than you did for the expense.

No one with the educated heart ever approached a clergyman, or a celebrity, or a long-absent visitor with the shocking greeting: "You don't remember me, do you?" No, he gives his name first. No one with the educated heart ever said, "Now do come and see me, sometime!" The educated heart's way of putting it is apt to be, "How about coming next Wednesday?" And strongly I doubt if the educated heart is ever tardy at an appointment. It knows that if only two minutes late a person has brought just that much less of himself.

You call once or twice at the hospital. Do you ever call again? Not unless you have the educated heart. Yet the patient is still perhaps quite ill. One there was who used to bring a scrapbook every morning, pasted in with funny items from the day's news.

Truly nothing is so rare as the educated heart. And if you wonder why, just show a kodak group picture — a banquet or a class photograph. What does every one of us first look at, talk about? Ourself. And that's the reason why most hearts are so unlearned in kindness.

If you want to enlarge that mystic organ whence flows true human kindness, you must cultivate your imagination. You must learn to put yourself in another's place, think his thoughts. The educated heart, remember, does kindness *with style.*

THREE DAYS TO SEE

Helen Keller

Condensed from
The Atlantic Monthly

I HAVE often thought it would be a blessing if each human being were stricken blind and deaf for a few days at some time during his early adult life. Darkness would make him more appreciative of sight; silence would teach him the joys of sound.

Now and then I have tested my seeing friends to discover what they see. Recently I asked a friend, who had just returned from a long walk in the woods, what she had observed. "Nothing in particular," she replied.

How was it possible, I asked myself, to walk for an hour through the woods and see nothing worthy of note? I, who cannot see, find hundreds of things to interest me through mere touch. I feel the delicate symmetry of a leaf. I pass my hands lovingly about the smooth skin of a silver birch, or the rough, shaggy bark of a pine. In spring I touch the branches of trees hopefully in search of a bud, the first sign of awakening nature after her winter's sleep. Occasionally, if I am very fortunate, I place my hand gently on a small tree and feel the happy quiver of a bird in full song.

At times my heart cries out with longing to see all these things. If I can get so much pleasure from mere touch, how much more beauty must be revealed by sight. And I have imagined what I should most like to see if I were given the use of my eyes, say, for just three days.

I should divide the period into three parts. On the first day, I should want to see the people whose kindness and companionship have made my life worth living. I do not know what it is to see into the heart of a friend through that "window of the soul," the eye. I can only "see" through my finger tips the outline of a face. I can detect laughter, sorrow, and many other obvious emotions. I know my friends from the feel of their faces.

How much easier, how much more satisfying it is for you who can see to grasp quickly the essential qualities of another person by watching the subtleties of expression, the quiver of a muscle, the flutter of a hand. But does it ever occur to you to use your sight to see into the inner nature of a friend? Do not most of you seeing people grasp casually the outward features of a face and let it go at that?

For instance, can you describe accurately the faces of five good friends? As an experiment, I have questioned husbands about the color of their wives' eyes, and often they express embarrassed confusion and admit that they do not know.

Oh, the things that I should see if I had the power of sight for just three days!

The first day would be a busy one. I should call to me all my dear friends and look long into their faces, imprinting upon my mind the outward evidences of the beauty that is within them. I should let my eyes rest, too, on the face of a baby, so that I could catch a vision of the eager, innocent beauty which precedes the individual's consciousness of the conflicts which life develops. I should like to see the books which have been read to me, and which have revealed to me the deepest channels of human life. And I should like to look into the loyal, trusting eyes of my dogs, the little Scottie and the stalwart Great Dane.

In the afternoon I should take a long walk in the woods and intoxicate my eyes on the beauties of the world of nature. And I should pray for the glory of a colorful sunset. That night, I think, I should not be able to sleep.

The next day I should arise with the dawn and see the thrilling miracle by which night is transformed into day. I should behold with awe the magnificent panorama of light with which the sun awakens the sleeping earth.

This day I should devote to a hasty glimpse of the world, past and present. I should want to see the pageant of man's progress, and so I should go to the museums. There my eyes would see the condensed history of the earth — animals and the races of men pictured in their native environment; gigantic carcasses of dinosaurs and mastodons which roamed the earth before man appeared, with his tiny stature and powerful brain, to conquer the animal kingdom.

My next stop would be the Museum of Art. I know well through my hands the sculptured gods and goddesses of the ancient Nile-land. I have felt copies of Parthenon friezes, and I have sensed the rhythmic beauty of charging Athenian warriors. The gnarled, bearded features of Homer are dear to me, for he, too, knew blindness.

So on this, my second day, I should try to probe into the soul of man through his art. The things I knew through touch I should now see. More splendid still, the whole magnificent world of painting would be opened to me. I should be able to get only a superficial impression. Artists tell me that for a deep and true appreciation of art one must educate the eye. One must learn through experience to weigh the merits of line, of composition, of form and color. If I had eyes, how happily would I embark on so fascinating a study!

The evening of my second day I should spend at a theater or at the movies. How I should like to see the fascinating figure of Hamlet, or the gusty Falstaff amid colorful Elizabethan trappings! I cannot enjoy the beauty of rhythmic movement except in a sphere restricted to the touch of my hands. I can vision only dimly the grace of a Pavlowa, although I know something of the delight of rhythm, for often I can sense the beat of music as it vibrates through the floor. I can well imagine that cadenced motion must be one of the most pleasing sights in the world. I have been able to gather something of this by tracing with my fingers the lines in sculptured marble; if this static grace can be so lovely, how much more acute must be the thrill of seeing grace in motion.

The following morning, I should again greet the dawn, anxious to discover new delights, new revelations of beauty. Today, this third day, I shall spend in the workaday world, amid the haunts of men going about the business of life. The city becomes my destination.

First, I stand at a busy corner, merely looking at people, trying by sight of them to understand something of their daily lives. I see smiles, and I am happy. I see serious determination, and I am proud. I see suffering, and I am compassionate.

I stroll down Fifth Avenue. I throw my eyes out of focus, so that I see no particular object but only a seething kaleidoscope of color. I am certain that the colors of women's dresses moving in a throng must be a gorgeous spectacle of which I should never tire. But perhaps if I had sight I should be like most other women — too interested in styles to give much attention to the splendor of color in the mass.

From Fifth Avenue I make a tour of the city — to the slums, to factories, to parks where children play. I take a stay-at-home trip abroad by visiting the foreign quarters. Always my eyes are open to all the sights of both happiness and misery so that I may probe deep and add to my understanding of how people work and live.

My third day of sight is drawing to an end. Perhaps there are many serious pursuits to which I should devote the few remaining hours, but I am afraid that on the evening of that last day I should again run away to the theater, to a hilariously funny play, so that I might appreciate the overtones of comedy in the human spirit.

At midnight permanent night would close in on me again. Naturally in those three short days I should not have seen all I wanted to see. Only when darkness had again descended upon me should I realize how much I had left unseen.

Perhaps this short outline does not agree with the program you might set for yourself if you knew that you were about to be stricken blind. I am, however, sure that if you faced that fate you would use your eyes as never before. Everything you saw would become dear to you. Your eyes would touch and embrace every object that came within your range of vision. Then, at last, you would really see, and a new world of beauty would open itself before you.

I who am blind can give one hint to those who see: Use your eyes as if tomorrow you would be stricken blind. And the same method can be applied to the other senses. Hear the music of voices, the song of a bird, the mighty strains of an orchestra, as if you would be stricken deaf tomorrow. Touch each object as if tomorrow your tactile sense would fail. Smell the perfume of flowers, taste with relish each morsel, as if tomorrow you could never smell and taste again. Make the most of every sense; glory in all the facets of pleasure and beauty which the world reveals to you through the several means of contact which nature provides. But of all the senses, I am sure that sight must be the most delightful.

Nature's Best

In *The Lost Woods*,* Edwin Way Teale, the naturalist, writes: "If I were to choose the sights, the sounds, the fragrances I most would want to see and hear and smell — among all the delights of the open world — on a final day on earth, I think I would choose these: the clear, ethereal song of a white-throated sparrow singing at dawn; the smell of pine trees in the heat of noon; the lonely calling of Canada geese; the sight of a dragonfly glinting in the sunshine; the voice of a hermit thrush far in a darkening woods at evening; and — most spiritual and moving of sights — the white cathedral of a cumulus cloud floating serenely in the blue of the sky."

* Published by Dodd, Mead

Thanks to recent research, medical schools are teaching doctors to trace and correct the mental states that cause bodily ailments

How Your Mind May Make You Ill

Condensed from Your Life

Elsie McCormick

FOR MORE THAN a decade a group of outstanding physicians has been investigating the strange influence that our minds have on our bodies. They have evidence even stronger than the medical profession previously suspected that mental conditions can upset normal physical functions, can weaken our resistance to infection, and, most remarkable of all, can actually cause physical change in vital organs. Dr. Flanders Dunbar and associates at the Columbia-Presbyterian Medical Center in New York City studied 1500 patients suffering from a variety of illnesses. An emotional upset lay at the root of more than half the cases.

At Johns Hopkins, Dr. G. Canby Robinson examined 50 patients who complained of nausea or stomach pains; he could find a definite organic reason in only six cases. The rest were literally worrying themselves sick. One man's symptoms began years before, on the day he lost his job. A woman confessed that hers developed after listening to a description of stomach cancer on the radio.

Few ailments show so clearly as stomach ulcer the close connections between mind and body. At the New York Hospital, Dr. Harold G. Wolff tested 205 patients to see how emotional upsets affected the flow of hydrochloric acid, which aggravates stomach ulcers. While making his tests he led the conversation around to topics he suspected would be painful. The acid count soared when the bankrupt business or the thwarted career was being discussed. It doubled at the mere mention of an estranged wife.

A study of mucous colitis patients made at Massachusetts General Hospital showed that 92 percent of them were harried by worry and emotional strain. One man had a colitis attack every day for two months on his way to work. When questioned, he explained that his easy-going boss had been replaced just two months before by an efficiency expert. A change in his own job cured him. A nurse recovered from severe mucous colitis on the day her family forgave her for marrying a man of a different religion.

For years it has been known that anger can send our blood pressure skyrocketing. And now doctors suspect that a prolonged state of anger bottled up inside ourselves is often responsible for "essential hypertension," a form of chronic high blood pressure which has no apparent physical cause. This discovery is particularly significant when we realize how many deaths after 50 are related to blood-pressure disturbances.

In the last few years, researchers have studied hundreds of essential-hypertension patients, and find that they tend to have the same character traits. On the surface these people appear to be typical Caspar Milquetoasts. But a fierce resentment usually smolders beneath this submissive façade. When shown how to release pent-up emotions their blood pressure drops like a plummet.

One meek little man, who belonged to a turbulent labor union, suffered from high blood pressure only during times of industrial peace. The moment a strike was declared and he could release his buried anger by shouting insults at strike-breakers, his blood pressure went down to normal.

A study of 100 tuberculous patients revealed that those who were emotionally disturbed had a swifter form of the disease than those free of strain. Other studies have shown that many cases of diabetes have suffered from severe emotional shock; that arthritic attacks frequently run parallel to acute mental upsets; that worry can accelerate tooth decay. There are many diseases still to be explored. But enough is already known to alleviate much unnecessary suffering.

Dr. Dunbar and her assistants treated 121 patients with heart trouble and spent from one to 36 hours with each of them, discussing their emotional difficulties and pointing out ways of living that would bring them peace. The genuinely damaged hearts were not miraculously repaired, but in nearly every case the painful symptoms ceased. Furthermore, the records of patients followed up for several years show no recurrence of attacks.

As a result of recent research which shows that knowledge of the patient's frustrations and worries is quite as important as chemical analyses and X-ray findings, medical colleges like those at Harvard, Cornell and Columbia now require intensive courses in the mental roots of illness, and a new medicine is being practiced, called "psychosomatic" from the Greek words for "mind" and "body."

Sometimes the emotional conflict is so deep-seated that the patient must be referred to a psychiatrist. But a general practitioner trained in mind-body relationships can usually uncover the difficulty — even when the patient has carefully hidden it from himself.

The doctor's approach is one of friendly interest. He knows that most of us bury distressing problems in a secret crypt of our minds. Then the peace we attain is bought at the price of poor health. He works on the modern belief that unless we give our emotions some conscious expression our bodies will express them in terms of flesh and blood. Bringing them into the light of day gives us a chance to work them out before they injure our vital organs.

There are, of course, problems which psychosomatic medicine cannot solve. Countless ailments are not caused by any mental state. Some difficulties, economic and physical, are not readily banished. In such cases the modern physician helps his patient face his problem squarely, accept it, and build up satisfactory compensations. When we stop fighting the inevitable we release energy which enables us to create a richer life, even in the face of poor health.

Young medical graduates of today are often able to help cases that baffle physicians of the old school. After older doctors had failed to cure a little girl of persistent vomiting, a recent graduate of the Cornell Medical Center was consulted. The laboratory reported no intestinal difficulty, but a friendly talk with the child revealed a painful emotional upset. She had remarked in a moment of pique that she wished her teacher would die. Three days later the teacher did drop dead of heart failure. The child, who felt sure that her wish had caused the tragedy, reacted with stomach trouble. When the doctor convinced her that she was not responsible for the teacher's death, she recovered.

"Once again," writes Dr. Franz Alexander, "the patient as a human being with his worries, fears, hopes and despairs, as an individual whole and not only as the possessor of organs, is becoming the legitimate object of medical interest." It is more important, progressive doctors now insist, to know what sort of patient has a disease, than what sort of disease the patient has.

Of all the things you wear, your expression is the most important. The next time you catch a glimpse of yourself in a store window or a counter mirror, skip the glance at your hat angle and check up on the expression just below. Then decide if it isn't worth a little time and effort to exchange that look of grim determination for something a little more appealing.

— Janet Lane in *Collier's*

"WE HAVE WITH US TONIGHT—"

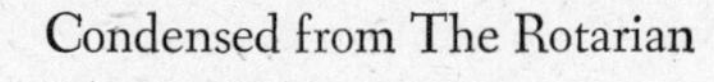

Condensed from The Rotarian

Dale Carnegie

Whose widely known course in public speaking has made self-confident speakers of over 55,000 business men and women

YOU HAVE been invited to make a speech, and have come to me with perplexing questions. I'll try to answer them.

"*Shall I accept the invitation?*" Yes. It will be a lot of fun, and prove one of the most thrilling experiences of your life. Indeed, if I were you, I wouldn't even wait for an invitation to make a speech. For the good of my soul, I'd seize the first opportunity to make one voluntarily — and every legitimate opportunity thereafter: office conference, club meeting, church gathering, Parent-Teachers meeting. For public speaking is a sure way to leadership. I know hundreds of men who have created more prestige by one five-minute talk than they had by five years of grinding work. Once successfully master an audience with a short talk and thereafter you'll be a better master of yourself.

You won't make a brilliant speech. But don't let that worry you. Few people do. If you doubt me, turn on your radio, or listen to the talks in the House or Senate at Washington.

"*But I never faced an audience in my life. I'm afraid I'll faint.*" Oh, no, you won't. I have watched 55,000 business men and women face audiences for the first time. Only one fainted. Of him I prophesied right then that within a few weeks he would actually enjoy talking in public. He did. He continued to meet with a public speaking group twice a week after that for years.

Of course you will be nervous at first. Everyone is. Bryan was. So were Theodore Roosevelt and Lloyd George. But there are certain things that will help you develop courage in advance. One is practice. Practice. Practice. Where? Anywhere. When I was riding horseback to college out in Missouri years ago, I used to go out in the barn and practice my talks to the horses and frightened pigeons. Talk to friends about the points you are going to discuss. Call in the neighbors and practice on them. Talk to any available group that will listen.

Don't imagine it is going to be difficult. You could make a good talk right now if somebody knocked you down. You have frequently made good talks at home when you were mad. Remember the heat and force and color you put into your talks then. All you have to do is to release that same intensity of feeling before an audience. Good public speaking is merely enlarged conversation. Nothing more.

Remember nothing is holding you back except your own thoughts. So stop thinking of yourself. Think of your subject, your audience. "Do the thing you fear to," said Emerson, "and the death of fear is absolutely certain."

"*What shall I talk about?*" Talk about what interests you — from pouter pigeons to Julius Caesar; speak with enthusiasm and you are sure to interest your audience. I have seen that happen thousands of times. I know a man who could hold you and 5000 other people spellbound by talking about his hobby of collecting Oriental rugs. You may know more about catfish or cyclones or cleaning fluids than anyone else in the audience. If so, that may be a good topic for you. Don't try to get a topic out of the newspapers or the encyclopedia or a book of speeches. Dig your topic — or, if your subject is assigned, your approach — out of your own head and heart.

"*How shall I prepare?*" That question takes us right into the secret chambers of good speaking. Three fourths of the success of your talk will depend on whether or not you are adequately prepared. Most speakers who fail do so because they wouldn't take the time to prepare. Harry Emerson Fosdick, one of the most eloquent speakers in America, used to say that it took him ten hours to prepare a ten-minute talk and 20 hours for a 20-minute talk.

You can stand up right now and talk about some childhood exploit or how you got started in business or the most exciting adventure of your life. You have lived through these things. The secret of preparation is to investigate your subject so thoroughly that it becomes for the time being as intimate a part of you as these vivid experiences. Suppose, for example, you have been asked to talk on the subject, "Is the public honest?" First, sit down and check up your own experiences. Then go to the merchants in your town who do credit business and ask them for their experiences. Ask your local dentists and doctors. If there is a Better Business Bureau in your town, interview the manager. Write the National Association of Credit Men asking where you can find material. Go to your public library. Spend an hour of preparation for every seven seconds you expect to talk. Get ten times as much material as you can use. You will then have an inner urge, a conviction — and your talk will almost make itself.

"*Shall I memorize my talk?*" No! Never! If you do, you are likely to forget; and the pangs of inflammatory rheumatism seem mild in comparison with the agonies endured by the speaker who suddenly forgets his "canned" speech. But even if you do remember your talk, you will be thinking of words, not ideas. Consequently, you will have a faraway look in your eyes and a faraway sound in your voice. The whole performance will lack life, color, intimacy. No one will pay much attention to it.

But if you *think* out what you are going to say — think it out over and over again, make a few notes and then trust to Allah to give you the words you need — your performance will be human and natural. True, your talk may be crude in spots, your phraseology may be awkward, you are almost certain to leave out some of the things you intended to say; but what you do say will get over far better than a memorized oration.

"*What gestures shall I make?*" As far as the audience is concerned, it won't be necessary to make any gestures. But gestures will help *you* to let yourself go. I use lots of gestures while speaking, especially when I am talking on the radio. I need them to help me warm up before the unresponsive mike. In the same way, you can force yourself to speak with enthusiasm before an audience by merely forcing yourself to make any sort of emphatic gestures. But don't plan them in advance. Don't let any elocutionist drill you to gesture with graceful curves in front of a mirror. Remember you are trying to instruct, entertain or move an audience to action. A speech is a psychological process, not a physical exhibition of grace; and you should no more be thinking of gestures than of words. You ought to be thinking only of your ideas, your message and your audience.

"*Shall I put my hands in my pockets?*" Theodore Roosevelt did, and so did William Jennings Bryan and Chauncey M. Depew. Of course, the best place for your hands is at your sides. They look well there, and they are in position to gesture easily when the urge comes. But if your hands feel like a bunch of bananas hanging at your sides, your mind won't be free and easy. And the condition of your mind is far more important than the position of your hands. So put your hands in your pockets if that gives you more ease. You are trying to make something happen in the other man's head and heart. If you can do that, it doesn't matter what you do with your hands.

"*How shall I deliver my talk?*" Speak sincerely, from the heart. You may make blunders, but you can hardly fail to make an impression. The most difficult problem I face in training men is to blast them out of their shells and inspire them to speak with genuine earnestness. That is probably the most important rule in delivery. Your audience must feel that you know what you are talking about, that you mean it and have an intense desire to tell about it.

"*How can I tell whether I am being heard?*" When Abraham Lincoln made, at Cooper Union in New York, the famous speech that he afterward said made him President, he posted a friend in the back row with instructions to signal with his cane if Lincoln couldn't be heard. Not a bad idea for you. Remember, your voice can't carry unless you have plenty of air in your lungs. So breathe deeply. Don't talk to the people in the front row. Talk to the people in the back row. Think your voice into the rear of the room. Speak with energy. Open your mouth. You don't have to shout. Even a whisper, when made correctly, will carry to the back of a large theater.

"*Shall I tell funny stories?*" No! By the beard of the prophet, No! In the whole realm of speechmaking, humor is the most difficult thing to achieve. If you aren't a natural humorist — if you *try* to be funny — you may easily fail. And if you fail, you will only afflict your audience with pity and embarrassment.

"*How long shall I talk?*" George Horace Lorimer once told me that he always stopped a series of articles in *The Saturday Evening Post* when they were at the peak of their popularity. That is a good time to stop a talk, too. Stop when people are eager to have you go on. Stop before they want you to. Lincoln made the most famous speech in the world at Gettysburg; and he did it with ten sentences and spoke less than five minutes. Unless you are very much better than you think you are, and unless your subject is extremely important, you had better not take more than twice as much time as Lincoln took.

To me, the conception of two people living together for 25 years without having a cross word suggests a lack of spirit only to be admired in sheep. Where there is spirit there must be sparks. Don't imagine that your first row in married life will be the end of everything. It is more likely to be the real beginning. — A. P. Herbert, quoted in *Ladies' Home Journal*

Women over Forty

Condensed from the book of the same title

Sarah Trent

OUR Aunt Mathilda probably shuddered at facing the middle years, with their prospects of changes, mental and physical; she dreaded them because she had heard women wail: "We're on the verge of the most difficult period of our lives!"

Nonsense! If a woman has done her share of the world's work, and has tasted life's responsibilities and experiences, she will find herself prepared to enjoy the rewards of maturity, in spite of this much-heralded "change." The situation is not tragic, as many women like to make it. The "female troubles" (obscure and terrifying ills which etched wrinkles into grandmothers' faces) need never plague our lives if we intelligently take advantage of modern knowledge.

But there must be no sitting back with folded hands, letting ourselves get flabby, mentally and bodily; we must acknowledge that the middle years do present to every woman peculiar problems, problems to be faced and solved.

This is the time for searching self-analysis. To live the forties as nature intended, full of energy and wisdom, at the peak of mental power, we must evaluate ourselves correctly. What, exactly, is it that nature does to us somewhere after the fortieth year?

In one simple sentence, she relieves us of the burden of child-bearing, and of periodic discomfort. Not overnight, but gradually, over a period of years, varying with the individual. Biologically, the process is simplicity itself and normally quite painless. The uterus, no longer needed for maternity, will gradually begin to atrophy. The ovaries, no longer parting with an ovum once a month for fertilization, will cease to function; gradually, too, the menstrual flow will become irregular and at last cease. With these major indications, there will be glandular changes (the physical basis for the mental instability), there may be disturbances of the vaso-motor system, resulting in the "hot flushes," perspirations, or palpitations.

There you have the menopause — before modern medicine, the most feared experience of woman's life, bristling with catastrophe, made hideous by superstition. Is there anything so fearsome about the process? Nature is saying, "you have up to this time lived for the race, now live for yourself."

For these women, there are, however, a few words of easily taken advice. First, avoid physical excesses of all kinds — too much fatigue, excitement, work, too little sleep or exercise. Simple, regular living is especially desirable at this time. Second, if during the menopause any marked physical symptoms are noticeable, then let the doctor be visited. The medical profession recommends that women put themselves in the doctor's hands during this period, just as for prenatal care. The patient is thus relieved of uncertainty and worry — she has shifted the responsibility for her health onto the shoulders of the family doctor. His word will do much to relieve nervousness and dread.

There will be certain emotional changes; but they need not be disturbing. These changes, like all processes of nature, will come gradually; no woman will wake up some morning and find herself mentally quite another creature from the one who turned out the light the night before. But the average emotionally stable woman, to whom tears are as alien as tantrums, may find herself inclined to weep without reason. Let her weep away. The outlet of a good crying spell does wonders. She may find herself annoyed by trifles — impelled to nag and scold; she may become moody, prone to self-pity, sunk often in an inexplicable slough of misery. In some cases, the uglier emotions may raise their heads; fear and jealousy may wreak havoc if the sufferer is not forewarned. Or one who has prided herself on her power of concentration may find her mind wandering, unable to make decisions, to think things through to logical conclusions.

But these deviations from the normal must not be taken too seriously. They merely mean that the ductless glands, in process of reorganization, are reacting on the nervous system, to make it jumpy. And they are by no means permanent. Only as this fact is understood and discussed frankly will many married couples be able to weather the period during which the wife is adapting herself to a new scheme of things. The husband must understand what is taking place in his wife's body, and the wife must know herself so thoroughly that she will be able to attribute any divergence from the norm to its proper causes. She must learn to laugh and reason herself out of the difficulties, secure in the knowledge that they will shortly adjust themselves. Dilemmas which seem insurmountable will become just what they are — ordinary problems; mental lassitude will pass into a new surging up of energetic, clear thinking.

Fears lest she lose her looks will change to a secure confidence that there can be no diminution of attractiveness and charm in a well-poised, serene, mature woman. Jealousy, closely associated with fear, can be cured by the same means. Both have their basic cause in sex.

And the woman over forty need not consider that her sex life is a thing of the past; she must realize that it is only a new phase of sex life beginning for her. Simply because a woman can no longer reproduce, it does not follow that sex drops out of her life or becomes negligible. On the contrary, she has a right to, and should have, as normal a sex life as a woman twenty years her junior. The menopause is a *pause*, not a halt. To bear out this statement — one of the most noted gynecologists in New York City found that in an imposing percentage of his cases the fullest sex life was attained *after the age of fifty.*

And finally, of these old wives' tales that are rampant in the feminine world — how women go insane during the adjustment period; of poor Mrs. So-and-So, suddenly gone quite out of her head — let it be said emphatically, nature never intended anything of the sort. If there are such cases, then age is only a contributing factor to a deep-seated abnormality, and not the primary cause. There is no "queerness" which the average woman cannot banish by self-control, sane living and a clear understanding of what is actually going on.

So we give you the woman over forty! Freed by nature from her duty of child-bearing, her family brought up, she is ready for the most mentally fruitful and socially profitable period of her career — for the luxury of living *for herself*. One sees such women everywhere — in the professions, in the arts, in public life — full of energy, full of accomplishment. Shortly, it will be the exceptional woman who deems that she has fulfilled her mission in life when she sees her children settled. It will be the usual thing for women to make a neat division of their lives — the years up to forty for growing, for learning, for marrying and bearing children; the later years for self-expression, for service, for all kinds of social and helpful activities. We give you the Woman over Forty.

The Tonic of Praise

Praise is not only gratifying — it is the source of fresh energy which can be measured in the laboratory.

Dr. Henry H. Goddard, in his years at the Vineland Training School in New Jersey, used the "ergograph," an instrument devised to measure fatigue. When an assistant said to a tired child at the instrument, "You're doing fine, John," the boy's energy-curve soared. Discouragement and fault-finding were found to have a measurable opposite effect.

— Gretta Palmer

A simple recipe for happiness which actually works

One Day Can Change Your Life

Condensed from Cosmopolitan

Henry James Forman

IN MY WORK as a personnel manager, I always tried to discourage the idea that any person in our office was indispensable.

One young woman, however, defeated that program completely. She did her work well, but others did it as unimpeachably when she was on vacation. She was not especially pretty, or possessed of any remarkable talents. Yet somehow she created an atmosphere that drew people to her. Everyone recognized that she had become the most necessary member of the staff.

I determined to find out why. After a conversation with her, the reasons appeared quite simple. Once, a few years earlier, she had chanced upon a brief magazine suggestion.

"Try religion for a day — a single day!" the writer had said. "Only twenty-four hours out of the more than half a million hours of your probable life span. All the great of all the ages have agreed as to the overwhelming benefits of religion as the supreme hygiene. Don't you think it's worth investing about one twenty-five thousandth of your time in giving it a trial?"

Up to that point religion had meant little to Miss Brown. Now suddenly she determined to try the experiment.

"Think," she exclaimed to me, once she had broken through her shyness, "think what it meant, a whole day spent without a trace of any *fear* — no fear of any person or any thing! No fear of life, no fear of death. No fear of old age or of sickness or my job or the future, or anything else. I felt *free* for the first time in my life."

Miss Brown had not discovered the supreme hygiene of living without some religious preparation, including a study of the Bible.

She had also read a little psychology. What she learned was that the *giant emotions*, the *destructive* ones, which religions refer to as deadly sins — anger, hatred, fear, greed, lust, cruelty and pride — all are deadly poisons. They poison us as they work within us, and they poison life and the world about us.

Not religion alone but science teaches the same thing. Physicians and psychiatrists are now demonstrating that the "deadly sins" are really major errors in the technique of living.

Dr. Carl Jung of Zurich, one of the great psychiatrists, says: "Every one of my patients in the second half of life — that is to say, over 35 — fell ill because he had lost that which the living religions of every age have given their followers; and none of them has really been healed who did not regain his religious outlook."

Your persistent fear is a persistent paralysis. Your anger and hatred today will make some life or lives darker — but chiefly your own life. Just as your tolerance and kindness this morning may affect the outlook and condition of persons you are hardly aware of, and certainly will affect your own condition, incalculably for good.

Health and *wholeness*, in other words, and that often despised partner, holiness, are really one and the same thing. That at least partly explains why religion is instinctive in all of us.

Those are things Miss Brown discovered for herself when she undertook to lead the religious life. Everything, she said, somehow began to flow toward instead of away from her. She seemed to have become positive instead of negative. She felt that she was at last a genuine human being. She tried it for a day, and so great was the joy she experienced that she tried it for another day.

Then something happened that wrecked her equanimity — an office tempest in which she was made the scapegoat. For bitter days she was filled with the old resentments: anger, hatred, intolerance toward people about her.

Then she recalled the two happy days when life had been pure joy. It had been like another world. All at once the force of this fact struck her.

The world was the same — the same identical world. It was *she* who had been new and young and happy during those all-too-brief hours. Now she understood that the turmoil she had yielded to was almost entirely within herself. If she fell back into her old attitude of suspicion, fear, anger and hatred, suffering and pain followed as certainly as night followed day. But so long as she kept to her faith that kindness, good will and love are not only virtues (which means strengths) but psychic and physical necessities for withstanding the shocks of daily life, then she could continue to be psychically, mentally, physically whole. For her, she knew, the way was to begin again — *begin and continue* — the oldest maxim in this field of making oneself over.

Success came to her increasingly, for in no domain is effort rewarded so richly. People about her noted the change in her.

I recall a friend asking her one day, "But what religion or creed do you really belong to, Miss Brown?"

"Belong?" she repeated. "I really don't know. Or rather," she added with a sudden luminous smile, "it must be that I belong to all of them."

When Oliver Wendell Holmes was still on the Supreme Court bench, he and Justice Brandeis took walks every afternoon. On one of these occasions Holmes, then 92, paused to gaze in frank admiration at a beautiful young girl who passed them. He even turned to look at her as she continued down the street. Then, turning to Brandeis, he sighed: "Ah! What wouldn't I give to be 70 again!"

— Drew Pearson and Robert S. Allen, *The Nine Old Men* (Doubleday)

KEEP OPEN the Windows of Your Mind

Condensed from The American Magazine

Merle Crowell

CARL LOMEN, the reindeer king of Alaska, told me this true story:

"A certain Greenland Eskimo," said Lomen, "was taken on one of the American North Polar expeditions a number of years ago. Later, as a reward for faithful service, he was brought to New York City for a short visit. At all the miracles of sight and sound he was filled with a most amazed wonder. When he returned to his native village, he told stories of buildings that rose into the very face of the sky; of streetcars, which he described as houses that moved along the trail, with people living in them as they moved; of mammoth bridges, artificial lights, and all the other dazzling concomitants of the metropolis.

"His people looked at him coldly and walked away. And forthwith throughout the whole village he was dubbed Sagdluk, meaning The Liar, and this name he carried in shame to his grave. Long before his death his original name was entirely forgotten.

"When Knud Rasmussen made his trip from Greenland to Alaska he was accompanied by an Eskimo named Mitek (Eider Duck). Mitek visited Copenhagen and New York, where he saw many things for the first time and was impressed. Later, upon his return to Greenland, he recalled the tragedy of Sagdluk, and decided that it would not be wise to tell the truth. Instead, he would narrate stories that his people could grasp, and thus save his reputation.

"So he told them how he and Doctor Rasmussen maintained a kayak on the banks of a great river, the Hudson, and how, each morning, they paddled out for their hunting. Ducks, geese and seals were to be had a-plenty, and they enjoyed the visit immensely. . . . Mitek, in the eyes of his countrymen, is a very honest man. His neighbors treat him with rare respect."

The road of the teller of new truths has always been rocky. Socrates sipping the hemlock, Christ crucified, Stephen stoned, Bruno burned at the stake, Galileo terrified into retraction of his solar verities — forever could one follow that bloody trail through the pages of history.

Too many of us resent the impact of new ideas and look with suspicion on whoever imparts them to us. We hate to be disturbed in the beliefs and prejudices that have been handed down with the family furniture. At maturity we seek the sterile comfort of mental hibernation, and live off the fat of ancient fetishes. If a new idea invades our den, we rise up snarling from our winter sleep.

The Eskimos, at least, had some excuse. Their simple minds were unable to visualize the startling pictures drawn by Sagdluk. But there is no adequate reason why the average man should ever close his mind to fresh "slants" on life. That's isolationism in its most tragic form.

An old farmer up in Vermont always used to wind up his prayers with this plea: "Oh, God, give me an open mind!" If more people followed his example, they might escape being hamstrung by prejudices. And what a pleasant place to live in the world would be!

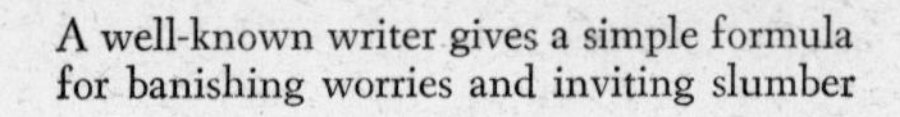

A well-known writer gives a simple formula for banishing worries and inviting slumber

You Can Sleep

Condensed from The Baltimore Sunday Sun

J. P. McEvoy

Do you lie awake at night, tossing and turning, hearing the clock strike two, three, four, before you finally drop off into exhausted slumber? I used to do that. But now I've learned the secret of quick, restful sleep. This is it: You *can* sleep — if you want to. It's as simple as that.

You lie awake because you *want* to. Don't tell me, "I go to bed and try to sleep but I just can't." Be honest with yourself. Do you really *try* to go to sleep? When worries crowd into your mind do you dismiss them — or dwell upon them? Do you think, "Gosh, that was a boner I made today. . . . I must remember to do such-and-such. . . . Maybe I'd better make a note of it. . . ." Honest now: are you wanting to go to sleep? Or are you wanting to stay awake and think?

Tonight try this experiment. Imagine you are taking down your thoughts in a notebook and that you must put them down carefully just as they come along. Start by trying to think of nothing but sleep and going to sleep. Then note how many other thoughts keep interfering, and how only by definite effort can you bring back the thought of sleep — that you want to sleep. You will be surprised to discover the tricks your mind will play to keep you thinking about your worries, how it will dodge and twist to throw off the notion of sleep.

Note one other thing — *the* most important thing. Whenever you think about your troubles you are not thinking about sleeping. Whenever you think about sleeping you are not thinking about

> I FOUND my recipe for falling asleep in *The Lives of a Bengal Lancer*. It is simply to draw 20 even breaths, then on the 21st hold the breath as long as possible. By the time I have done this three times I am drowsy.
>
> — Sophie Kerr

your troubles. You cannot think of two different things at the same time. Thus, by concentrating on the mere thought of sleep, you can drive your worries from your mind. But you must first *want* to sleep.

"But that isn't easy," you say. "Worries pop into my mind and then I can't get rid of them. If you had my troubles . . ."

If I had your troubles and were as proud of them as you are — if I took them to bed with me as a child takes her dolls and hugged them to me and wouldn't let them go — they'd keep me awake too. In fact, I used to do that very thing. I was writing and producing musical shows on Broadway, and anybody in that business will tell you there are tons of worries in it. They kept me awake night after night. And then I discovered that when I thought only of going to sleep I felt sleepy.

I used also a second and equally important technique. This is very simple too, though it took me a long while to become proficient. It is the technique of relaxing progressively. My psychologist friend Lucius Humphrey told me — and I can tell you — all you need to know in a couple of minutes. The rest is practice. Don't try it a few times and then give it up. With diligent practice you will become able to put yourself to sleep within five minutes whenever you wish.

Tonight when you go to bed make yourself as comfortable as you can. Take any position you like — the one in which you feel most completely relaxed. Close your eyes.

Now you are ready to start concentrating on the one thought of relaxation, progressing from one part of your anatomy to another. Think first of the muscles of your scalp, the top of your head. Relax those muscles. Now concentrate on the muscles of your forehead. Feel the muscles sag. Now your eyelids. Relax them. They are so heavy you can't lift them. Now the muscles of your face. Let the muscles go. Your jaws — let them sag. Note especially your neck. Move your head around until your neck is so relaxed your head feels like a dead weight. Drop it — let it roll until it comes to a stop of itself. Go right down your back. Feel the muscles let go.

Let your mind follow down each arm, relaxing the shoulders, the elbows, wrists, each finger. Now consider the muscles of your chest. Relax them. Then your stomach. Let everything sag. Heavy. Heavy.

Feel the heaviness of your hips — pushing against the bed. Now relax the muscles of each thigh, foot, toe. Slowly. Slowly. . . . You're asleep!

Maybe not the first time you do it. But if you are awake you won't be wide awake. And one more round trip from head to toe should put you under. Later, when you have practiced this technique faithfully night after night, you will never finish the whole route — you will be asleep long before that. Confidentially, I haven't got past my arms for years.

Don't give any thought to whether you forgot some part of the body. The magic lies not in any special order but in the fact that while you are consciously thinking of relaxing each part of your body you are not thinking about your troubles.

It works. I was once as proud an insomniac as you would ever meet. Now I can always put myself to sleep in a couple of minutes. You can do it too if you really want to.

The Gusher

Condensed from The Golden Book Magazine

Charles Battell Loomis

One meets many kinds of people at afternoon teas—the bored, the bashful, the intense — but for sheer delight nothing quite equals the gusher. She is generally very pretty. Nature insists upon compensations.

When you meet a real gusher — one born to gush — you can throw all bounds of probability aside and say the first thing that comes into your head, sure that it will meet with an appreciative burst of enthusiasm. But the attention of the Simon-pure gusher is purely subconscious. Her real attention is always on something else all the while — perhaps on the gowns of her neighbors, perhaps on the reflection of her pretty face — but never on the conversation.

You are presented to her as "Mr. Mmmm," and she is "delighted," and smiles so ravishingly that you wish you were 20 years younger. You do not yet know that she is a gusher. But her first remark labels her. Just to test her, for there is something in the animation of her face and the farawayness of the eye that makes you suspect her, you say:

"I happen to have six children —"

"Oh, how perfectly dee-ar! How old are they?"

She scans the gown of a woman who has just entered the room and, being quite sure that she is engaged in a mental valuation of it, you say:

"They're all of them six."

"Oh, how lovely!" Her unseeing eyes look you in the face. "Just the right age to be companions."

"Yes, all but one."

The eye has wandered to another gown, but the sympathetic voice says:

"Oh, what a pi-i-ty!"

"Yes, isn't it! But he's quite healthy."

It's a game now — fair game — and you're very glad you came to the tea!

"Healthy, you say? How nice. It's perfectly lovely to be healthy. Do you live in the country?"

"Not exactly the country. We live in New York, in Madison Square, under the trees."

"Oh, how perfectly idyllic!"

"Yes; we have all the advantages of the city and the delights of the country. The children bathe in the fountain every day when the weather is cold enough."

"Oh, how charming! How many children have you?"

"Only seven. The oldest is five and the youngest is six."

"Just the interesting age. Don't you think children fascinating?"

Again the roaming eye and the vivacious smile.

"Yes, indeed. My oldest — he's 14 and quite original — says that when he grows up he doesn't know what he'll be."

"Really! How cute! How old did you say he was?"

"Just 17, but perfectly girl-like and masculine."

She nods her head, and murmurs in musical, sympathetic tones:

"That's an adorable age. Did you say it was a girl?"

"Yes, his name's Ethel. He's a great help to her mother."

"Little darling."

"Yes; I tell them there may be city advantages, but I think they're much better off where they are."

"Where did you say you were?"

"On the Connecticut shore. You see, having only the one child,

Mrs. Smith is very anxious that it should grow up healthy." (Absent-minded nods indicative of full attention.) "He plays with the fisherman's child and gets great drafts of fresh air."

"Oh, you're quite a poet!"

"No; I'm a painter."

Now she is really attentive.

"Oh, do you paint? How perfectly adorable! Do you ever allow visitors in your studio?"

"Why, I never prevent them, but I'm so afraid it will bore them that I never ask them."

"Oh, how could anybody be bored at anything?"

"But everyone hasn't your enthusiasm. My studio is in the top of the Madison Square tower, and I never see a soul."

"Oh, then you're not married."

"Dear, no; a man who is wedded to his art mustn't commit bigamy."

"How clever. So you're a bachelor?" Again she is appraising a dress.

"Yes, but I have my wife for a chaperone and I'd be delighted to have you come and take tea with us some Saturday from six until three."

"Perfectly delighted!" Her eye now catches sight of an acquaintance just coming in, and you say:

"Hope you don't mind a little artistic unconventionality. We always have beer at our teas served with sugar and lemons, the Russian fashion."

"Oh, I think it's much better than cream. I adore unconventionality."

"You're glad you met me, I'm sure."

"Awfully good of you to say so."

Anything goes at an afternoon tea. But it's better not to go.

My Child Was Crippled

Condensed from The Forum

Anonymous

ADALINE was nearly two years old before we knew definitely that there was something wrong with her. At first she seemed to be just a healthy, bright infant. When she reached the end of her first year and showed no interest in trying to walk we didn't worry. But as the months wore on and still the baby made no effort, I took her to a pediatrician who told me that the child had probably received a head injury from the instruments used at birth, resulting in a spastic condition affecting the lower limbs. An orthopedic surgeon verified this diagnosis and told me frankly that, while spastic conditions often responded to treatment and surgery, they were never completely curable and that to some extent Adaline always would be crippled.

My first reaction was a fierce determination to shield my weakling, to make up for her disability by an overflowing love that approached hysteria. I almost resented my other children because they might lessen the completeness of my devotion. Fortunately I remembered one home where an invalid was the figure around whom the family revolved. The constraint on the well members was appalling and the effects upon the invalid far from desirable.

With so grim an object lesson in mind, I decided that my task was, first of all, to keep a normal, happy home, so that my three able-bodied children might have a sound environment and my handicapped child the outlook of a person normal physically. I would do all I could to see that her life was as full as it could be made, but Adaline would have to adapt herself to the world, since the world would never conform to her limitations.

I put Adaline's case in the hands of a leading orthopedic surgeon. He first operated on her when she was five. During the following 11 years his treatment changed Adaline from a child who could scarcely walk at all, who, as an adult would have been barred from almost every normal activity, to a person who, while she walks somewhat lamely, wears no brace, and can go anywhere alone, although she cannot dance or participate in active sports.

Such progress did not come overnight. It took four painful surgical operations, various types of massage and physiotherapy treatments, endless special exercises. The results from these exercises were imperceptibly slow and had to be pursued with unfaltering perseverance. I set aside a certain hour, never permitting anything to interfere, and during the remainder of the day we did not even mention those exercises.

My husband and I made it a rule never to discuss in the family circle Adaline's treatments and operations. We never behaved as though the surgical operations were spectacular events. The result was that Adaline and her two brothers and sister took the whole business with amazing juvenile composure. When Adaline was in the hospital the children took her toys and games, but all emphasis was placed on how glad we should be to have her home, never on how much we pitied her.

The greatest difficulty came from doting relatives. Although a complete cure was never promised, their head-shaking after each operation made me want to strangle them. They always exclaimed, "Another operation!" Their tone implied that we had tried surgery once, and, since it could work no miracle, we should abandon it.

As long as a lame child can get about to play at all, he seems pathetic neither to himself nor to his youthful friends. Time and again I have felt positively humble at the philosophical wisdom with which Adaline's contemporaries disposed of her limitation. There were certain things Adaline couldn't do, but that needn't matter too much, because there were other things she could do. When they organized games they gave her the parts she *could* do. When she fell, as she often did, they asked, "Are you hurt?" And when she wasn't, things went on as before. I kept an ample supply of games Adaline could enjoy, but I had also a table tennis set, three pairs of roller skates, and all the usual paraphernalia for active children, and I never, never was guilty of saying, "Oh, now, don't play *that;* play something Adaline can enjoy too."

Knowing that she would sorely need both physical and mental courage, I carried on an unobtrusive campaign to release Adaline from fear. The first step was pets — kittens and dogs. When she was eight we bought a Shetland pony. Adaline didn't ride very well, of course, but her control over that docile beast gave her added self-confidence. When she was 12 she was taught to swim. She's no wonderful swimmer, but she's capable of taking care of herself in water. And when she was 16 she learned to drive an automobile.

Often we harbor the erroneous impression that a lame child is essentially a saint. But a lame child has just as much talent for selfishness, conceit, untruthfulness, or any other unpleasant characteristic as a robust child. Adaline was no better and no worse than my other children, and I insisted upon exactly the same standards of behavior for her as for them.

For instance, in our home it has always been understood that each child puts away his playthings. Adaline loved dragging out every toy in the place and she hated clearing up after her play. Often I should have liked to put things away for her, because the actual work of putting them away required a lot more physical effort from her than from the others. I didn't succumb to this mistaken kindness. I believed that Adaline should have the same responsibility that the other children shouldered.

Here, again, relatives disapproved of my Spartan attitude. My mother said, "If she were my child, I'd give her anything she wants; there's time enough later on for her to suffer." In other words, let her grow up a spoiled hellion and, when she's an unbearable adult, she can find out to her sorrow that the world won't give her everything she wants just because she's lame.

Adaline was nearly ten before she could go to school. Until then I taught her at home. Because I knew that many interesting doors would always be closed to her, I was watchful to cultivate any special talents and interests she displayed. I saw to it that she had piano lessons, took her to children's concerts, bought her records of the simpler symphonies, and a child's book giving the stories of the operas. The only definite talent Adaline evidenced was in drawing. She did so well that I had trouble with her adult relatives. They decided she was a genius and began to point out the various geniuses who had maimed bodies!

I am extremely unsympathetic with such attitudes — I wanted Adaline to draw merely because she enjoyed it. If, later on, she could do something special with it, all right. But I wasn't going to permit her relatives to oblige her to be an artist. Relations grew pretty strained over this point just as, when Adaline came out with a high I.Q. in some intelligence tests at school, I had difficulty in restraining two of her aunts from convincing her that, although she was lame, she had the best brain in our family.

It was not until late adolescence that Adaline's lameness appeared truly tragic to her. Of course this was the time Adaline should have started going out with boys — and didn't. There were several who liked well enough to come in and work algebra problems with Adaline or play cards with her. But taking her out — a date — was another question, and missing out on the complete social popularity any young girl desires was a bitter dose to her.

There was almost nothing I could do to soften this blow. Let her popular sister see to it that Adaline had dates? Often my older daughter, in perplexed distress, asked if she should do this. My answer was an emphatic negative. I knew that Adaline would see through any such plan and that it would hurt her pride.

There was only one thing I could do, and that was to try to prevent the sensitiveness Adaline was acquiring from coloring her mental outlook. A scholastic competition gave me my entering wedge. Her only formidable rival was a pretty girl who was one of the school's social lights. Adaline's gloating at victory over this girl was alarming.

"Why are you so glad to win over Lucille?" I asked.

Taken off guard, she answered exactly what was in her heart: "She may be the most popular girl at school and all the boys may be crazy about her, but I showed her that she can't have everything."

That was all I needed. I had the long talk I'd been waiting for. I told Adaline that she must not let a lame body result in a lame mind, that her true victory would come when and if her reactions to life were those of a person without any physical disability. When I finished I wasn't certain I'd done any good. But I soon saw that I had. I believe that afterward Adaline never made faces at anything until she felt that her attitude was not prejudiced by her handicap.

Secretly I hoped Adaline would want to be self-supporting. I thought financial independence would give her an assurance nothing else could. But when my frail one, at the end of her second year at the university, announced that she'd prefer to go to New York for six months of art work, and then on to Paris to study design for a year, I was left mentally gasping. At the age of 20 she no longer felt the need to be near a protecting arm. This was a little more than I had bargained for. But I turned a deaf ear on my maternal instinct and the incredulous indignation of relatives, and helped her carry out her plans.

She had not been gone a month before I knew from her letters that her battle was won. Away from her family for the first time in her life, she was making friends, confident that they could like her for herself alone. Whatever social inhibitions she had harbored were dropping away. I shall always remember how very casually she wrote, "I went this evening with a boy from my class to see a French film." No further explanations, but she wanted me to know.

The year in Paris accented this healthful freedom. She had so many interests that there was no time to worry over those doors that must always be closed to her. When she returned, she was as poised and assured as any young woman of 22 could possibly be.

Today, at 27, Adaline does hard work that she enjoys in the interior decorating department of a large store. She's extremely capable in both her business and personal life. She isn't married but she has had proposals, and she will probably marry within the next few years. I feel saddened over nothing about her except the remembrance that I was not wise enough to find some way to make happy those years of her late adolescence.

Not long ago we were in a group where a thoughtless person referred scornfully to somebody as a cripple. Afterward I mentioned to Adaline the pain the remark had given me. She looked at me in astonishment. "You suffered for my feelings? Why, that remark was a triumph for me. The man who said that isn't intentionally unkind; he had forgotten all about my lameness." She was right. He had forgotten. And so do many people forget, because she forgets it so superbly herself.

The Art of Circumlocution

Dr. Granville Moody, a popular army chaplain during the Civil War, could forget the cloth, when necessary, with evangelic tact. At Lookout Mountain, the colonel of Moody's regiment went tearing up and down the lines, yelling to the troops, "Give 'em hell, boys!" The chaplain was at his heels, yelling, "Do as your Colonel tells you, boys! Do as your Colonel tells you!"

— Julia B. Foraker, *I Would Live It Again* (Harper)

Daniel Boone was asked if he had ever been lost in the woods. "No, I never got lost," Boone replied reflectively. "But I was *bewildered* once for three days."

— Constance Lindsay Skinner, *Pioneers of the Old Southwest* (Yale University Press)

MUSIC: *A Friend for Life*

Condensed from "Friends and Fiddlers"
Catherine Drinker Bowen

I HAVE four brothers and a sister, two children and four nieces and nephews. None of us are professional musicians. But strike A on the piano, and to a man we move to our fiddles as mechanically as we answer the telephone. People ask us constantly, "How comes all this music in your households?" And they add with a vague look of distress, "We used to play the piano, but —"

I cannot bear to hear this. It outrages me to see my friends go hungrily to concerts and come away with the hunger unappeased, for I know what these people want. They may not know it themselves, but they want music — music as it should be had, music at home, a part of daily life, a thing as necessary, as satisfying, as the midday meal. They want to *play*. And they are kept back by the wicked notion that to play an instrument one must be possessed by that bogey called Talent.

My children and nieces and nephews are intelligent and ambitious, but without musical gift — no perfect pitch, no golden voice, no limber wrist of magic. We are merely examples of how far the normal person may come into possession of music. And though my own musical reminiscences range from the age of seven to 37, I hasten to offer my affidavit that I have seen people begin to play the violin at 27, the viola at 32, the flute at 40, the cello at 62.

One quality music, alone among the arts, possesses: a warm, satisfying friendliness. Other arts are lonely — *my* picture, *my* poem, *my* novel. But in music (ensemble music, not soloism) we share — and we receive tenfold what we give. An instant flash of communication passes between strangers discovering a mutual love of ensemble playing. To know this warm, invisible bond; to break for an instant that hard protection with which every adult surrounds himself — what glorious indulgence!

Perhaps it is this warm yet impersonal friendliness of music that causes other people to look so wistfully upon our family quintets, our neighborly octets. *Ensemble*, that is the key to musical enjoyment! Your soloist is a bird of different feather, and your concert-goer, though he feed upon symphony as a lamb upon milk, is no true lover if he play no instrument. Your true lover does more than admire the muse — he sweats a little in her service.

It is an old story, the power of music — music that can drive men to war, to love, to God. Sometimes it does not drive at all, but lays hands upon the troubled spirit, to soothe and to heal. Music has done that for me — all my life music has been a healer. At unhappy moments I used to flee to the hills, to the woods, and find comfort there; but now, in my middle years, I need stronger enchantment. I am impatient with the wooded dark hills; I cry out to them, and they do not respond. But music has never failed me. Music speaks, and I reply. Slowly my cold blood warms; in my veins I feel it swell and quicken. Once more the heart leaps eagerly, once more I am blinded with the glory that surrounds me.

When people say, "How have you time for so much music, besides writing, tending children, and keeping house?" I now have a reply. "It is managed by a shrewd system of neglect." Neglect is truly an art. I began exercising it at music school. In my rented room, I learned to practice with an unmade bed. Other victories followed — not darning one's stockings until the holes got above the shoe, and then doing them on the foot. Four years of this prepared me beautifully for marriage, a maidless kitchen and, very soon, a nurseless nursery. Where then would I and my fiddle have been without that training in the art of neglect? Gradually, after admitted periods of failure, I made music part of the daily routine. Baby No. 2 taking his nap, Baby No. 1 jailed securely in her pen outside the window, I practiced 40 minutes while my sponge cake was baking. Children of three or four will coöperate in this kind of thing; though perhaps it is resignation rather than coöperation.

If only our children could discover music for themselves, and not be pulled to it, sulking under the harness! Verbal persuasion is unwise; exposure, repeated exposure, to good music is what turns the trick. But it must include more than listening.

The one key I have found to a child's heart, musically speaking, the one bait to which he will rise eagerly, is active participation in ensemble performance. Do not ask them to listen to Haydn; ask them to *play* Haydn, no matter how unskillfully. Tell a child that Beethoven is beautiful and he will not believe you until he has proved it by the repeated testimony of his own finger tips. But I never saw a child that was not bored by soloism — his own as well as another's. . . . What boy wants to sit on a piano stool and play pieces for mother's visitors? A child detects instantly a false situation; in the name of music or culture, he is being sacrificed to his mother's vanity; no wonder he bides his time to fling off music forever!

Musical participation cannot begin too early. Let the child sing nursery rhymes with his mother, turn pages for the pianist, or sound A for the fiddler to tune. Leave the nursery door open, for music that drifts upstairs to a child's room possesses a peculiar potency. Going to sleep to music, awaking to music — these are, in some unaccountable way, musical participation; they define music, for the child, as a thing natural and homely, like breakfast, dinner and supper.

Having sung with my children until we knew every song in the book, I bethought me of those other children who have no aunts or fathers to sing with them. I went to a place of spectacular bleakness which called itself Home for Friendless Children and asked the youngsters, "Would you like to come home with me Sunday, and sing with my children?"

On Sunday night, seven selected orphans sat very stiffly and said "No, thank you" to cake, and "No, thank you" to root beer. What was wrong with this party? Was it turning sour? Then we began to sing — my children, my nieces, nephews, my brother and his wife; and the orphans — all seven — burst into harmony. They sang, very loud and true. For sheer volume my orphans outsang everybody. Our pianist swung around on the stool, astonished. "Well," he said. "Well!" And the party began. They washed down liters of root beer; only crumbs were left on the cake plate. "Sure, we'll come again!" they told us.

Then they announced they wanted an orchestra, and I collected instruments for them. "Friendless Children" the sign read at the gate. Looking at the seven, I knew they were not friendless now. . . .

All around me I see homes where there seems to be nothing for the old to do. Old men especially sit and eat their hearts out in querulous discontent or sink into a premature senility that could have been long delayed had they been occupied. In an upstate town lived a man, a jeweler by trade, who played the flute until he got so old his lip cracked. Then he learned the violin, which he played until he died at 84. I knew another man, in his 70's, who was long bedridden, but nobody was sorry for him — nobody had a chance to be, because in bed he was always busy making violins. And when he got up he played upon them.

We who pride ourselves on our acceptance of fact — we have no excuse if we do not prepare our defenses against old age. Already I am preparing mine, and the greatest of these shall be music. If at 70 my chin must say a last farewell to that warm fiddle-hardness beneath the jawbone, even then I shall not be defeated. I have a last line of resistance, a never-ending resource: I can be listener.

I am preparing myself, now, to be listener. And it requires preparation. An enormous literature of music must be proved upon my fiddle before I can know it by ear alone! Then, at 70, I shall go furiously to concerts — many more than now, and I shall keep on going.

Thus far, music has been to me healer, friend, confidant. At 37 I am blinded by the world, busy with children — the fire of life rages hotly. But some day I shall cease conquering, cease being defeated, and shall begin to accept. Then I can study music as Euclid studied the circle; I can "see beauty bare." I shall have not more *time* for music but more room in my soul. When Beethoven comes I shall have, as it were, a house more spacious in which to receive him. It is a great, a pleasant thing to have a friend with whom to walk, untroubled, at peace — the heart all clean and quiet, ready for the spirit that may choose to be its guest.

Life Extension Plan

"WHEN a physician is compelled to predict death," says Dr. Irving S. Cutter, dean of the School of Medicine of Northwestern University, "he realizes that the reaction of the individual may upset his estimate. If the patient reacts morbidly, his distress disturbs physiological processes and shortens his life. But if he accepts his fate and resolves to make his last days more useful, he achieves a life-preserving philosophy and extends his own life.

"Many invalids could be up and about, enjoying days that they might prolong into years, if they had this will to live. Just as the well man, by wise living, can extend his years beyond the average span, so can the ill, the doomed, stretch and improve their existence through their mental outlook."

Turn Your Sickness into an Asset

By Louis E. Bisch, M.D.
Author of "Be Glad You're Neurotic"

ONLY YESTERDAY you were marching in health and vigor; sickness was a far-off shadow. Then suddenly illness unhinged your knees, brought you limply to bed. And now you are a horizontal citizen of the sickroom, an unwilling initiate in the fellowship of pain.

Your reaction is to rail against fate, to resent bitterly such untimely interference with life's routine. Yet your illness can confer substantial benefits — and not just in the realm of Job-like piety, either. An enforced holiday in bed blamelessly releases us from a too-busy world, sharpens our mental and spiritual perceptions, and permits a clearer perspective on our lives. Any serious illness should be regarded as an opportunity to gather dividends and generate energies that mere health cannot possibly bestow.

I am not speaking of those chronic sufferers whose illness dooms them to a life of invalidism, and whose heroic readjustments lift them above the rank of ordinary men. The great American historian Francis Parkman is a triumphant prototype of all such conquerors of pain. During the greater part of his life, Parkman suffered so acutely that he could not work for more than five minutes at a time. His eyesight was so wretched that he could scrawl only a few gigantic words on a manuscript. He was racked by major digestive trouble, terrific rheumatism and agonizing headaches. Physically, almost *everything* was wrong with him, yet he contrived to write nearly 20 magnificent volumes of history.

But our interest here centers on the ordinary mortal stricken for the first time. These sick-chamber casuals rarely learn to make the most of illness, regarding it only as a visitation of bad luck. Yet thousands actually have found themselves for the first time during sickness. The "beloved physician," Dr. Edward Livingston Trudeau, was sent, as a young doctor, to the mountains where he expected to die of tuberculosis. But he did not die. As he lay in bed he had a vision of a great hospital where he could rebuild other sufferers. Flat on his back, he examined patients not as ill as himself. He raised money and labored until his dream became the great sanatorium at Saranac that has helped thousands of tuberculosis patients. Trudeau's affliction turned an unknown doctor into a physician of world-wide fame.

Eugene O'Neill was an utter drifter with no plan of life until he was 25. A serious breakdown gave him the requisite leisure, he says, "to evaluate the impressions of many years in which experiences had crowded one upon the other, with never a second's reflection." It was in the hospital that he first began to write the plays that revolutionized American drama.

Like any major experience, illness actually changes us. How? Well, for one thing we are temporarily relieved from the terrible pressure of meeting the world head-on. Responsibility melts away like snow on an April roof; we don't have to catch trains, tend babies, or wind the clock. We enter a realm of introspection and self-analysis. We think soberly, perhaps for the first time, about our past and future. Former values are seen to be fallacious; habitual courses of action appear weak, foolish or stubborn. Illness, it seems, gives us that rarest thing in the world — a *second chance*, not only at health but at life itself!

Illness knocks a lot of nonsense out of us; it induces humility, cuts us down to our own size. It enables us to throw a searchlight upon our inner selves and to discover how often we have rationalized our failures and weaknesses, dodged vital issues and run skulkingly away. Mistakes made in our jobs, marriage and social contacts stand out clearly. Especially when we are a bit scared is the salutary effect of sickness particularly marked; typhoid and pneumonia have reformed drunkards, thieves, liars and wife-beaters. If a stiff bout of illness brings us near to death's door — perhaps so much the better. For only when the way straitens and the gate grows narrow, do some people discover their soul, their God, or their life work.

Florence Nightingale, too ill to move from her bed, reorganized the hospitals of England. Semi-paralyzed, and under the constant menace of apoplexy, Pasteur was tireless in his attack on disease. Innumerable illustrations might be cited. And the testimony from humbler sources is just as striking. A young man in a hospital for two weeks discovered that he had always wanted to be a research worker in chemistry. Till then he had been "too busy" as a drug salesman. Today he is making a splendid go of his new job. While recuperating from scarlet fever a woman in her 40's vanquished the terrors she had felt about approaching middle life. "I am not going to return to my former state of feeling superfluous," she resolved. "My children are married and can take care of themselves. I'm going to start a millinery shop and make them like it." She did, and needless to say, they do!

In talking with patients, I find that many who have sojourned in "the pleasant land of counterpane" say that for the first time they learned the true meaning of friendship, often undecipherable in the complex pattern of this modern world. They say also that they discovered secret depths of their own life-stream. "After a few days in bed," writes one of them, "time becomes an unimagined luxury. Time to think, time to enjoy, time to create, time at last to express the best and deepest part of human nature. Illness is one of the great privileges of life; it whispers that man's destiny is bound up with transcendental powers. Illness pares and lops off the outer parts of life and leaves one with the essence of it."

Even pain confers spiritual insight, a beauty of outlook, a philosophy of life, and understanding and forgiveness of humanity — in short, a quality of peace and serenity — that can scarcely be acquired by the "owner of pure horse flesh." Suffering is a cleansing fire that chars away much of the meanness, triviality and restlessness of so-called "health." Milton declared, "Who best can suffer, best can do." The proof is his *Paradise Lost* written after he was stricken blind.

In illness you discover that your imagination is more active than it ever has been; unshackled by petty details of existence, you day-dream, build air castles, make plans. As your physical strength returns, your fantasies are not dulled; rather they become more practical, and you definitely decide upon the things you will put into action when you recover.

Your concentration improves tremendously. You are astonished to find how easily you can think a difficult problem through to its solution. Why? Because your instincts of self-preservation are speeded up, and all nonessentials are eliminated. It is interesting too that your reactions to what you see and hear are more acute. A robin at the window, a fleeting expression on a friend's face are delicately savored as memorable experiences. Illness *sensitizes* you; that is why you may be irritable. You may even weep at the least provocation. But this sensitivity should be turned to better uses. Now is an excellent time to develop yourself along a special line, to read widely, or to create original ideas. Contrary to an old belief, a sick body does not necessarily make a sick mind, except in those who try to make their illness an excuse for laziness. No one honestly can use his illness, whatever its nature, as an excuse for ineffectualness or failure.

If you have never been sick, never lost so much as a day in bed — then you have missed something! When your turn comes, don't be dismayed. Remind yourself that pain and suffering may teach you something valuable, something that you could not have learned otherwise. Possibly it may change for the better the entire course of your life. You and those around you will be happier if you can look upon any illness as a blessing in disguise, and wisely determine to make the most of it. You *can* turn your sickness into an asset.

"WE LIVE IN THE SLUMS"

Condensed from The Forum

Norma Lee Browning

Russell hitchhiked 1800 miles to marry me. He came to New York, where I had been taking a Master's degree, with 75 cents in his pocket and a camera over his shoulders.

With the $15 I had saved from spare-time typing jobs and the $25 a pawnbroker lent on the camera, we were married.

We knew that after five short days of honeymoon we must come to grips with poverty again. But we had worked our way through college and those four years had taught us how to have happiness when we hadn't a cent.

Russell soon found a job, as I knew he would, but somehow I had not expected that he would be paid only $15 a week. Where could we live on $15 a week? Hopefully we plunged into the cheap districts. We saw noisy apartments for $80 a month; single rooms with gas burners in bathrooms and windows on air-shafts, for $50 a month. We could not afford them.

Then one afternoon we came to the slums. We walked slowly, curious to see the swarming tenements. Garbage cans were ranged along the cracked sidewalks. Behind the buildings, the sky was crisscrossed with lines of fluttering clothes. Women passed us with market bags on their arms. Swarms of children played hopscotch; babies tottered against our knees.

We saw faded little signs, "1, 2, 3 Rooms, White Sinks. Inquire Within." We looked into narrow, dark hallways, and up at the maze of fire escapes. The buildings were dingy and the woodwork crumbled, unpainted.

One old building interested us with its arched brick entrance; gingerly we went in, and a janitress greeted us. She was pretty, and intelligent. She said she had a two-room apartment for rent.

"How much?" we asked.

"Eight dollars a month."

I could hardly believe it. The rooms were large enough, with high ceilings, cross-ventilation, sunshine, even a forsaken fireplace. They were quiet, except for the voices of the children playing four flights below. There was gas, a sink with a cold-water faucet, and a modern toilet. We took it.

It made us panicky at first to think of what our families would say. What they said was worse than we expected. How could we think of living among dirty, ignorant, drunken slum dwellers? We had blundered into the old Gas House district; it would not be safe to walk those streets at night. We should be cut off from all our friends. What would Russell's boss think of such an address? Without central heat and a bath, we should pay far more in doctor bills than we saved in rent. All this, and more, our friends said.

For three weeks we slept on a narrow cot lent to us by the janitress. Someone had left a small table, layers of newspapers glued to its top with sugary coffee. We scraped. The table was solid walnut. It was our first furniture — beautiful!

We bought a coal stove secondhand for $5. Pots and pans and tableware came from the five-and-ten; furniture from junk shops, to be repaired and gaily painted by ourselves.

"But how do you manage without a bath?" our friends ask. We have baths, quite often. Bathing was invented long before plumbing. An enamelware bathtub cost $1; a teakettle supplies hot water.

A neighbor helped us remodel the fireplace. It is a cheerful friend in the evenings, blazing with wood salvaged from wrecked buildings — ten cents a big basket — and it says good night to us with the flickering of its last low flames.

Maybe you can fix up an apartment, our friends had said, but you can't do anything about the neighborhood. We did not intend to do anything about the neighborhood; we should ignore it. We were not slum people; we had been to college; we were not like our neighbors. In our unconscious snobbishness we even felt that we might be a good influence. Our apartment would be different; it would be clean; it would be attractively furnished.

Our Viennese neighbor from the floor below came to call. She complimented us on our apartment beamingly, but I felt a certain reservation. She remarked that it takes time to make a home; she had lived 19 years in hers. We went to see her. Walt Disney might have done her apartment, which expressed perfectly her neat, jolly, rosy self. Starchy white curtains embroidered in dark blue; a riot of happy-colored flowers done in cross-stitch on sofa and mantelpiece and bed and pillows. The final straw to my shame was the glitter of her linoleum and the shine of her windowpanes.

The weekly wash is unknown to our neighbors. The clotheslines crisscrossing the court flutter daily with drying clothes because our neighbors will not leave a soiled garment in their houses overnight. And every day they wash all the oilcloth that covers their shelves and window sills.

We couldn't keep even our intellectual superiority. Tony, the coalman, talks rings around us in history and government. A saleswoman in one basement shop knows more about the Elizabethan dramatists than I, an English Literature major. Through the community mailbox, I discovered that another tenant subscribes to my favorite literary review. He is a housepainter. Why did we, of all people, ever suppose that thinking depends on a bank account?

Tony brings the coal and the ice. We pay him for these things, but we do not pay him for bringing us the breakfast rolls, for emptying the drip pan, for fixing the fire when we are out. To offer Tony payment for these services would insult him. He does them as a friend. His wife invited us for Easter dinner in their five sunny rooms, ashine with polished furniture and waxed linoleum, full of the chatter of six rosy children.

All our neighbors are friendly. The Hungarian woman on the second floor brings us curious little biscuits she bakes. When I work long at my typewriter, the Italian signora anxiously brings in a cup of hot coffee. The little German lady who lives nicely on $30 a month showed me how to plant flowers and she keeps them watered when I'm out. Russell made her a window box of scrap lumber; she made an embroidered apron for me.

Not once in the whole year have I seen a drunk in our neighborhood or heard a vulgar word. Our neighbors are not only clean and friendly but mannerly. Why did we, of all people, ever suppose that morals and manners depend on a bank account?

The first time I came home alone after dark, I frightened myself into a panic; a horror lurked in every dark doorway. Somehow I reached our entrance and fled gasping up the stairs. The janitress heard me, came out to see what was wrong. I told her I was scared. "What are you scared of?" she asked. "Nobody's on the street now, they're all in bed. It's almost ten o'clock."

This neighborhood is a small town. Most of its people have lived here for years. For blocks around, everybody knows everybody else and women doing their marketing exchange gossip. If we buy so much that we sigh at the thought of carrying the package up five flights of stairs, some dealer offers to bring it up to us on his way home to dinner.

For almost nothing at all in the shops along First Avenue we buy delicious rye bread and plenty of cakes for tea, cakes that our guests are crazy about. For we have plenty of guests. Far from being cut off from our friends, we have never been so popular with them. They keep us busy explaining that our apartment isn't a miracle. It isn't, you know; we pay the standard rent for the neighborhood; it is all strictly business. There is a waiting list of people who want to sublet our apartment. One of them is Russell's boss.

TO BORE OR NOT TO BORE

Condensed from The Atlantic Monthly

Ralph W. Bergengren

"TAKE me away," said Thomas Carlyle at a dinner table where one of the diners had been monologuing to the extreme limit of boredom, "and put me in a room by myself and give me a pipe of tobacco!"

Many of us have felt this emotion; and some realize that we have occasioned it. The nice consideration for the happiness of others which marks a gentleman may even make him particularly susceptible to this haunting apprehension. Carlyle defined the feeling when he said, "To sit still and be pumped into is never an exhilarating process." But pumping is different. How often have I myself, my adieus seemingly done, my hat in my hand and my feet on the threshold, taken a fresh grip, hat or no hat, on the pump handle, and set good-natured, Christian folk distressedly wondering if I would never stop! And how often have I afterward recalled something strained and morbidly intent in their expressions, a glassiness of the staring eye and a starchiness in the smiling lip, that has made me suffer under my bed cover and swear that next time I would depart like a sky rocket.

The Bore Positive pumps; the Bore Negative compels pumping. Unlike Carlyle, he regards being pumped into as an exhilarating process; he sits tight and says nothing; he keeps his victim talking.

In the last analysis a bore bores because he keeps us from something more interesting than himself. Coleridge's Ancient Mariner, full of an unusual personal experience that the leisurely reader finds most horridly entertaining, bored the Wedding Guest because at that moment the Wedding Guest wanted to get to the wedding. But the Mariner was too engrossed in his own tale to notice this lack of interest, and so invariably is the Bore Positive: everything escapes him except his listener.

But no matter how well we know we are bored, none of us can be certain that he does not sometimes bore. On the very occasion when I have felt myself as entertaining as a three-ring circus, I may in effect have been as gay and chatty as a like number of tombstones.

The first virtue that we who do not wish to be bores must practice is abstemiousness of self. I know it is hard, but I do not mean total abstinence. A man who tried to converse without his I's would make but a blind stagger at it; he would become a Bore Negative of the most negative description. But one can at least curb the pronoun, and confine the personally conducted tour into and about Myself within reasonable limits. Let him say, "I will not talk about Myself for more than 30 minutes," then reduce it to 25; then to 20 — and so on to the irreducible minimum; and he will be surprised to feel how his popularity increases with leaps and bounds at each reduction — provided he finds anything else to talk about.

Your Complete Bore, however, is incapable of this treatment, for he does not know that he is a bore. There is, however, one infallible rule for not being a bore — or at any rate for not being much of a bore — and that is, never to make a call, or to talk to a person, for more than 15 minutes. But to apply this rule successfully one must become adept in the Fine Art of Going Away. Remember: *Two persons who do not part with kisses should part with haste.*

But the 15-minute call followed by the flying exit is at best an unsatisfactory solution, it is next door to always staying at home. Better far to come out of your cave, mingle, bore as little as may be — and thank Heaven that here and there you meet one whom you feel reasonably certain that you do not bore.

This recipe for carving out your career is almost too simple — but it works

YOUTH, GET YOUR TOE IN THE DOOR

Condensed from Forbes

J. P. McEvoy

FOR YEARS ambitious young men have been asking me, "How does a fellow get started?" I always say, well, it's so simple and it sounds so easy you probably won't do it. Take a few months to learn shorthand and typing. Then pick out the business you'd like to run or the profession you'd like to star in and get yourself a job in it as a secretary, stenographer or typist. Now you're on the inside with tools with which you can chew your way right up to the top.

"A likely story," says the young man. "Name three." So I haul off and say, how about Alexander Hamilton, Fulgencio Batista, Billy Rose? That usually staggers him. I follow up my advantage quickly: How about Irvin Cobb, Grover Whalen, Frank Vanderlip, Fiorello La Guardia, Vincent Bendix, Charlie Butterworth?

By this time I have my young friend pretty well in hand, so I give him a few details. Let's take Batista, president of Cuba. You wouldn't think a fellow would deliberately sit down and learn shorthand so he could take over a country, but that's just what Batista did. He was a farm boy with ambition. He knew that the man who controlled the army controlled Cuba. He learned shorthand and typing, got a job taking dictation from the officers who were running the army. As he told me himself, "I thought it a good way to find out how things were done." How well he learned was shown a few years later when he led a group of fellow sergeants in revolt, took over the army, and made himself dictator of the country.

You can't get your name on the door until you get it on the payroll, I tell my young friend. And the person who does the hiring always wants to know what you can do. If you say "Anything" the answer is "Good-bye." But if you can type or take dictation, you're qualified for all the many jobs that require those two skills.

Secretaries not only learn how. They learn who. The secretary to the president of a company meets other presidents. The secretary to a theatrical producer meets other producers, stars, writers, directors. Herman Shumlin, producer of *Grand Hotel*, started as secretary to Jed Harris, producer of *Dinner at Eight*. Lillian Hellman, author of *The Children's Hour* and *The Little Foxes*, started as secretary to Herman Shumlin. George S. Kaufman and Moss Hart, both successful playwrights, started as stenographers.

The names of industrial leaders who started as stenographers and secretaries would fill a telephone directory. Among them: George W. Perkins, Frank A. Vanderlip, John J. Raskob. Two presidents of Armour & Company, T. George Lee and George A. Eastwood, were secretaries, and so was Vincent Bendix, aviation magnate, who makes it a policy to hire young men as secretaries and push them along into important positions.

Bendix (who bought a shorthand book and taught himself) told me of an important conference he had in his office a few years ago with the heads of five other large corporations. "As the hours dragged we let the office force go, but before we adjourned we agreed that each of us would jot down his understanding of the decisions we had reached. To our mutual surprise we discovered that five of the six of us had been making a shorthand record of the conference and had all started as stenographers!"

Irving Thalberg was the outstanding leader of the motion-picture industry when he died in his 30's. At 18 he was working in a Brooklyn dry-goods store by day and studying shorthand and Spanish by night. He put an ad in the paper: "Secretary, stenographer; Spanish-English; high school education; inexperienced; salary $15." He got four answers, took a ten-hour-a-day job in a small trading establishment. Later he worked for an exporter, an executive who demanded painstaking accuracy. The training stuck to Thalberg when he went to work for Carl Laemmle, then president of Universal Pictures. In Laemmle's office he learned the inside details of production, sales and promotion. He learned how deals were made, stories were dreamed and stars were born. At 21 he was running Universal, at 30 he was running MGM. To make the story perfect, his wife, Norma Shearer, also started as a stenographer.

The political skies are studded with stars of every magnitude who started as pale but effectual secretarial glowworms. Alexander Hamilton, at 20, was George Washington's secretary. Coming down to our own time, we find George B. Cortelyou, who wound up in three Cabinets after starting as private secretary to a fourth assistant Postmaster General, stenographer to President Cleveland, assistant secretary to President McKinley, and secretary to Theodore Roosevelt. Later, when president of the Consolidated Gas Company, he called stenography "the handmaiden of opportunity," and gave it credit for his success, pointing out that instead of being marooned in the outer fringes of an organization a stenographer usually finds himself in the inner circle, attached to a higher executive, where he learns all the details of the business, has incomparable opportunities to gain intimate knowledge of a successful man's methods, and is the obvious candidate for promotion when an opening occurs.

New York's Mayor La Guardia launched his political career taking down immigration hearings in shorthand. Later, while serving in Congress, he hired a very good secretary named Marie Fisher. She is now Mrs. La Guardia.

Leon Henderson learned shorthand in high school. Ambitious for a college education and lacking funds, he was working for the Du Ponts as a day laborer when he learned that their safety engineer had recently fired three stenographers because they couldn't adapt themselves to the peculiar dictating habits of their boss. It seems the engineer, in addition to speaking with machine-gun rapidity, made inspection trips on horseback, shouting recommendations and memoranda on the fly. Henderson, like most kids of his age, could ride a bicycle with his hands off the handlebars. So he took the job and kept it all summer, taking dictation as he pedaled along beside his boss. When fall came he had the down payment on his college education and was on his way to the top.

Care for more shorthand experts in the political arena? Add Senators Barkley of Kentucky and Byrnes of South Carolina — and, skipping backward, John Hay, secretary to Lincoln and later Secretary of State.

Dickens was a court reporter in his youth. Peter B. Kyne started collecting background material for his famous "Cappy Ricks" stories as a secretary in the wholesale lumber and shipping business at $7 a week. *Mr. Deeds Goes to Town* and *Mr. Smith Goes to Washington* — and Robert Riskin, who wrote both of these movie scripts, goes to the bank with the largest weekly writing check in Hollywood. How did he start? You guessed it.

May I tuck in a personal item? Some years ago I started hiring as secretary each summer a bright college graduate who knew shorthand, typing, or both. I was writing for the magazines, the theater and radio, and figured they would not only get training but make valuable contacts for themselves. One of these lads became an important NBC man, another editor of a national movie magazine. One of the girls, Elspeth Eric, starred in *Dead End* and *Margin for Error*. She succeeded a sad young man whom I moved from the typewriter to the stage. His name was, and still is, Charles Butterworth.

So learn a skill, young man, a skill you can exchange for room, board, and that toe in the door known variously as luck, opportunity or the breaks. Learn shorthand, typing and simple accounting. The young man who doesn't know them today is as illiterate as his father would have been without Readin', 'Ritin' and 'Rithmetic. Shoals of young people are being educated to enjoy leisure. Too few are being taught to *earn* leisure. You can earn it only through work, and you can get work only if you are equipped.

CAN YOU LOAF?

Condensed from Hearst's International Cosmopolitan

Bruce Barton
Author of "The Man Nobody Knows," etc.

Coming down from Boston, I made a census of the 32 passengers in one chair car. It was as follows:

Here lie many hard-working men

Asleep (in various awkward positions)	13
At work (earnest-looking men with brief cases)	2
Looking straight ahead with bored expression	6
Reading fiction	5
Reading serious book	1
Doing cross-word puzzles	2
Playing solitaire	1
Applying lip-stick	2

Thirty-two Americans, each with five hours on his hands, and almost all of them bored. Here is another picture:

"I retired from business two years ago," said a middle-aged man. "All my life I had been planning that when my daughter was married and I had a sure income I would retire. So, at 52, I sold my business. You must remember that I had planned to retire for a long time. I was well equipped for the easy life. I enjoyed riding and swimming and golf. I fished and hunted and played a fair game of bridge. It looked safe enough, and you'll probably think I'm crazy when I tell you what happened.

"I began waking up with a terrible thought: 'Gosh, now I've got to get out to that first tee and plug around that same old golf course all day.' It was worse than going to work. One day, I couldn't stand it any longer. Do you know, I've taken another job now. Salary not half what I used to make, but I didn't care."

As an advertising man I go around among all sorts of industries, and everywhere I see more leisure. A factory that used to make a certain number of articles with 1000 workers is now making ten times that number with no more workers, and at shorter hours. Modern machinery isn't the only thing that has brought on this trouble. Education has intensified it. A trained mind inevitably does more and does it more quickly.

Then, along come the doctors to double our lives. In Shakespeare's time a man of 40 was ready to call it a day. He had lived. Montaigne retired to his tower at 38. Napoleon conquered Europe at 30, and died at 52. They moved fast, and passed out young.

Today, at 40 we are just beginning to go strong, and the average age of presidents and chairmen of boards is around 65. By hanging on, each of us is the equivalent of two men of the olden times.

What's going to become of us all? How can we endure living when we don't have to spend all our time making a living? What shall be done to combat this new disease of Leisure? Let me submit three suggestions:

1. Quite a bit of leisure could be used up if we were ever courteous to one another.

We are all so foolishly and inexcusably rude. We ride all day in a Pullman car, and when the train draws near the station we jump out of our seats and push and jostle in the narrow corridor. Why must we trample on each other's toes and poke each other in the ribs and exchange black looks? Only five minutes at the most is at stake.

The same sort of thing happens on the road. In and out of the line of cars we dodge, straining our nerves and endangering our lives to be a jump ahead. We lift the telephone receiver, and if Central does not answer on the instant we grow apoplectic. I have seen a woman nearly decapitated in trying to leap ahead of another woman into a revolving door. We jam into a streetcar as if it were the last car that would ever run. We dive for an elevator to save one tenth of a minute in getting to our desks. At the golf course, where we have gone for recreation, we tear the buttons off our clothes in the locker room. Why? Just to beat the other members to the first tee.

"Good manners require a great deal of time," said Emerson.

2. Leisure would hurt much less if we weren't so terribly afraid of being alone. Away from a crowd we itch.

> I hope in hell their souls may dwell
> Who first invented Essex Junction.

What's the matter with Essex Junction? Nothing, except that we don't know how to use it. There are other stranded passengers, each of whom must have had interesting experiences. There are books. There are trees that have looked down upon the petty busyness of humanity for generations. There is a bench where one may dream.

3. We might each adopt a hobby which would have some relation to the happiness of other people.

I have a pet college in the Kentucky mountains. A long time was consumed in hunting it out and adopting it. I wanted to find the place where one dollar was made to do more work than anywhere else in the United States. Some kids are there at my expense. I go down each year to talk with them, and ride horseback. Never do I feel that these students owe me anything. The obligation is on the other side. They have given me a fresh interest for my leisure.

Sooner or later we will take cognizance of the fact that hard work and profits are less than half of the business of living. Every school will have a course in Thoreau, who lived on $27 a year and had a wonderful time in the woods. Stevenson's essay in praise of idlers will be a required study.

"In Sickness and in Health"

Condensed from
"Strength out of Suffering"

France Pastorelli

WHEN SICKNESS first breaks out, the attention and care of the whole household are focused on the sufferer, who, whether man or woman, instinctively turns to the affection of loved ones for help. But when sickness persists, the paths of the invalid and those around diverge more and more.

The sufferer, who had previously felt that he was understood and surrounded with care, begins to feel isolated, though living in the midst of others. The healthy people around him get accustomed to seeing him always weak, and in pain, and confined. The renewed outbreaks of his complaint, the hours when his life is in danger, no longer awake in them that dismay which formerly he took as proof of their affection. Gradually they become blind to nearly all the details of life in a sickroom.

Healthy people can be very slow in understanding certain things concerning an invalid, things both great and small. How many find it difficult to adapt themselves to his restricted movements and the few positions he is able to take up! Sometimes they never succeed in doing so. Articles he needs, which should be just at hand, are placed out of reach, as inaccessible as if they were in the next room. Or perhaps questions are asked him from the farther end of the room, so that, tired as he is, he has to raise his voice to answer; if he does not speak loud enough, the questioner repeats without coming nearer. Or, again, someone may talk to him right at the head of the bed, so that he is obliged to answer without looking at the speaker, or else has almost to dislocate his neck trying to see; or, again, the visitor may take up a position at the foot of the bed and, while talking, lean on it, giving it little shakes and knocks most trying to the patient.

The invalid often finds it difficult to establish well-balanced relations with the healthy. If he complains, he will soon succeed in annoying them, however legitimate his complaints may be, and he will be quickly branded as a hypochondriac, accused of being absorbed in the contemplation of his ills. If he submits wholeheartedly to his medical adviser's most stringent regulations, he will be the invalid who is always watching himself, and looking out for opportunities to be coddled. If he scorns to complain, and goes so far as never to mention his physical sufferings or to speak of an interior life which he feels he must live in solitude, then it will be found that he is not so ill or unfortunate after all, and those around him will speedily neglect the attentions due his illness.

The invalid will be sorely tried by certain types of healthy people found at every bedside. There are those who make it understood that they look upon their own health not as an inestimable privilege for which they ought to be thanking God every hour of their lives but as some kind of superiority due in a measure to themselves and of which they have reason to be proud. As to sickness, they make it very evident that in their eyes it is an inferiority only to be despised. The manner in which such persons make sick people feel they are humoring them is as insulting as a slap in the face.

Then there are the sermonizers and givers of advice who make one feel that they are saying to themselves, though they dare not say it aloud: "Why have you made up your mind to be bedridden for the rest of your life?"

There are others the exact opposite. They do not disguise their pleasure and astonishment at finding an invalid alive after a dangerous crisis, and they give him to understand that they do not expect to have the same pleasure renewed if another one like it supervenes.

There are the persistent tellers of anecdotes who stupefy a sufferer with their insane chatterings. They abound among nurses and people who have had a chronic invalid in their own households. They do not spare the sick person a single detail of the terrible scenes of agony at which they have been present, or a single phase of the slow disintegrations of the body they have witnessed. They recount in detail the white lies and pious frauds they have fabricated to deceive their patients.

There are those who explain that sickness is far more trying to the people around the patient than to the patient himself, and who describe with a super-abundance of detail their own weariness, their own courage, in connection with an illness of one of their relations.

There are the restless people. They offer the patient any number of things for which he has no use. They show an excess of zeal, and bustle about when there is no occasion. They are noisy and obtrusive, yet absent when they could be of use; these are the people who wake an invalid to ask if he is asleep.

Again there are the visitors who make a great show of their sympathy for sick people and who boast that they "have a way" with them, from whose every pore ooze levity and ignorance of suffering. One soon awakes to the fact that for them invalids are but dolls to amuse themselves with, or stubborn children to be domineered over.

Finally there are those who really understand. We who are sick are indeed privileged if we have friends among these! No discordant words fall from their lips. Only certain rare affections, especially those of mothers, husbands and wives, daughters, and angelic Sisters of Charity, do not get hardened to the suffering of those they love, but identify themselves more and more with them with a love that goes on growing in understanding and strength, however long the trial. Only to such loving hearts as these does the illness of the loved one never become too painful or heavy a burden; it is a trial which the invalid and the loving friend or relation share with a reciprocal love, tender and passionate. But not everyone has the privilege of participating in such love as this.

It must be admitted that the role of you who are well is a terribly uncomfortable if not a tragic one to play. But, when you come to our bedside, whether it is pain or joy you have to share with us, bring it all to us. Talk to us frankly about anything you like, without letting yourself be cut short by the fear of accentuating too much the distance there may be between a normal life and ours. Of this distance many of us have taken full measurement, and can look at it without a shudder. Speak, then, freely of the joyous life we will know no more, of the activities in which we can never again take part, of the freedom which has gone forever from us. Make us understand your difficulties and the questions which puzzle you, even if they are of the kind from which illness absolves us. Be assured that what we have learned in illness keeps such fervent sympathy alive in us that it enables us to live our difficult life and to take a share in that of others, out of the very fullness of our hearts. And if the thought of our pain comes into your mind, never let it lead you to keep silence about your own suffering, but let it make you feel that it is just the long trial we have had as invalids that has made us able to understand all.

Window on the World

IN A little church in the far south of Ireland, every window but one is of painted glass. Through that single exception may be seen a breath-taking view: a lake of deepest blue, studded with green islets, and backed by range after range of purple hills. Under the window is the inscription: "The heavens declare the glory of God, and the firmament showeth His handiwork."

— Robert Gibbings, *Coming Down the Wye* (Dutton)

How parents have helped shape youthful lives, related in letters from readers

Children CAN Be Taught Life

It's Plain Thievery!

A GUEST said recently, upon leaving: "I like to come here. It's the one place I can say anything I want to, knowing it won't go further." The compliment should really have gone to my mother.

One day, when I was about eight, I was playing beside an open window while Mrs. Brown confided to my mother a serious problem concerning her son. When Mrs. Brown had gone, my mother, realizing I had heard everything, said: "If Mrs. Brown had left her purse here today, would we give it to anyone else?"

"Of course not," I replied.

Mother continued: "Mrs. Brown left something more precious than her pocketbook today. She left a story that could make many people unhappy. It is still hers, even though she left it here. So we shall not give it to anyone. Do you understand?"

I did. And I have understood ever since that a confidence or a bit of careless gossip which a friend has left at my house is his — not mine to give to anyone.

— Constance Cameron

Chalk This One Up

THERE WERE three of us boys — one year apart. We quarreled often. But Mother said: "Don't sleep on anger." She placed a small child's blackboard in the hall, and encouraged us to write on it things we wouldn't say to one another. Andy had fought with Raymond. In childish pride, neither wanted to apologize. But before going to bed, one would write, "I'm sorry."

We all felt better for writing out our apology, or erasing a message. "Sorry I lost my temper, Andy," expressed our love for each other, our family tie and respect. — Raymond Forer

Strategy for Justice

My brother and I always came home from school hungry. One day, when we asked for food, Mother set a small cake before us on the kitchen table. Placing a knife beside the cake, she said: "One of you divide it. The other has first choice."

My brother was quicker than I, and he started to cut the cake in unequal pieces. Suddenly he stopped, looked at Mother and then at me. Then he cut the cake in exact halves and stood back for me to help myself.

From then on whatever there was to be shared — pie, cake, bread and butter — was divided in the same way. It taught us lasting respect for the other fellow's rights. — Jessamine Paret Knight

Bursting with Pride

When my sister and I were about seven and nine, we received the highest grades of our classes in school. So we decided that our family was well above the average in brains and we lost no time letting our playmates know it. Father, who had overheard our boastings, summoned us.

He had blown up a toy balloon to the size of a man's head. Gravely he announced that this was Elmer. Then followed the story of Elmer's life. Each time Elmer did something magnificent, Father would blow the balloon up a little larger. As the story progressed, Elmer grew to such proportions that my sister and I edged away. Suddenly, when Elmer seemed unable to endure even the slightest extra success, the story ended.

"It isn't fun to be too close to Elmer any more, is it?" Father asked. "He is so conceited and has such a big head. That's the way your playmates felt. You were so proud that it wasn't fun to be with you."

To this day, when we do anything we're particularly proud of, the thought of Elmer keeps us from getting the "big head." — Adla Mickwee

Gentle Reminder

My mother's theory was that once a child was taught right from wrong any ensuing lapse should be handled subtly.

There were four in our family and she had four miniature doghouses placed conspicuously on the kitchen mantel. In front of each was a toy dog. I was represented by a cocker, my brother by a terrier, and so on.

Whenever a member of the family did anything unbecoming to the rules and regulations of behavior, Mother quietly put the representative offender "in the doghouse."

Seldom was it necessary to carry the rebuke beyond this simple gesture. When my own children came along I inaugurated the idea in our home. They soon caught on. The effect of silent rebuke has saved useless arguments, scoldings and unnecessary accusations, to say nothing of developing our sense of humor. — Mrs. Edna M. Ingmanson

"*Not a Sparrow Shall Fall . . .*"

I WAS 11 when my father gave me an air gun. My first victim was a thrush, and though elated at my marksmanship, I felt guilty. Later I found my father removing flies and insects from a spider's web and putting them into a matchbox.

"What are you doing, Daddy?" I asked.

"Come with me and I'll show you," he replied. He led the way to the garden and showed me a nest of four young birds. My father dropped the insects into the wide-open mouths. Early next morning he came into my room. In his hand was the body of one of the birds.

"It died during the night," he said. That evening we found another one dead. And a few mornings later he brought in the third body.

"That last one's a sturdy-looking little fellow," Father said later. "Looks as though he might try out his wings pretty soon." But, he explained, he was probably weak, for we hadn't been able to do the incessant feeding that young birds require.

One day we found him rocking precariously on a twig. To me it seemed the most important thing in the world that this bird must fly. There was a flutter and he was off the branch. For a second his wings beat vainly; then he fell to the ground. His legs kicked once — and he was dead.

"Oh, Daddy," I cried remorsefully, "it's all my fault. I killed his mother."

"I know, Son. Don't worry about it — it was a thing most normal boys do. But I wanted you to see how impossible it is to hurt anything or anybody without hurting others — often yourself most." — Aubrey Tidey

A little classic on the science of self-direction, suggesting an infallible antidote to mental flabbiness — a technique which assures added zest to all one's daily activity

HOW TO LIVE ON TWENTY-FOUR HOURS A DAY

A condensation from the book

BY

ARNOLD BENNETT

This book has made thousands of converts, and old friends are always glad to meet it again. Written early in the career of the late Bennett, it remains one of his best-known works; it offers a miniature of the excellently disciplined method by which the distinguished author governed his own life with such evident success.

HOW TO LIVE

ON TWENTY-FOUR HOURS A DAY

THE PROVERB that time is money understates the case. Time is the inexplicable raw material of everything. Without it nothing is possible. The supply of time is truly a daily miracle. You wake up in the morning, and lo! your purse is magically filled with 24 hours of the unmanufactured tissue of your life. It is yours. The most precious of possessions showered upon you in a manner as singular as the commodity itself!

For remark! No one can take it from you. It is unstealable. And no one receives either more or less than you receive. Wealth or genius is never rewarded by even an extra hour a day. And there is no punishment. Waste this precious commodity as you will, and the supply will never be withheld from you.

You have to live on this 24 hours of daily time. Out of it you have to spin health, pleasure, money, content, respect, and the evolution of your immortal soul. If one can't contrive to live on a certain income of money, one earns a little more, or one braces the muscles and balances the budget. But if one cannot arrange that an income of 24 hours a day shall exactly cover all proper items of expenditure, one does muddle one's whole life definitely.

Which of us has not been saying to himself all his life: "I shall alter this or that when I have a little more time?" Which of us is not haunted by the feeling that the years slip by, and slip by, and that we have not yet been able to get our lives into proper working order? We have, and we have always had, all the time there is. It is the realization of this profound and neglected truth that has led me to the minute practical examination of daily time-expenditure.

THE MOST important preliminary to the task of arranging one's life so that one may live fully and comfortably within one's daily budget of 24 hours is the calm realization of the extreme difficulty of the task, of the sacrifices and the endless effort which it demands. I cannot too strongly insist on this. If you are not prepared for discouragements, if you will not be content with a small result for a big effort, then do not begin. Lie down again and resume the uneasy doze which you call your existence.

It is very sad, is it not? And yet I think it is rather fine, too, this necessity for the tense bracing of the will before anything worth doing can be done. I feel it to be the chief thing that differentiates me from the cat by the fire.

"Well," you say, "assume that I am braced for the battle. How do I begin?" Dear sir, you simply begin. If a man at a swimming pool, wanting to jump into the cold water, should ask you, "How do I begin to jump?" you would merely reply, "Just jump. Take hold of your nerves and jump."

The chief beauty about the constant supply of time is that you cannot waste it in advance. The next day, the next hour are lying ready for you, as perfect, as unspoiled, as if you had never wasted a single moment in your career. Therefore no object is served in waiting till next week, or even till tomorrow. But before you begin, let me warn you against your own ardor. Ardor is a treacherous thing. You can't satisfy it at first; it is eager to move mountains and divert the course of rivers. And then, too often, it wearies all of a sudden and dies.

Beware of undertaking too much at the start. Allow for accidents. Allow for human nature, especially your own. A glorious failure leads to nothing; a petty success may lead to a success that is not petty.

Therefore, in setting out on the immense enterprise of living fully within the narrow limits of 24 hours a day, let us avoid at any cost the risk of an early failure.

Now let us examine the budget of the day's time. You say your day is already full to overflowing. How? You actually spend in earning your livelihood — how much? Seven hours, on the average? And in actual sleep, seven? I will add two hours, and be generous. And I will defy you to account to me on the spur of the moment for the other eight hours.

To come to grips with the situation, I must choose a typical case — say a Londoner who works in an office. Now the great mistake which my typical man makes in regard to his day is a mistake of general attitude which vitiates two thirds of his energies and interests. In the majority of instances he does not precisely feel a passion for his business. He begins his business functions with reluctance, as late as he can, and he ends them with joy, as early as he can. And his engines while he is engaged in his business are seldom at their full horsepower.

Yet in spite of all this he persists in looking upon those hours from ten to six as "the day," to which the ten hours preceding and the six hours following are nothing but a prologue and epilogue. Such an attitude of course kills his interest in the odd 16 hours, with the result that, even if he does not waste them, he does not count them; he regards them simply as margin. If a man makes two thirds of his existence subservient to one third, for which he has no feverish zest, how can he hope to live fully and completely? He cannot.

To live fully and completely he must arrange a day within a day. And this inner day, a Chinese box in a larger Chinese box, must begin at 6 p.m. and end at 10 a.m. During all these 16 hours he has nothing whatever to do but cultivate his body and his soul and his fellow men. During those 16 hours he is free; he is not a wage-earner; he is just as good as a man with a private income. This must be his attitude. And his attitude is all important. His success in life depends on it.

In examining the typical man's method of employing the 16 hours that are entirely his, I will merely indicate things which he does which I think he ought not to do, postponing my suggestions for "planting" the times which I shall have cleared — as a settler clears spaces in a forest.

In justice I must say that he wastes very little time before he leaves the house in the morning at 9:10. In too many houses he gets up at nine, breakfasts between 9:7 and 9:9½, and then bolts. But immediately he bangs the front door his mental faculties, which are tireless, become idle. He walks to the station in a condition of mental coma. Arrived there, he usually has to wait for the train. At hundreds of suburban stations every morning you see men calmly strolling up and down platforms while railway companies unblushingly rob them of time, which is more than money. Hundreds of thousands of hours are thus lost every day because my typical man thinks so little of time that it has never occurred to him to take quite easy precautions against the risk of its loss.

He has a solid coin of time to spend every day — call it a sovereign. He must get change for it, and in getting change he is content to lose heavily. For that is what he does when the company robs him of five minutes twice a day. . . . You say I am dealing with minutiæ. I am. And later on I will justify myself.

Now will you kindly buy your paper and step into the train?

YOU GET into the morning train and you calmly give yourself up to your newspaper. Your air is the air of a leisured man, wealthy in time, of a man from some planet where there are 124 hours a day instead of 24. I am an impassioned reader of newspapers. Hence it is not prejudice when I say that since they are produced with rapidity, to be read with rapidity, there is no place in my daily program for them. I read newspapers as I may in odd moments. As for devoting to them 30 or 40 consecutive minutes of wonderful solitude, I cannot possibly allow you to scatter priceless pearls of time with such Oriental lavishness. You are not the Shah of time.

Let me respectfully remind you that you have no more time than I have. No newspaper reading in trains! I have already "put by" about three quarters of an hour for use.

Now you reach your office. And I abandon you there till six o'clock. I am aware that you have an hour in the midst of the day, less than half of which is given to eating. But I will leave you all that to spend as you choose. You may read your newspapers then.

I meet you again as you emerge from your office. You are pale and tired. At any rate, your wife says you are pale, and you give her to understand that you are tired. You don't eat immediately on your arrival home. But in about an hour or so you feel as if you could sit up and take a little nourishment. Then you smoke, seriously; you see friends; you putter; you play cards; you flirt with a book; you take a stroll; you caress the piano. . . . By Jove! a quarter past 11. Time to think about going to bed! You then devote quite 40 minutes to thinking about it, and at last you go to bed, exhausted by the day's work. Six hours have gone since you left the office — gone like a dream, gone like magic, unaccountably gone!

That is a fair sample case. But you say: "It's all very well for you to talk. A man *is* tired. A man must see his friends. He can't always be on the stretch." Just so. But when you arrange to go to the theater (especially with a pretty woman) what happens? You spare no toil to make yourself glorious in fine raiment; you rush back to town; you keep yourself on the stretch for four hours, if not five; you take her home; you take yourself home. You don't spend three quarters of an hour in "thinking about" going to bed. You go. Friends and fatigue have equally been forgotten, and the evening has seemed exquisitely long (or perhaps too short!) And do you remember that time when you were persuaded to sing in the chorus of the amateur operatic society, and slaved two hours every other night for three months? Can you deny that when you have something definite to look forward to at eventide, something that is to employ all your energy — the thought of that something gives a glow and a more intense vitality to the whole day?

What I suggest is that at six o'clock you look facts in the face and admit that you are not tired (because you are not, you know), and that you arrange your evening so that it is not cut in the middle by a meal. By so doing you will have a clear expanse of at least three hours. I do not suggest that you should employ three hours every night of your life in using up your mental energy. But I do suggest that you might, for a commencement, employ an hour and a half every other evening in some important and consecutive cultivation of the mind. You will still be left with three evenings for friends, bridge, tennis, domestic scenes, odd reading, pipes, gardening and pottering. You will still have the terrific wealth of 45 hours between 2 p.m. Saturday and 10 a.m. Monday. If you persevere you will soon want to pass four evenings, and perhaps five, in some sustained endeavor to be genuinely alive. And you will fall out of that habit of muttering to yourself at 11:15 p.m., "Time to be thinking about going to bed." The man who begins to go to bed 40 minutes before he opens his bedroom door is bored; that is to say, he is not living.

But remember, at the start, those 90 nocturnal minutes thrice a week must be the most important minutes in the 10,080. They must be sacred, quite as sacred as a dramatic rehearsal or a tennis match. Instead of saying, "Sorry, but I have to run off to the tennis club," you must say, ". . . but I have to work." This, I admit, is intensely difficult. Tennis is so much more urgent than the immortal soul.

IN THE AVERAGE case I should say: Confine your formal program to six days a week. If you find yourself wishing to extend it, extend it; but count the time extra as a windfall, not as regular income, so that you can return to a six-day program without the sensation of being poorer, of being a backslider.

Let us now see where we stand. So far we have marked for saving out of the waste of days half an hour at least on six mornings a week, and one hour and a half on three evenings a week. Total, seven hours and a half a week.

"What?" you cry. "You pretend to show us how to live, and

you only deal with seven hours and a half out of 168! Are you going to perform a miracle with your seven hours and a half?" Well, not to mince the matter, I am — if you will kindly let me! My contention is that the full use of those hours will quicken the whole life of the week, add zest to it, and increase the interest which you feel in even the most banal occupations.

It is not really a trifling effort to "clear" even seven hours and a half from the jungle. One may have spent one's time badly, but one did spend it. To do something else means a change of habits. And habits are the very dickens to change! Some sacrifice, and an immense deal of volition, will be necessary. Hence I iterate and reiterate: Start quietly, unostentatiously.

Before coming to the method of using the indicated hours, I have one final suggestion to make. That is, to allow much more than an hour and a half in which to do the work of an hour and a half. Remember the chance of accidents. Remember human nature. And give yourself, say, from 9 to 11:30 for your task of 90 minutes.

PEOPLE SAY: "One can't help one's thoughts." But one can. The control of the thinking machine is perfectly possible. And since nothing whatever happens to us outside our own brain, the supreme importance of being able to control what goes on in that mysterious brain is patent. For without the power to concentrate — that is to say, without the power to dictate to the brain its task and to insure obedience — true life is impossible. Mind control is the first element of a full existence. Hence, it seems to me, the first business of the day should be to put the mind through its paces. It is for this portion of the art and craft of living that I have reserved the time from the moment of quitting your door to the moment of arriving at your office.

"What? I am to cultivate my mind in the street, on the platform, and in the train?" Precisely. Nothing simpler! No tools required! Not even a book. Nevertheless, the affair is not easy.

When you leave your house, concentrate your mind on a subject (no matter what, to begin with). You will not have gone ten yards before your mind has skipped away under your very eyes and is larking round the corner with another subject. Bring it back by the scruff of the neck. Ere you have reached the station you will have brought it back about 40 times. Do not despair. You cannot by any chance fail if you persevere. It is idle to pretend that your mind is incapable of concentration. Do you not remember that morning when you received a disquieting letter which demanded a very carefully worded answer? How you kept your mind steadily on the subject of the answer until you reached the office: whereupon you instantly sat down and wrote the answer? That was a case in which *you* were roused by circumstances to such a degree of vitality that you were able to dominate your mind like a tyrant. You insisted that its work should be done, and its work *was* done.

By the regular practice of concentration (as to which there is no secret — save perseverance) you can tyrannize over your mind every hour of the day, and in no matter what place.

Now you are saying to yourself: "This fellow had begun to interest me. But what he says about thinking on trains, and on concentration, and so on, is not for me. It may be well enough for some folks, but it isn't in my line."

It *is* for you, I passionately repeat. Indeed, you are the very man I am aiming at. Throw away the suggestion, and you throw away the most precious suggestion that was ever offered to you. Try it. Get your mind in hand. And see how the process cures half the evils of life — especially worry, that miserable, avoidable, shameful disease — worry!

THE EXERCISE of concentrating the mind (to which at least half an hour a day should be given) is a mere preliminary, like scales on the piano. Having acquired power over that most unruly member, one has naturally to put it to the yoke. A course of primary study is indicated.

Now as to what this course of study should be there cannot be any question. It is the study of one's self. Man, know thyself. These words are so hackneyed that I blush to write them, yet only the most sagacious put them into practice. I don't know why. I am convinced that what is more than anything else lacking in the life of the average well-intentioned man of today is the reflective mood.

We do not reflect. I mean that we do not reflect upon genuinely important things; upon the problem of our happiness, upon the main direction in which we are going, upon what life is giving to us, upon the share which reason has (or has not) in determining our actions, and upon the relation between our principles and our conduct. For happiness does not spring from physical or mental pleasure, but from the development of reason and the adjustment of conduct to principles.

Do not fear that I mean to thrust certain principles upon your attention. All I urge is that a life in which conduct does not fairly well accord with principles is a silly life; and that conduct can only be made to accord with principles by means of daily examination, reflection and resolution. The less we reflect, the less reasonable we shall be. The next time you get cross with the waiter because your steak is over-cooked, ask reason to step into the cabinet-room of your mind, and consult her. She will probably tell you that the waiter did not cook the steak, and had no control over the cooking; and that even if he alone was to blame, you accomplished nothing by getting cross; you merely lost your dignity, looked a fool and soured the waiter, while producing no effect whatever on the steak.

The result of this consultation with reason (for which she makes no charge) will be that when once more your steak is over-cooked you will treat the waiter as a fellow creature, remain quite calm, and politely insist on having a fresh steak. The gain will be obvious and solid.

In the formation of principles, and the practice of conduct, much help can be derived from books. I suggest Marcus Aurelius and Epictetus. I may also mention Pascal, La Bruyère and Emerson.

But no reading of books will take the place of a daily, candid, honest examination of what one has recently done, and what one is about to do — of a steady looking at one's self in the face (disconcerting though the sight may be).

When shall this important business be accomplished? The solitude of the evening journey home appears to me to be suitable for it. A reflective mood naturally follows the exertion of having earned the day's living. Of course, if, instead of attending to an elementary and profoundly important duty, you prefer to read the paper (which you might just as well read while waiting for your dinner) I have nothing to say. But attend to it at some time of the day you must. I now come to the evening hours.

MANY PEOPLE remain idle in the evenings because they think there is no alternative to idleness but the study of literature; and they do not happen to have a taste for literature. This is a great mistake. There are enormous fields of knowledge quite outside literature which yield magnificent results to cultivators. For example, you go to concerts. You smoke your cigarette (and I regret to say that you strike your matches during the soft bars of the "Lohengrin" overture), and you enjoy the music. But you say you cannot play the piano or the fiddle. What does that matter?

Surely your inability to perform "The Maiden's Prayer" on a piano need not prevent you from making yourself familiar with the construction of the orchestra to which you listen. As things are, you probably think of the orchestra as a heterogeneous mass of instruments producing a confused agreeable mass of sound. You do not listen for details because you have never trained your ears to listen to details.

If you were asked to name the instruments which play the great theme at the beginning of Beethoven's C minor symphony — which has thrilled you — you could not name them for your life's sake. All that you can positively state about the C minor symphony is that it is a "jolly fine thing." Now, if you have read, say, Mr.

Krehbiel's *How to Listen to Music* (which contains photographs of all the orchestral instruments and plans of the arrangement of orchestras) you would next go to a concert with an astonishing intensification of interest in it. Instead of a confused mass, the orchestra would appear to you as what it is—a marvelously balanced organism whose various groups of members each have a different and an indispensable function. You would spy out the instruments, and listen for them. You would know the gulf that separates a French horn from an English horn, and perceive why a player of the hautboy gets higher wages than a fiddler, though the fiddle is the more difficult instrument. You would *live* at a concert, whereas previously you had merely existed there in a state of beatific coma, like a baby gazing at a bright object.

"But I hate music!" you say. My dear sir, I respect you.

What applies to music applies to the other arts. I might mention Mr. Clermont Witt's *How to Look at Pictures*, or Mr. Russell Sturgis's *How to Judge Architecture*, as beginnings (merely beginnings) of a systematic vitalizing knowledge in other arts.

"I hate all the arts!" you say. My dear sir, I respect you more and more. I will deal with your case next, before coming to literature.

ART IS a great thing. But it is not the greatest. The most important of all perceptions is the continual perception of cause and effect — of the continuous development of the universe.

It is hard to have one's watch stolen, but one reflects that the thief became a thief from causes of heredity and environment which are as interesting as they are scientifically comprehensible; and one buys another watch, if not with joy, at any rate with a philosophy that makes bitterness impossible. One loses, in the study of cause and effect, that absurd air which so many people have of being always shocked by the curiousness of life. Such people live amid human nature as if human nature were a foreign country. But, having reached maturity, one ought surely to be ashamed of being a stranger in a strange land.

The study of cause and effect, while it lessens the painfulness of life, adds to its picturesqueness. The man to whom evolution is but a name looks at the sea as a grandiose, monotonous spectacle. The man who is imbued with the idea of continuous cause and effect perceives in the sea an element which in the day-before-yesterday of geology was vapor, which yesterday was boiling, and which tomorrow will inevitably be ice. Nothing will afford a more durable satisfaction than the constantly cultivated appreciation of this tremendous, changeful picturesqueness of life.

Perhaps you happen to be an estate agent's clerk, and you hate the arts, and you want to foster your immortal soul, and you can't be interested in your business because it's so humdrum. Nothing is humdrum. The tremendous, changeful picturesqueness of life is marvelously shown in an estate agent's office. There was a congestion of traffic in Oxford Street; to avoid the congestion people actually began to travel under the cellars and drains, and the result was a rise of rents in Shepherd's Bush! And you say that isn't picturesque! Suppose you were to study, in this spirit, the property question for an hour and a half every other evening. Would it not give zest to your business, and transform your whole life?

You are a bank clerk, and you have not read that breathless romance (disguised as a scientific study), Walter Bagehot's *Lombard Street?* Ah, my dear sir, if you had begun with that, and followed it up for 90 minutes every other evening, how enthralling your business would be to you, and how much more clearly you would understand human nature.

You are "penned in town," but you love excursions to the country and the observation of wild life — certainly a heart-enlarging diversion. Why don't you walk out of your house door, in your slippers, to the nearest gas lamp of a night with a butterfly net, and observe the wild life of common and rare moths beating about it, and coördinate the knowledge thus obtained and build a superstructure on it, and at last get to *know* something about something?

You need not be devoted to the arts, nor to literature, in order to live fully. The whole field of daily habit and scene is waiting to satisfy that curiosity which means life, and the satisfaction of which means an understanding heart.

I now come to the case of the person, happily very common, who *does* "like reading."

NOVELS are excluded from the "serious reading" — of 90 minutes three times a week — for the reason that bad novels ought not to be read, and that good novels never demand any appreciable mental application on the part of the reader. A good novel rushes you forward like a skiff down a stream, and you arrive at the end, perhaps breathless, but unexhausted. The best novels involve the least strain. Now in the cultivation of the mind one of the most important factors is precisely the feeling of strain, of difficulty, of a task which one part of you is anxious to achieve and another part of you is anxious to shirk; and that feeling cannot be got in facing a novel.

Imaginative poetry produces probably the severest strain of any form of literature. It is the highest form of literature. I say this with the sad consciousness of the fact that the majority of people do not read poetry. If poetry is what is called "a sealed book" to you, begin by reading Hazlitt's famous essay on the nature of "poetry in general." It is difficult to imagine the mental state of the man who, after reading this essay, is not urgently desirous of reading some poetry before his next meal.

If you are antagonistic to poetry, then there is history or philosophy. Herbert Spencer's *First Principles*, for instance, simply laughs at the claims of poetry and refuses to be accepted as aught but the most majestic product of any human mind. I do not suggest it as a work suitable for a tyro in mental strains. But I see no reason why any man of average intelligence should not, after a year of continuous reading, be fit to assault the supreme masterpieces of history or philosophy. The great convenience of masterpieces is that they are so astonishingly lucid.

I offer two general suggestions for self-improvement through reading. The first is to define the direction and scope of your efforts. Choose a limited period, or a limited subject, or a single author. Say to yourself: "I will know something about the French Revolution, or the rise of railways, or the works of John Keats." And during a given period confine yourself to your choice. There is much pleasure to be derived from being a specialist.

The second suggestion is to think as well as to read. I know people who read and read, and for all the good it does them they might just as well cut bread-and-butter. They fly through the shires of literature on a motorcar, their sole object being motion. They boast of how many books they have read in a year.

Unless you give at least 45 minutes to careful, fatiguing reflection (it is an awful bore at first) upon what you are reading, your 90 minutes of a night are chiefly wasted. This means that your pace will be slow. Never mind. Forget the goal; think only of the surrounding country; and after a period, perhaps when you least expect it, you will suddenly find yourself in a lovely town on a hill.

I CANNOT TERMINATE these hints upon the full use of one's time to the great end of living (as distinguished from vegetating) without referring to certain dangers which lie in wait for the sincere aspirant towards life. The first is the danger of becoming that most odious of persons — a prig. A prig is a pompous fool who has gone out for a ceremonial walk, and without knowing it has lost an important part of his attire, namely, his sense of humor. A prig is a tedious individual who, having made a discovery, is so impressed that he is capable of being gravely displeased because the entire world is not also impressed by it. Hence, when one sets forth on the enterprise of using all one's time, it is just as well to remember that it is one's own time, and not other people's time, with which one has to deal; that the earth rolled on pretty comfortably before one began to balance a budget of the hours.

Another danger is of being tied to a program like a slave to a chariot. I know men whose lives are a burden to themselves and to their relatives and friends simply because they have failed to appreciate the obvious fact that while a program must be respected it must not be worshiped as a fetish. "Oh, no," I have heard a martyred wife exclaim, "Arthur always takes the dog out for exercise at eight o'clock and he always begins to read at a quarter to nine. So it's quite out of the question that we should . . ." etc., etc. And the note of absolute finality in that plaintive voice reveals the unsuspected tragedy of a career. On the other hand, a program is a program. And unless it is treated with deference it ceases to be anything but a poor joke.

There is still another danger of developing a policy of rush, of being gradually more obsessed by what one has to do next. The only cure is to reconstitute one's program, and to attempt less. But an excellent palliative is to pass with exaggerated deliberation from one portion of the program to another; in other words, to waste five minutes with consciousness of wasting them.

The last, and the chiefest danger is one to which I have already referred — the risk of failure at the start. This may easily kill outright the newborn impulse toward a complete vitality, and therefore every precaution should be observed to avoid it. The impulse must not be overtaxed. Let the pace of the first lap be even absurdly slow, but let it be as regular as possible. And, having once decided to achieve a certain task, achieve it at all costs of tedium and distaste. The gain in self-confidence of having accomplished a tiresome labor is immense.

Finally, in choosing the first occupations of those evening hours, be guided by nothing whatever but your taste and natural inclination. It is a fine thing to be a walking encyclopedia of philosophy, but if you happen to have no liking for philosophy, and to have a liking for the natural history of street-cries, much better leave philosophy alone, and take to street-cries.

About Arnold Bennett

As a poverty-stricken clerk in a London law office, Arnold Bennett took for his motto: "The best is good enough for me." And by the best he meant the material as well as the spiritual rewards of success. To achieve these ends he took stock of himself and "realized the three qualities I possessed; on these I have traded ever since. First, an omnivorous memory that remembers how much London spends in one day on cab fares just as easily as the stock anecdotes of Shelley and Byron. Second, a naturally sound taste in literature. And third, the invaluable journalistic faculty of seeming to know much more than one does."

It was this last quality that started him writing. When his first attempt won a 20-guinea prize he broke away from the law office, which bored him, and became a free lance in London's literary Fleet Street, working "obstinately." At the age of 31 his first novel, *A Man from the North*, was published, and a year later he was able to record in his diary: "This year I have written 335,340 words, grand total: 224 articles and stories."

So well planned was his time that, in spite of his prodigious literary output throughout life, he did not neglect other interests: water-color painting, the piano, first-nights at the opera and theater, and his weekly book column in the London *Standard*. "I do all my work in my head," he remarked. "I never begin to write until everything is in order." He spent years of research before writing such a novel as *Imperial Palace*, a book of some 240,000 words with 85 characters, in which a great "luxury hotel" is the real protagonist.

Arnold Bennett was always an honest critic of his own work. Recollecting the "pot-boiling" period when he wrote to stave off poverty, he said: "My soul glances back furtively with loathing at that period of emotional and intellectual dishonor." On the other hand, he frankly believed that such works as *The Old Wives' Tale*, *Clayhanger* and *Riceyman Steps* — books that brought him one of the great names in the literary world — would live.

At the time of his death in 1931 it was said that Arnold Bennett's books had earned him more readers and more wealth than those of any other British author; and so great was his prestige that his praise alone could almost insure the popular success of a book in England.

My Adventures with a Paint Brush

Condensed from "Amid These Storms"

Winston S. Churchill

World-famous British statesman and soldier

TO HAVE REACHED the age of 40 without ever handling a brush, to have regarded the painting of pictures as a mystery, and then suddenly to find oneself plunged in the middle of a new interest with paints and palettes and canvases, and not to be discouraged by results, is an astonishing and enriching experience. I hope it may be shared by others.

For to be really happy and to avoid worry and mental overstrain we ought all to have hobbies, and they must all be *real*. Best of all, and easiest to take up, are sketching and painting. They came to my rescue at a most trying time. When I left the Admiralty at the end of May 1915, I still remained a member of the Cabinet and of the War Council. In this position I knew everything and could do nothing; I had vehement convictions and no power to give effect to them; I had enforced leisure at a moment when every fiber of my being was inflamed to action.

And then it was, one Sunday in the country, that the children's paint box came to my aid. My first experiments with their toy water colors led me to secure, next morning, a complete outfit for painting in oils. The next step was *to begin*. The palette gleamed with beads of color; fair and white rose the canvas; the empty brush hung poised, heavy with destiny, irresolute in the air. Very gingerly

I mixed a little blue paint with a very small brush, and then with infinite precaution made a mark about as big as a small bean upon the affronted snow-white shield. At that moment a motorcar was heard on the drive and from it there stepped none other than the gifted wife of Sir John Lavery, the distinguished portrait painter. "Painting! But what are you hesitating about? Let me have a brush, a big one." Splash into the turpentine, wallop into the blue and white, frantic flourish on my palette, and then several large, fierce strokes of blue on the absolutely cowering canvas. The spell was broken. My sickly inhibitions rolled away. I seized the largest brush and fell upon my victim with berserk fury. I have never felt any awe of a canvas since.

This beginning with Audacity is a very great part of the art of painting. We must not be too ambitious. We cannot aspire to masterpieces. We may content ourselves with a joy ride in a paint box. And for this, Audacity is the only ticket.

I write no word in disparagement of water colors. But there is really nothing like oils. First of all, you can correct mistakes more easily. One sweep of the palette-knife "lifts" the blood and tears of a morning from the canvas; the canvas is all the better for past impressions. Secondly, you can approach your problem from any direction, beginning if you will with a moderate central arrangement of middle tones, and then hurling in the extremes when the psychological moment comes. Lastly, the pigments are so nice to handle. You can build them on layer after layer if you like and can change your plan to meet the exigencies of time and weather. Matching them with what you see is fascinating. Try it, if you have not done so — before you die.

As one slowly begins to escape from the difficulties of choosing the right colors and laying them on in the right places and in the right way, wider considerations come into view. One is astonished to find out how many things there are in the landscape one never noticed before. And there is a tremendous new pleasure that invests every walk or drive with an added object. So many colors on the hillside, each different in shadow and in sunlight; such brilliant reflections in the pool, each a key lower than what they repeat; such lovely lights gilding or silvering surface or outline. I found myself instinctively as I walked noting the tint and character of a leaf, the dreamy purple shades of mountains, the exquisite lacery of winter branches, the dim, pale silhouettes of far horizons. And I had lived for over 40 years without ever noticing any of them except in a general way, as one might look at a crowd and say, "What a lot of people!"

I think this heightened sense of observation of nature is one of the chief delights that have come to me through trying to paint. And if you do observe accurately and with refinement, and record what you have seen with tolerable correspondence, the result follows on the canvas with startling obedience.

Then, the art galleries take on a new and — to me at least — a severely practical interest. You see the difficulty that baffled you yesterday; and you see how easily it has been overcome by a great painter. You look at the masterpieces of art with an analyzing and a comprehending eye.

Chance one day led me to a secluded nook near Marseilles where I fell in with two disciples of Cézanne. They viewed nature as a mass of shimmering light in which forms and surfaces are comparatively unimportant, indeed hardly visible, but which gleams and glows with beautiful harmonies and contrasts of color. I had hitherto painted the sea flat, with long, smooth strokes of mixed pigment. Now I must try to represent it by innumerable small separate patches of pure color. Each of these little points of color sets up a strong radiation of which the eye is conscious without detecting the cause. Look at the blue of the sea. How can you depict it? Certainly not by any single color that was ever manufactured. The only way in which that luminous intensity of blue can be simulated is by this multitude of tiny points of varied color all in true relation to the rest of the scheme. Difficult? Fascinating!

I was shown a picture by Cézanne of a blank wall of a house, which he had made instinct with the most delicate lights and colors. Now

I often amuse myself when I am looking at a wall or a flat surface of any kind by trying to distinguish all the different tints which can be discerned upon it, and considering whether these arise from reflections or from natural hue. You would be astonished the first time you tried this to see how many and what beautiful colors there are even in the most commonplace objects.

Obviously, then, armed with a paint box, one cannot be bored or left at a loose end. How much there is to admire and how little time there is to see it in! For the first time one begins to envy Methuselah.

It is interesting to note the part memory plays in painting. When Whistler guided a school in Paris he made his pupils observe their model on the ground floor, and then run upstairs and paint their picture on the floor above. As they became more proficient he put their easels up a story higher, till at last the *élite* were scampering up six flights into the attic.

All the greatest landscapes have been painted indoors, and often long after the first impressions were gathered. In a dim cellar the Dutch or Italian master recreated the gleaming ice of a Netherlands carnival or the lustrous sunshine of Venice. Here, then, is required a formidable memory of the visual kind. So painting may be a very useful exercise for the development of a trained, accurate, retentive memory.

Again, there is really nothing like painting as a spur to travel. Every day is provided with its expedition and its occupation — cheap, attainable, absorbing, recuperative. The vain racket of the tourist gives place to the calm enjoyment of the philosopher. Every country you visit has a theme of its own and even if you cannot portray it as you see it, you know it, you feel it, and you admire it forever. But after all, if only the sun will shine, one does not need to go beyond one's own country. The amateur painter wanders and loiters contentedly from place to place, always on the lookout for some bright butterfly of a picture which can be caught and carried safely home.

Painting is complete as a distraction. I know of nothing which, without exhausting the body, more entirely absorbs the mind. Whatever the worries of the hour or the threats of the future, once the picture has begun to flow there is no room for them in the mental screen. They pass out into shadow and darkness. All one's mental light becomes concentrated on the task. When I have stood up on parade, or even, I regret to say, in church, for half an hour at a time, I have always felt that the erect position is not natural to man and is only with fatigue and difficulty maintained. But no one who is fond of painting finds the slightest inconvenience in standing to paint for three or four hours at a stretch.

Buy a paint box and have a try. It would be a sad pity to shuffle along through one's playtime with golf and bridge, when all the while, if you only knew, there is waiting for you close at hand the wonderful new world of thought and craft, a sunlit garden gleaming with color. Inexpensive independence, new mental food and exercise, an added interest in every common scene, an occupation for every idle hour, an unceasing voyage of entrancing discovery — these are high prizes. I hope they may be yours.

When Charles M. Schwab was 72 years old he was sued for a large sum of money. It was the kind of case most prominent men would have settled out of court, to avoid publicity; but Charlie went through with it and won. Before he left the witness stand, he asked and received permission to make a statement.

"I am an old man," he said, "and I want to say that 90 percent of my troubles have been due to my being good to other people. If you younger folk want to avoid trouble, be hard-boiled and say *no* to everybody. You will then walk through life unmolested, but" — and here the old-time smile lit up his face — "you will have to do without friends and you won't have much fun."

— Otto Eisenschiml, *Without Fame* (Alliance)